African Arguments

Written by experts with an unrivalled knowledge of the continent, African Arguments is a series of concise, engaging books that address the key issues currently facing Africa. Topical and thought-provoking, accessible but in-depth, they provide essential reading for anyone interested in getting to the heart of both why contemporary Africa is the way it is and how it is changing.

African Arguments Online

African Arguments Online is a website managed by the Royal African Society, which hosts debates on the African Arguments series and other topical issues that affect Africa: http://africanarguments.org

Published by Zed Books and the International African Institute with the support of the following organizations:

International African Institute promotes scholarly under-standing of Africa, notably its changing societies, cultures and languages. Founded in 1926 and based in London, it supports a range of seminars and publications, including the journal *Africa*.

www.internationalafricaninstitute.org

Royal African Society is Britain's prime Africa organization. Now more than a hundred years old, its in-depth, long-term knowledge of the continent and its peoples makes the Society the first stop for anyone wishing to know more about the continent. RAS fosters a better understanding of Africa in the UK and throughout the world – its history, politics, culture, problems and potential. RAS disseminates this knowledge and insight and celebrates the diversity and depth of African culture.

www.royalafricansociety.org

The World Peace Foundation, founded in 1910, is located at the Fletcher School, Tufts University. The Foundation's mission is to promote innovative research and teaching, believing that these are critical to the challenges of making peace around the world, and should go hand in hand with advocacy and practical engagement with the toughest issues. Its central theme is 'reinventing peace' for the twenty-first century.

www.worldpeacefoundation.org

About the author

Michael Deibert is an author and journalist, whose writing has appeared in the *Washington Post*, the *Guardian*, the *Wall Street Journal*, the *Miami Herald*, *Le Monde diplomatique* and *Folha de São Paulo*, among other publications. He has been a featured commentator on international affairs for the BBC, Channel 4, Al Jazeera, National Public Radio, WNYC New York Public Radio and KPFK Pacifica Radio. In recent years, Michael has worked to increase and sustain dialogue on international peace-building and development issues, with a particular focus on Africa and Latin America. He is the author of *Notes from the Last Testament: The Struggle for Haiti* (2005).

THE DEMOCRATIC REPUBLIC OF CONGO

BETWEEN HOPE AND DESPAIR

Michael Deibert

Zed Books
LONDON | NEW YORK

in association with

International African Institute
Royal African Society
World Peace Foundation

The Democratic Republic of Congo: between hope and despair was first published in association with the International African Institute, the Royal African Society and the World Peace Foundation in 2013 by Zed Books Ltd, 7 Cynthia Street, London N1 9JF, UK and Room 400, 175 Fifth Avenue, New York, NY 10010, USA

www.zedbooks.co.uk
www.internationalafricaninstitute.org
www.royalafricansociety.org
www.worldpeacefoundation.org

Set in Monotype Plantin and FontFont Kievit by Ewan Smith, London
Index: ed.emery@thefreeuniversity.net
Cover designed by Rogue Four Design
Printed and bound by the CPI Group (UK) Ltd, Croyden CRO 4YY

Distributed in the USA exclusively by Palgrave Macmillan, a division of St Martin's Press, LLC, 175 Fifth Avenue, New York, NY 10010, USA

A catalogue record for this book is available from the British Library
Library of Congress Cataloging in Publication Data available

ISBN 978 1 78032 346 6 hb
ISBN 978 1 78032 345 9 pb

CONTENTS

ACKNOWLEDGEMENTS

Since I began the research five years ago that would result in the book you hold in your hands, I have been helped along the way by many people.

In Congo itself, I was immeasurably assisted by the insights and, when I was lucky, the companionship of Charles Mushizi, Pastor Marrion P'Udongo, Andrew McConnell, David Nthengwe, Ivo Brandau, Joe Bavier, Marcus Bleasdale, Alfred Buju and Natalia Pizzatti. The staff at HEAL Africa in Goma provided me with a little oasis on the shores of Lake Kivu in which to transcribe my notes during my final reporting trip there, and the staff at the United Nations High Commissioner for Refugees in Masisi, North Kivu, were of invaluable assistance as I tried to piece together the tangled histories of the population there.

In Northern Uganda, where I researched key facts about the Lord's Resistance Army, both Father Joseph Okumu and Ron Atkinson shared their great wealth of experience of the Acholi region with me and made me feel like a welcomed guest. Francis Odongyoo of Human Rights Focus patiently discussed the context and history of the Acholi experience with me in much the same way the group has documented recent history in their meticulously detailed reports. Ojara Sunday Braxton shared a long motorcycle ride out into the countryside with me that helped give me a taste of rural Acholi life.

My colleagues in journalism over the years helped maintain my faith in the value of independent reporting even in the face of the increasingly harsh financial demands put on the reporters themselves, and for that I would like to thank Gerry Hadden, Nomi Prins, Natasha Del Toro, Jacklynne Hobbs, Howard

French, Jean-Claude Louis, Mariane Pearl, Thos Robinson, Jan Voordouw and Mike Tarr.

During the long and financially difficult years that helped produce this book, I have been grateful for the friendship of some truly special people. In Paris, Martín de la Serna, Pedro Rodriguez, Etelle Higonnet, and the denizens of Château Rouge, who gave me a glimpse of Africa before I ever set foot there and helped shape my experience of a city that is somehow always tied to my time in Congo. In Spain, Richard Boncy and Manuel Vazquez-Boidard never lost faith in the value of what I was doing. In New Orleans, where this book went through a critical phase, I valued the friendship of Erin Gandy, Greg Kelly and Jac Brubaker, and the presence of two great independent bookstores, Arcadian Books and McKeown's Books, both of which helped provide me with literary sustenance in between Congo-related reading. In Miami, where this book was completed within sight of the blue-green waters of Biscayne Bay, Charles Manus, Katherine Coder, Anna Edgerton and Kaveh Karandish kept me good company. I would like to thank some of the gifted writers, film-makers, visual artists and others whom I have been lucky enough to know, and who have supported my work so generously over the years, particularly Ben Fountain, David Searcy, Eirin Mobekk, Francesca Romeo and Hilary Wallis for inspiring me with their examples. To my old friends Sutton Stokes, Justin Cappiello, Philip Schnell and Ana Kitova, I hope we have many more years together.

My editor at Zed Books, Ken Barlow, Stephanie Kitchen at the International African Institute and Alex de Waal of the World Peace Foundation were all very supportive of this book in its initial stages, and the International Peace Research Association helped make my last research trip to central Africa possible with its generous grant.

Although this book touches on eras of history predating Joseph Kabila's assumption of the presidency of the Democratic

Republic of Congo, it is by no means meant to be the definitive record of those periods. Authoritative histories of the First and Second Congo Wars already exist, and readers interested in a more detailed account of the intricacies of these earlier conflicts than that which is provided here are urged to consult them. Likewise, I would have been perfectly adrift when navigating the development of central Africa's pre-colonial history were it not for the invaluable contributions of historians such as John K. Thornton, Jan Vansina, Alison des Forges and Adam Hochschild. For details of the mass grave that was the Congo Free State, I am forever in the debt of the work and courage of E. D. Morel and Roger Casement, who, at great personal sacrifice and peril, rang the alarm for the world to hear in a way that should still afflict our conscience today.

I have watched my brothers, Benjamin Deibert and Christopher Deibert, grow into fine men over the years, and I am thankful for their support. My grandfather, James Breon, likewise has never failed to give thoughtful and wise advice. My father, Caleb Deibert, and my grandmother, Elizabeth Deibert, first helped put me on the road years ago with their stories of life in Argentina.

Two of the people dearest to me – my old friend Sebastian Montiel Quezada and my mother Jann Marie Deibert – did not live to see this book's completion, but the warmth of their memory propelled it forward.

Finally, to all of the people whose faces I looked into in displaced persons camps such as those at Kibumba, Bihito, Kalinga and countless others; to the survivors of terrible violence at places such as Bogoro and Mongbwalu; to the enduring Acholi people of northern Uganda; to the shegue who chatted with me and shared bread with me on the streets of Kinshasa – this is your story, not mine. I only hope that I have done you justice.

Michael Deibert, Miami, March 2013

ABBREVIATIONS

ABAKO	Alliance des Bakongo
Abir	Anglo-Belgian India-Rubber Company
ADF	Allied Democratic Forces
ADP	Alliance Democratique des Peuples
AFDL	Alliance des Forces Démocratiques pour la Libération du Congo-Zaïre
AGK	AngloGold Kilo
ALiR	Armée pour la Libération du Rwanda
AMP	Alliance pour la Majorité Présidentielle
ANC	Armée Nationale Congolaise
ANR	Agence Nationale de Renseignements
APC	Armée Populaire Congolaise
APCLS	Alliance des Patriotes pour un Congo Libre et Souverain
AU	African Union
BDK	Bundu dia Kongo
CAR	Central African Republic
CCTV	Canal Congo Télévision
CDR	Coalition pour la Défense de la République
CENI	Commission Électorale Nationale Indépendante
CIAT	Comité International d'Accompagnement de la Transition
CND	Centre Nationale de Documentation
CNDP	Congrès National pour la Défense du Peuple
CNRD	Conseil National de la Résistance pour la Démocratie
CNS	Conférence Nationale Souveraine
CONAKAT	Confédération des Associations Tribales du Katanga
DSP	Division Spéciale Présidentielle
EGMF	Entreprise Générale Malta Forrest

EU	European Union
FAC	Forces Armées Congolaises
FAP	Forces Armées Populaires
FAR	Forces Armées Rwandaises
FARDC	Forces Armées de la République Démocratique du Congo
FAZ	Forces Armées Zaïroises
FDLR	Forces Démocratiques de Libération du Rwanda
FNI	Front des Nationalistes et Intégrationnistes
FNL	Forces Nationales de Libération
FNLA	Frente Nacional de Libertação de Angola
FNLC	Front National pour la Libération du Congo
FOCA	Forces Combattantes Abacunguzi
FPJC	Front Populaire pour la Justice au Congo
FRODEBU	Front pour la Démocratie au Burundi
FRPI	Forces de Résistance Patriotique d'Ituri
Gécamines	Générale des Carrières et des Mines
GFI	George Forrest International
GSSP	Groupe Spécial de la Sécurité Présidentielle
HSMF	Holy Spirit Mobile Force
ICC	International Criminal Court
IDP	internally displaced person
IMF	International Monetary Fund
JMPR	Jeunesse du Mouvement Populaire de la Révolution
JUFERI	Jeunesses de l'Union des Fédéralistes et des Républicains Independents
JUNAFEC	Jeunesse de l'Union des Nationalistes Fédéralistes du Congo
LRA	Lord's Resistance Army
M23	Mouvement du 23 Mars
MCDDI	Mouvement Congolais pour la Démocratie et le Développement Intégral
MCK	Mining Company Katanga
MDR	Mouvement Démocratique Républicain
MLC	Mouvement pour la Liberation du Congo
MNC	Mouvement National Congolais
MONUC	Mission de l'Organisation des Nations Unies en République Démocratique du Congo

MONUSCO	Mission de l'Organisation des Nations Unies pour la Stabilisation en République Démocratique du Congo
MPLA	Movimento Popular de Libertação de Angola
MPR	Mouvement Populaire de la Révolution
MRND	Mouvement Révolutionaire National pour le Développement
MSF	Médecins Sans Frontières
MSR	Mouvement Social pour le Renouveau
NGO	non-governmental organisation
NRA	National Resistance Army
OKIMO	Office des Mines d'Or de Kilo-Moto
ONUC	Opération des Nations Unies au Congo
PALIPEHUTU	Parti pour la Libération du Peuple Hutu
PALU	Parti Lumumbiste Unifié
PARECO	Coalition des Patriotes Résistants Congolais
Parmehutu	Parti du Mouvement de l'Emancipation Hutu
PNC	Police Nationale Congolaise
PPRD	Parti du Peuple pour la Reconstruction et la Démocratie
PRP	Parti de la Révolution du Peuple
RALIK	Radio Liberté Kinshasa
RCD	Rassemblement Congolais pour la Démocratie
RCD-G	Rassemblement Congolais pour la Démocratie-Goma
RCD-K	Rassemblement Congolais pour la Démocratie-Kisangani
RCD-ML	Rassemblement Congolais pour la Démocratie-Mouvement de Libération
RCD-N	Rassemblement Congolais pour la Démocratie-National
RDF	Rwanda Defence Force
RPA	Rwandan Patriotic Army
RPF	Rwandan Patriotic Front
RTLM	Radio Télévision Libre des Mille Collines
RTNC	Radio-Télévision Nationale Congolaise
SNIP	Service National d'Intelligence et de Protection
SOKIMO	Société des Mines d'Or de Kilo-Moto

SOMIGL	Société Minière des Grands Lacs
Sominki	Société Minière du Kivu
SPLA	Sudan People's Liberation Army
UDEMO	Union des Démocrates Mobutistes
UDPS	Union pour la Démocratie et le Progrès Social
UFERI	Union des Fédéralistes et des Républicains Indépendants
UMHK	Union Minière du Haut Katanga
UN	United Nations
UNAFEC	Union Nationale des Démocrates Fédéralistes du Congo
UNAMIR	United Nations Assistance Mission for Rwanda
UNC	Union pour la Nation Congolaise
UNDP	United Nations Development Programme
UNHCR	Office of the United Nations High Commissioner for Refugees
UNITA	União Nacional para a Independência Total de Angola
UNLA	Uganda National Liberation Army
UPC	Union des Patriotes Congolais
UPDA	Uganda People's Democratic Army
UPDF	Uganda People's Defence Force

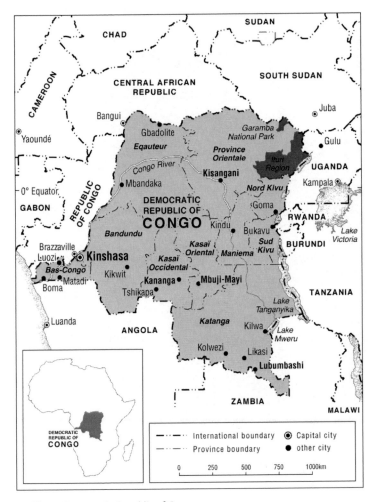

Map 1 Democratic Republic of Congo

Map 2 Eastern Democratic Republic of Congo

RAMA: What's a deserter?

MARK: A deserter is a uniformed soldier who says Libertashio is dead.

RAMA: But it's true. Papa is dead.

MARK: That's merely civilian truth.

Sony Labou Tansi, *La parenthèse de sang*

In memory of my mother, Jann Marie Deibert, who taught me to care.

PROLOGUE: THE KILLING FIELDS

We were wading through chest-high grass, which undulated like a green sea on the slopes of the hillside, when we came upon the bones still bleaching in the sun.

'I was living just down here in the valley,' said the farmer, dressed in tattered black pants and a frayed blue shirt. 'They were killing people with guns, with machetes, with spears and arrows. I escaped because I saw people running in my direction. Three of my children were killed in my own house.'

The farmer was named Mathieu Nyakufa, a 52-year-old member of the Hema ethnic group, many of whom live in the eastern reaches of the Democratic Republic of Congo that abut the Ugandan border. Despite the passage of time – the attack on Bogoro occurred in February 2003, five years before we found ourselves in the field – the pain of the farmer's loss was obviously still fresher than the human remnants we now looked down upon.

The three of us – Nyakufa, my driver and translator Pastor Marrion P'Udongo and myself – had come to this field in a remote part of eastern Congo to try to piece together how the region was recovering from the conflict that had raged there for much of the first decade of the twenty-first century, a struggle that had pitted several ethnic groups against one another amid a backdrop of mineral theft and the destructive military ambitions of Congo's neighbours and the government of Congo's President Joseph Kabila. The young Kabila, who had taken over the reins of the state in January 2001 following the assassination of his father, Laurent-Désiré Kabila, seemed a distant, aloof figure here on the other side of this vast country. But he had nevertheless maintained his proxies here, much the same as any other warlord.

The pastor and I had driven over windswept green hills from the dusty, dilapidated provincial capital of Bunia. Every night, Bunia was plunged into blackness save for the generator-powered lights at the Hotel Bunia, a small inn owned and operated by a crew of Indian cousins from the state of Maharashtra who provided guests with fiery Indian fare, and the lights that came from the compound of the local contingent of the United Nations peacekeeping mission, known by its French-language acronym MONUC. Despite being the largest such force in the world, with some 17,000 soldiers at the time, the mission was still spread incredibly thin over an expanse of jungle, churning rivers and mountains the size of Western Europe.

Like much of Congo, Ituri (since 1966 part of the country's vast Orientale province) was a patchwork of ethnic groups and subgroups. The Hema could be broken down into the northern Gegere and the southern Hema, while another ethnic division in Ituri, the Lendu, were made up of the northern Lendu and the southern Ngiti.[1] While the Lendu were mainly composed of farmers who arrived from southern Sudan in the sixteenth century, the Hema were a Nilotic grouping that came to the area around the late seventeenth century.[2] Standing in the shadows, and sometimes fighting side by side with the ethnic militias that grew out of these divisions, was a panoply of other armed groups, each with its own competing, overlapping and colliding agendas, and a civilian population, including a substantial number of Mbuti pygmies, made to suffer the consequences of the mad scramble for power and riches.

Often portrayed solely as an ethnic feud, the Hema–Lendu conflict was in fact more complex. In many ways, it resulted from policies that poisoned relations between two communities that had previously coexisted, albeit uneasily, for many years. Prior to colonial rule, Lendu farmers leased out large tracts of land to

Hema herders. This changed with the arrival of the Belgians in the 1880s. In an echo of their policy in nearby Rwanda, which elevated the Tutsi ethnic group over the Hutu in areas of administration, education and business, the Belgians in this part of Congo favoured the pastoral Hema over the agriculturalist Lendu, leading to resentment on the part of those left on the downside of this arrangement.[3] Nevertheless, the region remained largely peaceful. In the early 1950s, the British anthropologist Colin Turnbull lived in Ituri's lush forests among the pygmies, conducting the research that would eventually help form his book *The Forest People*. At the time, Turnbull characterised the region's jungles as appearing as a 'dense, damp and inhospitable-looking darkness' to outsiders, whereas they were in fact a 'cool, restful shady world' for their inhabitants.[4]

It was also a rich world, or should have been, for Ituri had been blessed with abundant timber, fertile soil and gold deposits that many experts believed to be among the most promising ever located. After the Belgians departed in 1960, the dictator Mobutu Sese Seko – who renamed Congo as Zaire and ruled it from 1965 until 1997 – launched his *authenticité* campaign, whose stated aim was to rid the country of colonial vestiges and create a true national identity. Significantly, the assumption of control over Ituri farmland previously owned by Europeans was overseen by Mobutu's minister of agriculture, Zbo Kalogi, himself a Hema. Kalogi favoured his own ethnic group in reallocating the land, deepening feelings of marginalisation among the Lendu.[5] A land ownership law – popularly known as the *loi Bakajika* after the deputy (Bakajika Bantu) who proposed it – was enacted in 1966, just as Mobutu was consolidating his power, and was followed by additional legal measures in 1971 and 1973 to solidify the government's control over what had been ancestral lands, and ensure the regime's continued access to the country's mineral resources.[6]

At the same time, the colonial Société des Mines d'Or de Kilo-

Moto became the Office des Mines d'Or de Kilo-Moto (OKIMO), an immense parastatal company that oversaw the mining of Ituri's vast gold deposits. By the time Mobutu was overthrown in a Rwandan-organised invasion of Congo, the resources of Ituri and elsewhere – festering under decades of Mobutu's divide-and-rule strategy and agitated by outside forces – were ripe for the plunder.

Like much of the violence that would consume Congo, some of the trails for what happened in Ituri meandered back to Uganda and Rwanda. When a Rwandan/Ugandan-backed rebel movement, the Rassemblement Congolais pour la Démocratie (RCD), splintered amid a falling-out of its foreign patrons in the central city of Kisangani in 1999, one of its leaders, Antipas Mbusa Nyamwisi, decamped northwards towards Ituri in September of that year and eventually took over a Uganda-aligned faction of the movement, the RCD-Mouvement de Libération. Although ostensibly subordinate to another leader, Ernest Wamba dia Wamba, Nyamwisi was a member of the Nande ethnic group and came from the nearby Ruwenzori area of North Kivu, about 200 kilometres south of Bunia. His presence in the region therefore was not totally unexpected, and, as Wamba dia Wamba sat ensconced in the Ugandan capital of Kampala, his influence proved to be more pervasive.

Once in Bunia, Nyamwisi alternately courted local Hema and Lendu supremacists as a land dispute in Ituri's Djugu district between Hema and Lendu spiralled into violence.[7] Fanning the flames still further, that same month Uganda's national army, the Uganda People's Defence Force (UPDF), which had maintained a base in Bunia since November 1998,[8] and specifically Brigadier General James Kazini, felt secure enough of their power to announce the re-creation of the province of Kibali-Ituri (which had existed from 1962 until 1966) and the appointment of a Gegere Hema businesswoman as its governor.[9]

By early 2001, clashes between Hema and Lendu militias had killed more than 200 people around Bunia alone.[10] Nyamwisi installed his own puppet governor from another area of Congo in Bunia in early 2002, and, after acting as party to the April 2002 Sun City agreement to end Congo's war, Nyamwisi's forces essentially became proxies for the Kabila government. Nyamwisi himself remained in his home area of Beni. The match had been lit, though, and – agreement or no – the Ituri conflict would burn on and on.

The 2003 raid on Bogoro – which had killed an estimated 200 civilians[11] – was committed by the Forces de Résistance Patriotique d'Ituri (FRPI), a militia dominated by the Ngiti that was then acting in concert with another Lendu organisation, the Front des Nationalistes et Intégrationnistes (FNI).[12] A scattered collection of thatched-roof huts and mud dwellings, Bogoro was a stronghold of the Hema-centric Union des Patriotes Congolais (UPC), the first party formed on an ethnic basis in Ituri when it was created in July 2001 by Thomas Lubanga.[13] The UPC's military wing was commanded by Lubanga's deputy, Bosco Ntaganda, who was not even Hema but rather a Rwandan Tutsi who had fought with Rwandan President Paul Kagame's Rwandan Patriotic Front rebels in the early 1990s before returning to Congo.

'The UPC told me, "Papa, run away, don't wait, because the Lendu are killing your people",' the farmer Nyakufa told me, breaking into my thoughts with the memory of his experience.

Bogoro was not exceptional. Other towns – Mambasa, Drodro, Nyakunde, Bunia itself – all saw similar massacres, some with far greater casualties, committed by one or other of the armed groups operating in the region. Between January 1999 and March 2003, one human rights organisation estimated that at least 55,000 civilians were killed in direct violence in Ituri.[14] The region's riches poured across the border towards Uganda and Rwanda, and, in its rich gold fields, international mining companies entered into relationships with armed groups that were, at best, of questionable ethical standing.

By the time of my visit to Ituri, although militias still skirmished with MONUC peacekeepers and government soldiers from time to time, the guns had paused. Several prominent leaders of ethno-supremacist politics – the FNI's Mathieu Ngudjolo, the FRPI's Germain Katanga and the UPC's Thomas Lubanga – had been arrested and transferred to the Netherlands for trial by the International Criminal Court (ICC) in the Hague, while a fourth militia leader, the FNI's Floribert Njabu, was being held in the Congolese capital Kinshasa under murky circumstances. Another target of international prosecutors, Bosco Ntaganda – whose arrest warrant by the ICC was unsealed[15] almost at the moment of our visit to Bogoro – remained tantalisingly out of reach.

Ntaganda had left Ituri to wage war in the province of North Kivu, immediately to Ituri's south, in a rebellion he and his commander Laurent Nkunda claimed was launched to defend the rights of Congo's Tutsis, but which bore all the hallmarks of the ethnic warfare-for-profit modus operandi of Ntaganda's time in Ituri.

In Bunia, a local priest, discussing the former fighters still in the district, told me that 'they recognise that they were manipulated and used for the interests of some people, including their leaders. They now see that everyone was a loser in that situation. They are not ready to start that adventure again.'[16]

At the Bunia headquarters of the FNI, now a registered political party, the group's political co-ordinator, Sylvestre Sombo, sat behind a battered desk with a few other men. He was dismissive of international efforts in Ituri, and of the arrests on behalf of the ICC, saying 'if we have peace in Ituri today, it's not because of international or local justice, but because the children of Ituri decided to create a way to peace for themselves'.[17]

Days later, en route to the town of Mongbwalu (itself the scene of a ghastly massacre), the pastor and I found ourselves gazing down upon some 200 mud-covered men panning for traces of gold in the muddy brown waters of the Manyidaa mining camp. Working for the mine's Congolese owners and trying to rid the area of water bubbling up from underground with a primitive pump, the prospectors were following an old map of the site made by the Belgians before they left the region almost 50 years before.

Adamo Bedijo, a 32-year-old university graduate, stating the obvious, said that it was 'very difficult, punishing work'.

'We are not paid, we work until we hit the vein of gold and hope that will pay us,' he told me, sweat beading on his brow under a blast furnace-hot tropical sun, his comrades engaged in their seemingly Sisyphean task below us. 'The government has abandoned us, so I am forced to endure all this suffering.'[18]

The conflict in Ituri may not have been the bloodiest episode in Congo's long immolation, but in all its particulars Ituri served as an apt microcosm of what had happened and would continue to happen around the country as it passed into the new millennium: the elements of ethnic cleansing and supremacy in the violence; the lure of untapped mineral riches following the Congolese state's implosion in the late 1990s; the nefarious and destructive influence of Congo's neighbours; the fitful interest of some sections of the international community combined with the active collusion with evil of others; and a 'peace' process and political reform that did little but favour one group of criminals over another. Ituri also offered a glimpse of the human toll of the Congo wars, and the lasting scars the people of Congo felt long after the guns theoretically fell silent. Indeed, for many of them, they never did. For nearly a decade, Joseph Kabila and a small cadre of advisers had been lording over the areas of Congo under their command, adroit, media-savvy, but with an iron fist ready to be brought down at a moment's notice on those who threatened their grip on power. Drifting and myopic policies drawn up by a succession of international leaders were most often forged in the context of imagined grand geo-politics rather than the realities on the ground, allowing both the Kabila government and Congo's neighbours to operate with brutality and impunity. Predatory and unscrupulous foreign business practitioners stepped into the void left by corruption and nepotism and continue today to bleed the country dry of its mineral riches.

Though far from a paradise before the advent of Europe's colonial adventure there, Congo became a place as deeply scarred and deformed by colonialism as any state in Africa, and the bloodshed that has befallen the country since then is not the result of some sort of indigenous, irresistible, immemorial blood lust on the part of the Congolese, but rather has been a tool used by individuals and governments to advance their own political and economic goals throughout the territory Congo occupies, a state of affairs that has been true for the last 140 years. These intertwining destinies – financial and political – have remained largely obscure to the general public despite the great loss of life in Congo. This book aims to change that and to, in the words of E. D. Morel, 'flood their deeds with day'.

Back in Ituri, as we stood with him in the gathering twilight, overlooking the accursed field outside Bogoro during that late afternoon in early 2008, the farmer Mathieu Nyakufa fished a single cigarette out of his fraying top shirt pocket and lit it as he looked over the expanse of green holding what was left of the departed.

'Sometimes I feel so bad about what happened to my children,' he told us. 'But now that we are reconciled, what can I do?'

1 | KINGDOM OF KONGO TO FIRST CONGO REPUBLIC

Despite its present image as a place of endless war, the people occupying the area that today comprises the nation of Congo were members of a myriad state-like entities that governed their various realms, sometimes for centuries, with varying degrees of sophistication and competence. These empires and statelets extended over 2.3 million square miles, of which some 60 per cent consisted of jungle cover. The mighty Congo River cut through the expanse, flowing 2,700 miles (4,344 kilometres) from its headwaters to the estuary, and spanning some 7 miles across at its widest point. Buffalo, cheetahs, elephants, leopards, lions, rhinoceros and zebras roamed its savannahs and mountain gorillas clung to the slopes of its densely forested mountains.

Spreading eastward from the Atlantic Ocean and encompassing parts of present-day Angola, Congo-Brazzaville and Gabon as well as Congo itself, the Kingdom of Kongo was the dominant coastal kingdom in central Africa from roughly 1482 until 1550.[1] Its political structure was centred around M'banza-Kongo, where the king (Mwene Kongo or 'Lord of Congo') resided and around which the gravitational pull of central power revolved for the surrounding provinces. Kongo had an extraordinarily strong central state, with provinces ruled by governors appointed by the king,[2] and a shield-bearing infantry supported by thousands of lightly armed troops.[3]

At some point in 1482 or 1483, the Portuguese explorer Diogo Cão came ashore from the Atlantic near the mouth of the Congo River, initiating the first recorded contact between Europeans and the Bakongo people, several of whom Cão promptly seized as hostages and took back to Portugal. He returned to Africa again in 1485, bringing these hostages with him, and initiated further contact with the local people that resulted in his leaving some of his party behind in Africa as he returned to Europe with still more locals, including several Kongo nobles. After a third visit in 1487, Kongo's king, Nzinga Nkuwu, sent the kingdom's spiritual leader and several other high-ranking officials back to Portugal. In 1491, Ruy de Sousa led the first official Portuguese diplomatic mission to the kingdom.

Nzinga Nkuwu would rule until 1506, even going so far as to accept Christian baptism as João I before lapsing back into traditional religion.[4] Upon Nzinga's death, his Catholic son, Afonso, won a battle to succeed his father and Kongo's links with Lisbon deepened.[5] Under Afonso's own son, Diogo I Nkumbi a Mpudi, who assumed the throne in 1545, tensions with the Portuguese flared up and relations alternated between war and collaboration for much of the rest of the century.

By the 1530s, more than 5,000 slaves per year were being sent across the Atlantic from Kongo; by the 1600s, that number was 15,000.[6] From 1561 until 1576, Kongo experienced lawlessness and revolt amid invasions from the east by the mysterious Jaga.[7] Cannibalistic, palm wine-drinking and cattle-killing, the Jaga invaded Kongo in 1568 and succeeded in destroying M'banza-Kongo before being beaten back with Portuguese assistance.[8] With dissension rife within the monarchy, Kongo experienced civil war throughout much of the 1700s,[9] and by the late 1770s armies loyal to royal pretenders dotted Kongo territory.[10]

It was during this time that the messianic strain within the spiritual/political life of the Bakongo first came to prominence, as exemplified by Dona Beatriz, a woman born of noble Kongo parentage under the name Kimpa Vita in what is today Angola. Given to receiving visions of a spiritual and religious nature, she ventured forth in the early 1700s at a time when the kingdom was in the grip of seemingly endless civil war. Claiming to be possessed by the spirit of Saint Anthony in what was by then one of the most heavily Catholicised regions of Africa, Beatriz preached in favour of the unification of Kongo under one ruler. She developed her own, idiosyncratic brand of religion, which she sought to take to the territory's far corners before being captured and burned as a heretic in 1706.

Immediately to the east of Kongo, in an area encompassing much of the present-day state of Kasai and bordered by the Kasai, Lulua and Sankuru rivers, the Kuba kingdom subsumed several local ethnic groups and flourished due to its control of the ivory trade.[11] The Kuba formed a multilingual, multi-ethnic kingdom with the king based in Nsheng, from where he governed in tandem with various consultative royal councils over a political system that fanned out through thousands of (some quite diminutive) villages.[12] During the late 1800s, cessionary struggles among the monarchy somewhat diminished the coherence of the state structure, but the aged Kuba king, Kwet a Mbewky, still felt sufficiently in charge to levy a sentence of death on anyone who showed a foreigner the path to his royal court.[13]

South of the dense rainforests, on the savannah, the Luba empire existed in what was historically a sparsely populated region. The empire, 'a homogenous religious culture',[14] stretched across north-central Katanga province to the border of Kasai. The Luba had a complex, episodic genesis myth full of courtly and familial intrigue and characters such as Nkongolo Mwamba Muiya Nkololo ('Nkongolo Mwamba who dances with the nkololo knife').[15] Like the deity of the Old Testament, the creation myth of Nkongolo displays a marked sadism, with Nkongolo frequently killing those who displease him. While the Luba's 'sacred villages' spread outward from Lake Boya in a manner linked to Luba cosmology, and although there was a strong Luba state in what today is the province of Katanga by the sixteenth century, slavery of the Luba was still practised by the Kuba well into the

1890s.[16] The system of government was a melding of *balopwe* (sacred kingship) and rule by consultative council. Via migration, the Luba would eventually introduce their language to central Kasai.[17] By the 1860s, the Luba and Bemba were solid allies of Arab slavers operating in the region.[18]

Although its greatest king, Ilunga Tshibinda, was a Luba, the Lunda empire was a distinct kingdom stretching over much of what is now Katanga, despite being far less a military force than Kongo to the west.[19] By the late 1700s, the Lunda empire was huge,[20] and by the 1800s the kingdom was warring (with little effect) against Kongo.[21]

Things began to change significantly during the second half of the nineteenth century, with the driving catalyst the British-born explorer Henry Morton Stanley. Born John Rowlands in Denbigh, Wales and reared in a workhouse of Dickensian grimness before fleeing to the United States at 18, he arrived in New Orleans, took the name of a merchant he met there and subsequently ended up fighting in both the Confederate and Union armies during the American Civil War. After the war, Stanley carved out a new career as a journalist, and in this guise he first travelled to Africa at the head of an expedition to locate the Scottish explorer David Livingstone, who had disappeared while travelling there. Against all odds, Stanley succeeded. Returning to Africa in an attempt to map the Congo River underwritten by his contacts in the newspaper business – an endeavour that would take nearly three years and during which more than half of his expedition would die – Stanley traversed nearly the entire waist of Africa. Setting the template for other foreign invading powers in years to come, Stanley's expeditions through the heart of the continent have been described as:

> small armies ... [that] cut through Africa with mean efficiency,
> blasting away at troublesome native settlements, flogging
> porters to death, leaving his expeditions' sick and lame to die
> on the trail and the deserters hanging in the trees.[22]

About the time Stanley's Civil War exploits were coming to an end, King Leopold II (Léopold-Louis-Philippe-Marie-Victor) was crowned in Belgium. The product of an ice-cold relationship with his mother and father, Leopold's attitude towards the country he presided over as a constitutional monarch was one of barely concealed contempt, as a famous comment he once made – *petit pays, petit gens* (small country, small people) – illustrated.[23]

Driven by visions of empire and an obsession with maps, surrounded by a Europe in the throes of the Industrial Revolution and hungry for raw materials, Leopold cast about for suitable colonial holdings before finally convening a conference in Brussels in September 1876 that focused on central Africa. During the conference he expounded upon the supposedly civilising mission behind his interest in Congo, and convinced the attendees – explorers, geographers, scientists and others – to endorse a chain of 'bases' to be set up in 'unclaimed' central Africa. The conference resulted in the founding of the Association Internationale Africaine (International African Association). Leopold would go on to form a succession of similarly named, quasi-scientific 'societies' whose main aim seemed to be to aid him in camouflaging the true nature of his interest.

A year after Leopold's Brussels conference, Stanley emerged from the African brush. To Stanley, death was the only suitable response to any form of insult or 'mocking' from those he encountered en route, and those within his party were treated little better.[24] Leopold recognised Stanley's brutal effectiveness and summoned the explorer to a meeting in Brussels. Leopold wanted Stanley to lead his project in Congo, a task for whose public aims Stanley could hardly have been more ill-suited. Both men, however, understood what the other wanted. Stanley accepted.

Upon returning to Africa in 1883, Stanley set furiously to work building the foundations of Leopold's empire along the Congo River, signing 'treaties' with local chiefs that most could neither read nor understand. It was decided that the colonial capital would be in Boma, a somnolent town of rough-hewn Portuguese traders and local Africans some 50 miles inland from the Atlantic coast. The American businessman and diplomat Henry Shelton Sanford, who had acted as the initial liaison between Leopold and Stanley, then persuaded US President Chester A. Arthur to recognise Leopold's claim to Congo in early 1884, and the Berlin Conference in November of that year entrusted an expanse the size of Western Europe to the whims of a king who had never set foot there. The next year the État Indépendant du Congo (Congo Free State) was born.[25]

The 1885 to 1908 existence of the Congo Free State was and remains one of history's great crimes, but at the time the rape and pillage of the prostrate land continued with much approbation from the world at large. Leopold was even elected president of the (British) Aborigines' Protection Society.

Leopold's Congo was connected through a series of river-boat stations along its mighty aquatic arteries, but how was the commerce that flowed outward from its interior accomplished? To keep recalcitrant locals in line as his agents searched for ivory and rubber, Leopold formed the Force Publique in 1886. Largely made up of white officers and African foot soldiers, often press-ganged into service, the Force Publique would become an object of terror for the Congolese. Barely disciplined troops harassed civilians with abandon and the *chicotte* – a razor-sharp leather whip – was the favoured tool for chastising those who fell foul of the authorities, often resulting in permanent injuries. The amputation of limbs became the norm as a means to instil fear among local people, while slaves latched together by chains around their necks and forced to work for the colonial authorities became a regular sight in the so-called 'Free State'.

The Congo had become a vast gulag of slave labour. Leopold formed the Anglo-Belgian India-Rubber Company (Abir) in August 1892 in collaboration with British businessman John Thomas North, and the Compagnie du Kasai was formed in

1901. Gold was discovered in Ituri in 1903, and Katanga was viewed as sufficiently rich to be administered separately by the Comité Spécial du Katanga from 1894 until 1910. In a fairly typical mission, in April 1899 a Belgian commander led a band of looters to sack Nsheng, which the Belgians attacked again in July of the following year, spelling the effective end of the Kuba empire.[26] From 1891 until 1892, the Canadian officer Captain William Stairs led a military campaign on Leopold's behalf in Katanga which succeeded in crushing the Yeke kingdom and killing its leader, the king Msiri.

Most of the meetings between whites and Africans were tragic during this period, and none more so than that of Ota Benga, an Mbuti pygmy whose entire immediate family was slain by the Force Publique while he was away on a hunting expedition. 'Discovered' by the American missionary Samuel Phillips Verner, Benga was shipped along with several other Congolese to the 1904 St Louis World's Fair, where he was displayed as a curiosity to gaping crowds. Returning to Congo after the fair, Benga felt out of place and subsequently returned with Verner to the United States where he lived as a kind of human exhibit at the Museum of Natural History and then at the Bronx Zoo in New York. Unable to return home, in March 1916, after building a ceremonial fire, Benga shot himself in the heart with a stolen revolver in Virginia.[27]

By July 1890, the American missionary George Washington Williams, who had travelled throughout the country, authored an open letter to Leopold in which he accused the king of appalling brutality and Stanley of tyrannical megalomania and called for the international community to investigate the atrocities. Another visitor, the African-American minister William Henry Sheppard, spent significant time among the Kuba in Kasai, one of the areas of Congo most violated by Leopold's thirst for rubber. Sheppard was among the first outsiders to witness and report the policy of dismemberment practised by Leopold's forces.[28] The Polish author

Joseph Conrad was sufficiently disturbed by his experiences in Leopold's Congo in 1890–91 that he was inspired to write *Heart of Darkness*, which would become his most famous work, nearly a decade later. Despite justified criticism of its portrayal of Africans, the book remains perhaps the most searing portrait of Leopold's conquest and rape of Congo and those who facilitated it.

In 1891, E. D. Morel began working as a shipping clerk for the Liverpool-based Elder Dempster Lines, which was contracted for shipping between Antwerp and Boma on behalf of the Congo Free State. What he saw at the docks in Antwerp disturbed him. In exchange for the rubber and ivory flowing into Belgium, only firearms, ammunition and chains were flowing back to Congo. Morel's logic was clear, his conclusion terrifying: 'How then, was the rubber and ivory being acquired? Certainly not by commercial dealing. Nothing was going in to pay for what was coming out.'[29]

Given the publicity generated about the horrors taking place in Congo, in 1903 the great Irish patriot and statesman Roger Casement, then the British consul in Boma, was commissioned by the British government to look into the allegations of abuse in the Congo Free State. Casement, a brilliant intellect who had in fact met Leopold in Brussels in 1900, travelled throughout the territory and his report, published the following year, caused a sensation. It makes for unrelentingly grim reading even today.

Casement encounters towns devoid of goats, sheep and fowl, which have been stolen by the authorities, where the grindingly poor inhabitants flee in terror at the approach of his steamer.[30] He observes the aftermath of a punitive expedition by the authorities against locals in Chumbiri who have been lax in remitting goats and fowl, which has resulted in the 'disappearance' of 17 people.[31] At Ifomi, he sees 15 local women – five nursing children and three pregnant – imprisoned because their husbands have failed to deliver the requisite amount of rubber, and tied together 'neck to neck or ankle to ankle' when they try to sleep at night.[32] Casement also finds that military operations – often using 'local' (i.e. Congolese) soldiers under white Belgian command – have been conducted during which 'there had been much loss of life, accompanied ... by a somewhat general mutilation of the dead'.[33] By mutilation of the dead, Casement meant the cutting off of hands and feet, practised upon the living as well as the dead, children as well as adults, in places such as Bikoro.[34]

Casement's private diary is even more disturbing. On 13 August he records '5 people from Bikoro with hands cut off', and the following day at Banzaka notes that 'all [the] villages destroyed for rubber'. On 22 August the expedition 'passed deserted site of Bokutea ... people were all taken away by force'. At Bongandanga on 29 August he finds 'nothing but guns ... 242 men with rubber all guarded like convicts'. The following day at Abir there are '16 men women & children tied up'.[35]

Morel and Casement would help found the Congo Reform Association, a body that would eventually come to include such luminaries as Sir Arthur Conan Doyle and Mark Twain. In 1905, a Belgian parliamentary committee confirmed the details of Casement's report, and in November 1908 the Congo Free State was annexed by the Belgian government. Leopold was gone, but the colonial creation he envisioned would continue for another 52 years under the name Congo Belge or the Belgian Congo.

It remained an extraordinarily rich prize for Brussels. The rubber boom would eventually peter out, but, in 1907, the first diamond found in Congo was discovered in Kasai. By 1929, the Belgian Congo was the world's second largest diamond producer, surpassed only by South Africa. In 1911, the Union Minière du Haut Katanga (UMHK) began producing copper in Katanga.

The transfer of Congo from Leopold's private business concern to the Belgian state saw something of a radical reorientation of the country's economic model. Rather than existing solely for the benefit of one man and a small cadre of partners, Congo was now thrown open to independent business concerns. An immense colonial bureaucracy was created and, in 1926, the capital was moved from Boma to Leopoldville, further inland and just across the river from Brazzaville, the capital of the French Congo.

In a move that would have a significant future impact, Belgium changed the ethnic make-up of whole regions and, where the ethnic template itself did not change, favoured some groups over others to promote its colonial enterprises. During the late 1930s, the Belgians imported thousands of Rwandans to work the farm and cattle plots of North Kivu.[36] At the same time, the Belgians created the Mission d'Immigration de Banyarwanda to move people from Rwanda to the Kivus (mostly for farming purposes) and Katanga (for mining). These immigrants would become known as Banyarwanda in North Kivu and Banyamulenge in South Kivu. Many Luba also emigrated from Kasai to Katanga during this period.

The Force Publique was reformed somewhat and helped fight against German forces in East Africa during World War I and again during World War II; the irony of being asked to defend freedom while they themselves remained enslaved to Brussels was not lost on the Congolese. Some on the ground realised this, and Pierre Ryckmans, who served as governor-general from 1934 to 1946, was perhaps one of the most far-sighted of the administrators, declaring at the end of his tenure that 'the days of colonialism are over' and urging Brussels to work to prepare the colony for its independence.[37]

The Belgian political establishment – narcissistic, petty and vengeful – had no intention of doing any such thing, however, and Brussels systematically denied the Congolese 'access to the more profitable sectors of the economy and to credit'.[38] The Union pour la Colonisation was founded by whites in Katanga to keep the region's political and economic power concentrated in white hands for decades to come. When the Belgian academic Jef van Bilsen set out his '30-year plan' for an independent Congo in December 1955, a Congolese political organisation, the Alliance des Bakongo (ABAKO), largely drawing its strength from the areas of western Congo where the kingdom of Kongo once reigned, responded in June 1956 with its own, far more radical, *Manifeste Conscience Africaine*. Largely the work of Joseph Iléo, the manifesto would help put ABAKO, headed by schoolteacher Joseph Kasa-Vubu, on the national political map.

One of ABAKO's chief rivals in the vanguard of the independence movement was the Mouvement National Congolais (MNC), whose driving force was a mercurial former postman and beer salesman from Kasai named Patrice Lumumba. A member of the Tetela ethnic group, Lumumba had spent much of his working life in Stanleyville, the large city located on a northern bend of the Congo River, and in Leopoldville itself. After arriving in the capital in 1957, Lumumba met Joseph-Désiré Mobutu, a former Force Publique member and journalist who would become Lumumba's aide-de-camp. In Katanga, the businessman Moïse Tshombe formed the Confédération des Associations Tribales du Katanga (CONAKAT), a political grouping that the Belgians regarded as more sympathetic to their interests.

As the movement for Congo's independence gathered steam, the world copper price plunged in 1957 and continued to fall the following year, prompting increased unemployment. During the Leopoldville Riot of 4–6 January 1959, several Europeans were attacked and the Force Publique used brutal methods to suppress the unrest, which eventually led to the deaths of at least 34 Congolese.[39] Meanwhile, infighting in the MNC led to a split, with one faction backing Lumumba and another veering off under the leadership of Albert Kalonji, a Luba nobleman who, like Lumumba, hailed from Kasai. In October of that year, more unrest hit Stanleyville, with over 20 people killed.[40] Lumumba, who was in Stanleyville at the time, was arrested shortly afterwards.

In May 1960, Lumumba's MNC won the largest number of seats for the upcoming National Assembly, with Antoine Gizenga's Parti Solidaire Africain and Kasa-Vubu's ABAKO obtaining second and third place respectively. Negotiations led to Lumumba being placed in the role of prime minister while Kasa-Vubu would serve as president, a less powerful position.

This should have been a great triumph for the country's diverse and disparate liberation movement, but instead the birth of the independent République du Congo was accomplished amid chaos, acrimony and relentless foreign interference that commenced at the very moment of the new state's birth.

At the independence ceremony on 30 June 1960, Belgium's King Baudouin delivered a speech that struck many as smug and paternalistic, referring to the criminal King Leopold as a 'genius'. Kasa-Vubu then followed with an innocuous and forgettable speech. Lumumba, for his part, although he had not been on the list of scheduled speakers, stood and delivered a rousing rebuttal, directed not at Baudouin himself but at the Congolese people, speaking of the 'indispensable struggle to put an end to the humiliating slavery which was imposed on us by force' and asking:

> Who will forget the rifle-fire from which so many of our
> brothers perished, or the jails into which were brutally thrown
> those who did not want to submit to a regime of oppression
> and exploitation, which were the means the colonialists
> employed to dominate us?[41]

He was interrupted eight times by furious applause. It was a harsh and perfectly accurate speech, and strong medicine the Belgians would have done well to take. But take it they would not.

Although the post-colonial Congolese elite 'lacked education, administrative and managerial experience and wealth', it would attempt to base 'its power on control of the state'.[42] But the Belgians would not relinquish that power so quickly, and the economy remained in the serpentine grip of the foreigners.

Trouble was not long in coming. In July 1960, General Émile Janssens (who had overseen the brutal January 1959 repression in Leopoldville), serving as the Congolese army's commander-in-chief, famously wrote on a blackboard before his local underlings

'After Independence = Before Independence', prompting a revolt that saw attacks against Europeans in Leopoldville. The revolt ended in Janssens' replacement by Victor Lundula as head of the Armée Nationale Congolaise (ANC) and the appointment of Joseph-Désiré Mobutu as the ANC's chief of staff.

With the support of the Union Minière, the slippery Belgian Prime Minister Gaston Eyskens, Foreign Minister Pierre Wigny and later Minister for African Affairs Harold d'Aspremont Lynden, Moïse Tshombe led Katanga into declaring independence from the Congolese state on 11 July 1960. Albert Kalonji would do the same, declaring South Kasai independent on 8 August. Far from being a disinterested observer as he is sometimes portrayed to have been, throughout the rest of 1960 the offended King Baudouin lauded the Tshombe regime in public and pilloried Congo's elected government.[43]

The day that Katanga seceded, Congolese and Belgian troops exchanged fire in Matadi, and unrest also gripped nearby Thysville. The following day, the Congolese government requested military assistance from the UN. On 13 July, Belgian troops occupied the Leopoldville airport and the European-populated parts of the city, which included, provocatively, the area where parliament was located.

Following UN Security Council Resolution 143 on 14 July 1960, UN Secretary-General Dag Hammarskjöld chose the Indian diplomat Rajeshwar Dayal to head the Opération des Nations Unies au Congo (ONUC), the first of several UN missions in the country. As the last Belgian troops left Leopoldville on 23 July 1960, ONUC troops arrived, though initially not deploying in Katanga, where white Belgian military personnel continued to support Tshombe's secessionist state.

The Congo government forces, however, were kept on a tight leash. Lumumba flew to the UN headquarters in New York, arriving on 24 July, and afterwards visited Washington and Ottawa and was told that all aid to Congo would go through the UN.[44]

Spurned by the West, Lumumba turned to the Soviet Union for assistance, and Soviet advisers and military equipment flooded into the country. During a reception held in Hammarskjöld's honour on 31 July, Lumumba's deputy prime minister, Antoine Gizenga, asked why, as the victims of Belgian aggression, Congo's democratic government was 'systematically and methodically disarmed while the aggressors, the Belgians, who are in our conquered country, still have their arms and all their firepower'.[45] For years, Brussels had done everything it could to cleave Katanga from Congo, and by the time of the mid-August deployment of UN troops there (after Tshombe had solidified his hold on power), the effect was to make the reunification of the country more difficult, not less, with the UN acting as a buffer between the powers in Kinshasa and Elizabethville. The ANC's re-taking of Bakwanga in the Kalonji heartland during the night of 26–27 August was very bloody and resulted in the deaths of many Luba. On 1 September – without permission from Lumumba – ANC chief Mobutu announced an end to military operations in Kasai.

Lumumba, whose relations with Kasa-Vubu were never more than cautiously cordial at the best of times, was thrown into an extraordinarily difficult situation. Many in the United States intelligence apparatus viewed Lumumba, while not a Communist himself, as a useful tool for the Soviets as they sought to expand their influence throughout Africa, and the view held by some of those at the UN was not much brighter.[46] Pierre Mulele, Lumumba's minister of education, was viewed with particular suspicion. Throughout the summer of 1960, the United States government used its contacts among Lumumba's opponents to finance demonstrations against him,[47] and the CIA explored ways to physically eliminate Lumumba by poisoning. Amid these tensions, an informal group of like-minded individuals – that is to say plotters – began to powwow among themselves about the direction in which the country was heading. Referred to as the Binza Group after the Leopoldville suburb in which most of the members lived, the group included Lumumba's Foreign Minister Justin Bomboko, the head of the new state's security service Victor Nendaka Bika and Lumumba's former aide Joseph-Désiré Mobutu. The United States made it clear to Mobutu that it would support a coup.[48]

On 5 September, Kasa-Vubu announced that he was dismissing Lumumba as prime minister. Lumumba in turn announced that he was dismissing Kasa-Vubu as president. Finally, on 14 September, Mobutu struck, going on the radio to state that he was 'neutralising' the country's politicians until the end of the year and announcing the formation of a college of commissioners to help govern the country. This college included a young Luba lawyer named Étienne Tshisekedi.[49] During a brief interim period, Joseph Iléo served as prime minister, succeeded eventually by Bomboko, Lumumba's former deputy Antoine Gizenga, Iléo again, and finally former MNC official Cyrille Adoula, who would serve until June 1964. For his part, Congo's legitimate prime minister, Lumumba, was placed under arrest at his residence, the building surrounded by one cordon of UN troops for his 'protection' and another of Congolese troops trying to prevent his escape. Gizenga eventually fled to Stanleyville where he attempted to rally nationalist forces to resist the coup. The stand-off at Lumumba's home continued until, under cover of lashing rain on the night of 27 November 1960, he escaped and headed towards Stanleyville.

Had he reached the jungle city, Lumumba could very well have rallied the nationalists. But Lumumba was delayed en route by both inclement weather and his desire to make speeches. One wonders what went through his mind as he looked out on the countryside of Congo. On 1 December, at roughly the midway point between Leopoldville and Stanleyville, he was overtaken by his pursuers at the town of Lodi. Lumumba nearly made it across the Sankuru River to the strong nationalist base on the other side when, crossing back for his family, he was seized by

ANC soldiers.[50] The UN force in nearby Mweka, apprised of Lumumba's situation by his driver, refused to offer the prime minister protection. ONUC's overall commander, General von Horn, even went so far as to issue the order that 'no action is to be taken … in respect of Lumumba'.[51]

What happened next is no less grim for being well known. Two days after being captured, Lumumba was flown back to Leopoldville where he was displayed at the airport like some sort of hunting trophy brought low in front of jeering soldiers and gawking journalists. Taken to Thysville, west of the capital, Lumumba was subsequently put on a plane to Elizabethville along with two supporters, former minister Maurice Mpolo and former vice-president of the Senate Joseph Okito. Tortured en route, at the airport he was delivered into the hands of his enemy Tshombe under the eyes of Swedish UN peacekeepers, who made no attempt to intervene.

In these events and in those that followed, a cast of characters with a direct line back to the Eyskens government in Brussels – Belgian major and Katangan gendarmerie commander Jules Loos, Mobutu adviser Louis Marlière, Belgian national and Katangan gendarme officer Gérard Soete – played their respective roles with aplomb. The three prisoners were alternately beaten by their guards and mocked by officials of Tshombe's government, and, on the evening of 17 January, Lumumba, Mpolo and Okito were taken to a remote, swampy area. At least two Belgians – police commissioner Frans Verscheure and Captain Julien Gat – were present along with assorted police and soldiers as well as Tshombe himself and several members of his cabinet. The men were shot one at a time, and their bodies buried. The bodies were later dug up, dismembered, burned and then dissolved in acid by two Belgian soldiers.[52] In a documentary filmed about the murder four decades later, one of the Belgians most closely associated with the crime, Gérard Soete, proudly displayed a pair of Lumumba's teeth that he had saved. Lumumba's daughter,

Juliana, who would go on to serve as minister of culture in the government of Joseph Kabila, later stated that 'this image recalls the Holocaust ... Their bodies were burnt, their body fat was used as fertilizer, their gold teeth were taken as war booty. That's called a crime against humanity.'[53]

Lumumba, the figure who more than any other single person symbolised Congo's independence and its refutation of foreign domination, was dead. Shortly before his murder, he had managed to smuggle a letter out to his family, in which he tried to explain his motives, stating that 'what we wanted for our country, its right to an honourable life, to a spotless dignity, to independence without restrictions, was never desired by the Belgian imperialists and their Western allies'. It went on:

> Dead or alive, free or in prison on the orders of the colonial-
> ists, it is not myself that counts. It is the Congo, it is our poor
> people, whose independence has been transformed into a cage,
> from whose confines the outside world looks on us ... To my
> children whom I leave and whom I may never see again, I
> would like them to be told that it is for them, as it is for every
> Congolese, to accomplish the sacred task of reconstructing our
> independence and our sovereignty, for without dignity there
> is no liberty, without justice there is no dignity, and without
> independence there are no free men.[54]

The murder of Lumumba hardly brought a halt to the chaos in Congo. By early 1961, Mobutu and his civilian allies controlled the western part of the country, Tshombe and his Belgian mercenaries (some led by the Frenchman Bob Denard and known as Les Affreux or the Dreadful Ones) controlled Katanga in the south, Albert Kalonji lorded over South Kasai, and Antoine Gizenga and the Lumumbaists controlled Stanleyville.

By late August 1961, ONUC launched Operation Rumpunch, a mission designed to disarm Katanga troops and arrest foreign mercenaries, but its success was largely scuttled by Belgian inter-ference. In September 1961, the UN launched Operation Morthor, which had the same objective, but it also proved ineffective. That same month, Dag Hammarskjöld was killed when the plane he was travelling in went down near the Rhodesian border; he was succeeded in his post at the UN by the Burmese diplomat U Thant. By the end of the year, a re-emboldened ANC reinvaded South Kasai and arrested Albert Kalonji, putting an end to the secession there.

Kasa-Vubu continued to preside over a series of weak govern-ments, with Mobutu largely pulling the strings behind the scenes, until finally, in late December 1962/January 1963, ONUC's Operation Grand Slam succeeded in ending the Katanga seces-sion. Moïse Tshombe fled to Rhodesia and, eventually, Spain. After tortuous negotiations, Kasa-Vubu succeeded in convincing Tshombe to return to Congo and take up the post of prime minister in a coalition government in July 1964.

Although Tshombe was now inside the government, Lum-umba's followers were far from neutralised. Lumumbaist rebels led by several former government ministers, including Pierre Mulele and Christophe Gbenye, seized nearly half the country as well as Stanleyville during mid- to late 1964. In the latter success, the ANC fled from the rebels, who then seized several hundred foreign hostages. The rebels were referred to as Simbas, from the Swahili word for lion.

The ANC, fighting with white foreign mercenaries led by the Irish soldier of fortune Mike Hoare, worked hard to dislodge the Simbas from the territory they controlled. Stanleyville itself fell on 24 November 1964 to Belgian troops operating with US air support.[55] Many dozens of the hostages were killed and most of the rebel leaders fled. Among those who had participated in the Simba rebellion was a young rebel leader named Laurent Kabila. Born in Jadotville (later called Likasi) in northern Katanga in 1939, Kabila's own father would be killed in the uprising and, throughout 1965, his forces in the east of the country would continue to do battle with Hoare's mercenaries. Despite the presence of the Argentina-born Cuban revolutionary Ernesto 'Che' Guevara in their ranks, Kabila's forces were routed and withdrew to a heavily forested portion of South Kivu.

The relationship between Tshombe and Kasa-Vubu remained as poisonous as it had ever been, with each seeking to undermine and gain political advantage over the other. Kasa-Vubu dismissed Tshombe as prime minister, in an echo of his earlier dismissal of Lumumba. Mobutu, sensing the time was ripe to act, met with 14 members of the army high command in Kinshasa in late November 1965 to decide upon another coup.[56] On 25 November, Mobutu struck for a second time, ousting Kasa-Vubu and declaring himself president.

A new era had begun.

2 | FIRE IN HIS WAKE

The rise and decline of Joseph-Désiré Mobutu

The man who led the coup, and who had been directing the action behind the scenes since 1960, was a curious character. Born in 1930 in Lisala in Équateur province in the north-western part of the country, Mobutu was an ethnic Ngbandi, a group that spills across the border between northern Congo and the southern Central African Republic. His father had passed away when he was quite young, and his mother had eventually sent him to Coquilhatville (present-day Mbandaka), a city on the banks of the Congo River, for his education at a Catholic boarding school run by Flemish Belgian priests. At around the age of 19, he was enrolled in the Force Publique after having been expelled from school for spending a three-week break carousing (against the rather puritanical school policy) in Leopoldville.[1] Like the Haitian dictator François Duvalier, in his early years Mobutu authored pseudonymous articles (against Force Publique regulations) that would eventually, once he left the army in 1956, earn him full-time work as an editor with two Congolese newspapers.[2] His life in the capital would put him in touch with Lumumba and eventually see him back in the fold of the new Congolese army.

Given his garish later public persona, it is hard now to imagine Mobutu as he was in those early years, an alternately flattering and grave military officer in a country that was in a constant state of violence and upheaval. It is tempting to invest his role at the outset of his career with the omnipotence that would come later. But, at the beginning, he was simply one of a number of bright, ambitious potential leaders who appeared in Congo's post-independence political firmament, and his success was by no means assured. Mobutu's rivals may have been just as ruthless, but none was as canny in playing off potential enemies and patrons against one another, and in securing what he needed from each of them, fitting together the complex ethno-political jigsaw that would finally lead to supreme power. Also, despite his many other flaws, Mobutu did, at least in the early years, display considerable bravery, personally confronting bands of mutinous soldiers on several occasions.[3]

Mobutu would rule Congo for 32 years, longer than Leopold or any other ruler. His impact, and the template for divide-and-rule governance he set up, would define Congo for many years to come. During his long tenure, he charted an idiosyncratic course, alternating between a not-entirely-convincing pan-Africanism and a cynical courting of both Western and Communist bloc powers. Suffused through it all was a cult of personality to rival anything Africa had seen before or since.

The coup was initially welcomed by many Congolese exhausted by five years of interminable political strife and violence.[4] On 28 November, Mobutu declared that, as 'it took five years for the politicians to lead the country to its ruin', political party activity would be suspended for five years.[5]

The following two years were pivotal for Congo. Mobutu's forces would crush two mutinies of varying pro-Tshombe colourations in Kisangani. In April 1966, Mobutu reduced Congo's provinces from 21 to 12; by December he would reduce them still more from 12 to 8, further centralising state control. In June, in the first display of the kind of ruthlessness that would come to define the regime, and which would lead to Mobutu being referred to as Bula Matari ('Breaker of Rocks', a sobriquet first applied to Henry Morton Stanley), four former cabinet ministers were tried for treason, convicted and then publicly hanged.

Over the course of the next year, Mobutu's nationalisation drive, which foreign powers may have thought they had derailed with the assassination of Lumumba, saw its first flowering. The Société des Mines d'Or de Kilo-Moto (SOKIMO), which had worked the gold fields of Ituri and Haut-Uélé, became the Office des Mines d'Or de Kilo-Moto (OKIMO). The Union Minière was reconfigured to create a massive state-owned mining enterprise, the Générale des Carrières et des Mines (Gécamines). The *loi Bakajika* land measure – the fount of so much conflict in the future – was also enacted that year. The following year, in March and May respectively, Mobutu oversaw the dissolution of Congo's parliament (parliament would not sit again until 1970) and the formation of the Mouvement Populaire de la Révolution (MPR), a political entity designed to shore up his regime and in which all Congolese would automatically become members. The same year, the state subsumed trade unions into a single, government-controlled body. In June 1967, a referendum was held on a new constitution establishing a presidential system and a one-chamber legislature, limiting the number of political parties and giving women the vote. It passed not solely due to fraud.[6]

After this triumph, Mobutu succeeded in luring one of his chief rivals, Lumumba's former minister of education and the former Simba leader Pierre Mulele, back to Congo from exile in Brazzaville with a promise of amnesty. Upon arrival, Mulele was tortured, convicted of treason and executed.

By 1969, Mobutu could look with satisfaction on the deaths of his two last remaining major rivals when Joseph Kasa-Vubu died in March and Moïse Tshombe, who had been held in an Algerian prison since June 1967, died in his cell in mysterious circumstances in June. As perhaps befitted a man who had done so much to aid the foreign agenda in Congo, Tshombe was buried in Belgium.

Nor was it only the powerful who felt the sharp end of Bula Matari. On 4 June 1969, Mobutu's security services opened fire on a demonstration by university students in Kinshasa, killing a number of people. Following the incident, many student leaders were arrested and the government-aligned Jeunesse du Mouvement Populaire de la Révolution (JMPR) was declared the nation's only legal student group.[7] The same year, seeking to further tighten his grip on the country, Mobutu created the Centre Nationale de Documentation (CND), his successor to Belgium's pre-independence Sûreté Nationale. In the years that followed, the CND would become an organ of state repression that would routinely imprison, torture and kill dissenting citizens.

As the new decade dawned, Mobutu's power over the country seemed ever ascendant, to such a degree that, with bitterly ironic symbolism, Belgium's King Baudouin returned for the June 1970 tenth anniversary of Congo's independence. It was his first visit since his hectoring speech and Lumumba's fiery rebuttal of 1960. In August, Mobutu was fêted at the White House by US President Richard Nixon.

In April 1971, Mobutu announced the launch of *authenticité*, a campaign that he said would help link Congo to its historical, pre-colonial past and bind the country together in a single national identity. By October, both the nation itself and its namesake river had been renamed Zaire, after a Portuguese corruption of the Kikongo word *nzere*, meaning 'the river that swallows all rivers'. Mobutu announced that henceforth all Christian first names would be shunned, and to set an example changed his own name from Joseph-Désiré Mobutu to Mobutu Sese Seko Kuku Ngbendu Wa Za Banga ('the all-powerful warrior who, because of endurance and inflexible will to win, goes from conquest to conquest, leaving fire in his wake'). Zaire's provinces were also renamed, with Katanga, for example, becoming Shaba. The Congolese military became the Forces Armées Zaïroises (FAZ). In the future, the government would outlaw all ethnic associations.[8]

William T. Close, an American surgeon (and father of the actress Glenn Close) who ran the Mama Yemo Hospital in Kinshasa (named after Mobutu's mother) from 1968 until 1977 and served as Mobutu's personal physician, came to know Mobutu well. Close remarked that, when they first met in 1960, Mobutu was a man of immense charm but concluded that, by the early 1970s, the dictator had grown increasingly megalomaniacal and 'could not admit error, and doubt played no part in his thinking'.[9]

This period also marked the ascendancy of Barthélémy Bisengimana, a Rwandan Tutsi who would serve as a Mobutu adviser from 1967 to 1977. Bisengimana was instrumental in helping to craft a 1971 law granting Zairian citizenship to all Rwandans and Burundians who had been in Congo since 1960, an act that contributed to the Rwandaphone communities, in North Kivu especially, coming to symbolise for some locals something of a loathed elite.[10]

Following his announcement of *authenticité*, Mobutu began espousing what was perceived as a more 'radical', though still opportunistic, rhetoric of pan-Africanism. In January 1973, he was received by Mao Zedong during a visit to China and received a US$100 million credit line for rural development.[11] In October of that year, Mobutu announced Zaire's decision to break off diplomatic relations with Israel at the United Nations, telling the assembled diplomats that 'between a brother and a friend, the choice is clear'. (Though not, as it happened, eternal, as relations between the two countries were restored in 1982.) The next month, it was announced that *authenticité* would enter a new phase, that of Zairisation.[12] Mobutu's attempt to reshape the country was also evidenced by the passage of the General Property Law of 1973, after which Banyarwanda in the Kivus bought off 'large chunks of land, especially in Masisi and Rutshuru' in murky circumstances.[13]

By the end of 1973, the more narcissistic aspects of Mobutu's personality had come to the fore and he strode across the country as an absolute monarch. By then, Mobutu had developed an impressive cult of personality centred around himself and full of the usual praise songs, synchronised dancing and pageantry.[14] Although he had, since 1965, largely succeeded in quelling the rebellions that had plagued the nation post-independence, this had come at the cost of the advent of a deformed and rapacious autocracy. Mobutu revised the 1967 constitution in 1974 so that the president of the MPR – Mobutu – became the president of the republic. It was again reiterated that membership in the MPR itself was compulsory, as was 'support of the revolution'. Mobutu's lavish egotism was bankrolled to a large degree by high copper prices between 1967 and early 1974 and the fact that, along with copper, for many years Zaire was the world's leading producer of cobalt. (When the bottom fell out of the cobalt market in 1978, the development hit the Zairian economy hard.) Until 1980, Zaire was also the world's largest germanium producer, with the Kipushi deposit operating at full capacity.[15]

The American author Norman Mailer, who visited Kinshasa in 1974 to witness the boxer Muhammad Ali's historic defeat of George Foreman during their famous 'Rumble in the Jungle', found Mobutu's person so inextricably entwined with the state that it was 'like a snake around a stick'.[16] With Mobutu always portraying himself as a 'father' to his people, the role of 'mother' alternated between his first wife, the jarringly named Marie-Antoinette, and his mother, Marie Madeleine 'Mama' Yemo. The regime adopted some of Lumumba's rhetoric and symbols (five years after Lumumba's assassination, Mobutu made him a national hero) while declining to act on Lumumba's more radical policies. For all the pomp and symbolism, very few of the benefits accrued from these high mineral prices filtered down to the Zairian people, and, as the 1970s dragged on, Mobutu himself became ever more distant and dissolute.

Neither the inadequacy of wages relative to prices nor the size of its parallel economy was unique to Zaire by the African standards of the time. What was, however, unique was the enormous ineffectiveness of the state in providing the sort of basic institutions – administration, judiciary, public services – that most countries take for granted as their responsibility in order to be conferred with a semblance of legitimacy.[17] The vast parallel economy in Zaire came to be known as Système D.

Although Mobutu lavished attention on the jungle outpost of Gbadolite – building a palace there and a runway capable of landing large jet aircraft – elsewhere in his native Équateur the rural poor lived in squalor and desperation similar to their countrymen in the Kivus and Kasai.[18] Amid the rhetoric of empowerment surrounding Zairisation (a process that one analysis referred to as 'an exceptional opportunity for enlarging the wealth of the politico-commercial class' via an 'astonishing frenzy of predatory expropriation'[19]), a term was even coined – *acquéreur* – to describe those who benefited from the process. It was not a term of noble praise.

By the middle of the decade, Mobutu's efforts to indigenise Zaire's industries were plunged into crisis through greed and mismanagement, most of it coming from within his own ruling clique. The economic downturn of 1974–75 hit Zaire brutally and, by late 1975, Zairisation was generally accepted to be a failure. In 1976, several Belgian mining firms merged to form the Société Minière du Kivu (Sominki), focusing on gold, cassiterite and coltan in the eastern provinces of the same name.[20] During the late 1970s, Mobutu was allowing foreign investors to run Gécamines' state-owned mines, and the ailing state was propped up by sputtering mineral revenues and foreign aid. By the late 1970s, Zaire was receiving nearly half of all the aid money the administration of US President Jimmy Carter allocated for sub-Saharan Africa.[21] Mobutu himself even felt the need to address the state's predatory nature in a 1977 speech during which he referred to corruption as *le mal zaïrois* (the Zairian sickness).

Zaire also received this aid despite an increasingly appalling human rights record. Throughout the 1970s it had become evident that the real job of entities such as the FAZ, the CND and the JMPR was to 'foster and maintain a pervasive climate of fear'.[22] Mass killings of regime opponents became ever more common.

Perhaps no single individual's career encapsulated the vagaries of Mobutuism more than that of Jean Nguza Karl-i-Bond. A Lunda from Katanga, Nguza had served as Mobutu's foreign minister from 1972 until 1974 and again from 1976 until 1977, as well as serving as the political director of the MPR. He fell out badly with Mobutu at the end of his second tenure as foreign minister, however, and was arrested, tortured and sentenced to death. He was freed a year later only to again become foreign minister and then prime minister until he fled into exile in 1981, at which point he testified in front of the US House of Representatives subcommittee on Africa, describing the situation of domestic terror among the regime's opponents within Zaire.[23] After an interim period in Belgium (during which he wrote a book about the Mobutu regime), somewhat unbelievably, he returned to Kinshasa, serving as Mobutu's ambassador to Washington. Such sadomasochistic patterns in the relationships between Mobutu and his ostensible supporters were by no means unique.

The state's general weakness was on dispiriting display during two invasions of Katanga (Shaba) from Angola in 1977 and 1978. Ever desirous of playing regional kingmaker, Mobutu had backed the losing side in the Angolan civil war, supporting the Frente Nacional de Libertação de Angola (FNLA) and the União Nacional para a Independência Total de Angola (UNITA) against Agostinho Neto's Movimento Popular de Libertação de Angola (MPLA). Once he came to power, to repay the favour, Neto was more than happy to play host to the Front National pour la Libération du Congo (FNLC), a group largely made up of former Tshombe gendarmes. The FNLC invaded Shaba in March 1977, and Mobutu succeeded in beating them back only with the aid of Moroccan troops and French aircraft. When the FNLC invaded again in May 1978 (killing many civilians in the city of Kolwezi), it was the turn of French and Belgian mercenaries to defend the government.

With the FAZ, Mobutu had created a system based not on

competence but on mutual dependency and complicity. The Shaba invasions revealed the FAZ for what it was, a tool of internal repression, not external defence. To add insult to injury for the long-suffering Zairian people, in December 1977 Mobutu staged farcical presidential elections in which he ran as the only candidate and in which the only choice was a vote of 'yes' or 'no'. State media trumpeted their master's 98.2 per cent favourable vote.

Following the Shaba debacle, the last significant pocket of resistance to Mobutuist hegemony was in the territory of Fizi in South Kivu province. Here, the former Lumumbaist rebel Laurent Kabila (as it happened, himself a Katangan Luba with whom the FNLC never bothered to co-ordinate) ruled over a dystopian fiefdom in, if not exactly harmony, then a modus vivendi with government forces sent to crush him. Beginning in 1967, Kabila and his Parti de la Révolution du Peuple (PRP) had created a state within a state marked by Maoist doctrine in rhetoric and brigandage in practice.[24] The PRP had few relations with the domestic opposition in Zaire, and, following Mobutu's 1973 visit to China, the PRP lost its main source of external funding. The military branch of the PRP, the Forces Armées Populaires (FAP), had shown itself to be neither very popular nor much of a fighting force. While his forces smuggled gold and ivory out of South Kivu, Kabila himself spent much of his time in Tanzania and Uganda, briefly earning notoriety when his forces kidnapped three Americans and one Dutch researcher and held them for ransom.

Slouching towards the abyss

By 1980, the state was in crisis. After 15 years of near-absolute power, Mobutu could look around a Zaire in which the signs of rot were strong. By the early 1980s, at the vaunted Mama Yemo Hospital in the capital, foreign journalists witnessed patients dying for lack of bandages, sterilisation equipment, oxygen and X-ray machines.[25] Even as his personal link to *le mal zaïrois* became more pronounced, Mobutu received a friendly hearing by world leaders such as US President Ronald Reagan and French Presidents Valéry Giscard d'Estaing and François Mitterrand. His period of radicalism long since eschewed, the dictator was welcomed back into the fold of reliable anti-Communist leaders.

In Zaire itself, however, many were deciding that enough was enough. An opposition movement, the Union pour la Démocratie et le Progrès Social (UDPS) was founded in 1982 by a diverse group of dissenters both from within and outside the Mobutuist political process. These included Étienne Tshisekedi, the Luba politician from Kasai who had briefly served on Mobutu's college of commissioners following the removal of Lumumba, and Frédéric Kibassa Maliba, who had served as a deputy in Zaire's parliament and then as the State Commissioner for Sports and Recreation.[26]

In November of that same year, Mobutu announced that he was appointing Léon Kengo Wa Dondo as prime minister. Born Leon Lubicz in 1935 to a Polish Jewish father and a Rwandan Tutsi mother, Kengo had changed his name during Mobutu's *authenticité* campaign. Conversely, in 1981, Mobutu rewrote the 1971 citizenship law, making proof of familial lineage in Zaire back to 1885 the new benchmark for the Rwandaphone peoples of the Kivus. By this point, both North and South Kivu had become 'densely populated and ethnically fragmented provinces'.[27]

A brief occupation of the town of Moba by Kabila's FAP in November 1984 led to ghastly reprisals against civilians by the FAZ. By 1985, Sominki was largely moribund in the Kivus,[28] and by the middle of the decade the army had sold off much of its best weaponry and equipment as the clique of commanding officers became a textbook example of corrupt entrepreneurialism.

Sensing that the disintegration of the armed forces might have no small impact on his longevity, in 1985 Mobutu created another elite military force responsible for his personal security. The force, which would become the Division Spéciale Présidentielle (DSP), was trained by Israeli security experts, and would later be headed by Mobutu's much-feared son, Kongulo, whose nickname – Saddam Hussein – spoke for itself.[29] Yet another security service, the Service National d'Intelligence et de Protection (whose acronym, SNIP, was the subject of much hilarity) would also be formed.

No one captured the *douleur* and absurdity of living in Mobutu's Congo during this period better than author and playwright Sony Labou Tansi, a native son despite his long residence in Brazzaville across the river. In novels such as *L'anté-peuple* (1983) and *Les sept solitudes de Lorsa Lopez* (1985), Tansi drew a vivid picture of a land overtaken by violence and despair. In perhaps his masterpiece, the 1981 play *La parenthèse de sang*, Tansi sketched a brilliant satire of tyranny in microcosm as a group of ruthless and ignorant soldiers search for a rebel leader who is already dead.

The Third Republic: old wine in a new bottle

During the year 1990, the process of Zaire's decomposition accelerated rapidly. Beginning in January, Mobutu commenced a two-month tour of the entire country, and in April he declared a 'Third Republic', one that would allow activity by political parties other than the MPR.

As he had often been, Mobutu proved to be ahead of the curve. Two months later, French President François Mitterrand hosted a Franco-African summit in La Baule, France, at which he suggested to the African leaders present that further aid would be tied to at least cosmetic attempts at democratisation. But, Mobutu being Mobutu, it was perhaps not ironic that, after the legalisation of opposition political parties, the human rights situation in Zaire began to decline precipitously. If there was to be an opening of the political process, the Mobutuist forces decided that first the opposition must be crushed with all the subtlety of an anvil, and Zaire witnessed 'the use of automatic firearms and other lethal weapons, such as bombs, against largely unarmed civilians'.[30]

Signs of decay were everywhere. By 1990, inflation in Zaire was running at 233 per cent (up from 56 per cent in 1989).[31] That same year, the vast Kamoto cobalt and copper mine in Katanga collapsed after years of state neglect. Although Mobutu was ostensibly 'opening up' Zaire's political process (he had little choice following the collapse of the Soviet Union and the withdrawal of his favourite trump card to play against the West), repression in Zaire, if anything, got worse.

In April 1991, in Mbuji-Mayi in southern Kasai-Oriental province, government troops killed at least nine people when they fired on UDPS activists protesting about the behaviour of security forces.[32] In May, after their campus was surrounded by security forces, students protesting against what they saw as government infiltration of the University of Lubumbashi were the victims of an appalling massacre in which many dozens died. The attack had a marked ethnic dimension, as many of the DSP personnel were Ngbandis, while many of those killed came from Kasai, the Kivus or Katanga.[33]

After a tense spring and early summer, the Conférence Nationale Souveraine (CNS) convened in early August 1991 to discuss the fate of the nation. During its first weeks, some 2,850 delegates from 200 political parties drew up both the terms of transition to democracy and a draft constitution.[34]

But the security situation in the country was becoming more and more volatile. In late September, the 31st brigade of the FAZ mutinied, and roiling violence and widespread looting consumed Kinshasa and other cities. More than 200 people were killed.[35] Despite Mobutu's televised address ordering the soldiers back to their barracks, to this day there is much suspicion in Kinshasa that the president had a hand in at least allowing the looting to 'punish' the *Kinois* (residents of Kinshasa) for their support of the opposition.

Amid the rioting, the CNS was suspended, but, by the end of September, Mobutu consented to accept Étienne Tshisekedi of the UDPS as prime minister. Tshisekedi was finally sworn in in mid-October, commencing a working relationship that lasted less than a month and saw Tshisekedi replaced at the beginning of November by Bernardin Mungul Diaka and then, in quick succession, by Mobutu's lackey Jean Nguza Karl-i-Bond. Further complicating the situation, by 1991 the UDPS had split into two parties with one led by Tshisekedi and the other headed by Kibassa Maliba.[36]

After being shuttered for a time, in early December the CNS resumed. On 4 December 1991, Mobutu's term in office was supposed to come to an end, but the president refused to leave. A *journée ville morte* – a general strike – was called in the capital for 7 December, a call to which the population generally adhered, but which had little effect.

By 1992, the lack of Mobutu's seriousness to open up Zaire's political system in any meaningful way became obvious. On 14 January, the CNS was again suspended, provoking yet another crisis. That same month, Jean-Marie Katonga Kabuluku, a former UDPS member of the National Assembly, was kidnapped, never to be seen again, and, in Kinshasa, 37 people were killed when soldiers attacked a demonstration calling for a resumption of the CNS.[37] On 16 February, various Christian denominations, but most prominently the Catholic church, staged a *marche d'espoir* (march of hope) through Kinshasa which ended when state security forces attacked the crowd and killed several dozen people.

The summer dragged on sullenly, but finally, in mid-August 1992, Mobutu replaced Prime Minister Jean Nguza Karl-i-Bond (a Lunda from Katanga, after all) with Étienne Tshisekedi (a Luba), prompting violent outbreaks in Shaba as Lunda attacked Luba, with at least 500 people killed and over 100,000 displaced.[38] Over the next year, the Katanga purges – as Mobutu stirred the ethnic pot against Tshisekedi – would kill at least 5,000 people and drive 1.3 million from their homes. Far from keeping order, the security forces only served to further terrorise the population. A December 1992 bout of looting by soldiers in Kisangani killed at least 50 people.[39]

As 1993 wore on, outbreaks of violence, both within the cities and among the country's various ethnic groups, were becoming ever more frequent. In January 1993, another explosion of looting by troops killed nearly 1,000 people in the capital. Among those slain was Berthos Kibassa, the son of UDPS leader Kibassa Maliba, killed when soldiers attacked his father's home.[40] Another bout of looting took place in the capital from 28 January until 2 February 1993, during which the French Ambassador Philippe Bernard was killed by gunfire.

On the other side of the country, beginning in March 1993 and with the encouragement of local officials, Nyanga, Nande and Hunde attacked Banyarwanda in North Kivu in assaults that lasted several days, with the violence spreading northwards from Walikale to Rutshuru. By June 1993, at least 3,000 people, the majority of them Banyarwanda, had been killed and 200,000 displaced.[41] Unfortunately, the issue of Banyarwanda and Banyamulenge was not addressed in any substantive way during the CNS.

As 1994 dawned, developments in Zaire itself, particularly in the east, gave the country's citizens plenty of cause to be worried. Adding to the tension was the fact that, however anarchically Zaire was (mis)governed, most of its neighbours, many of which would play decisive roles in its coming conflict, were in little better shape.

To Zaire's south, Angola had been in a nearly continuous state of war since a nationalist independence movement against the Portuguese had begun in 1961. By 1994 the country was immersed in a ghastly round of siege fighting as UNITA rebels – with financial and military support from apartheid-era South Africa and the United States – encircled and bombarded towns and cities. President José Eduardo dos Santos, in office since 1979, financed the government's side of the war with oil exports, while

UNITA's bizarre and enigmatic leader Jonas Savimbi bankrolled its part in the conflict through diamond smuggling.[42]

Across the river from Kinshasa in the neighbouring Republic of Congo (Congo-Brazzaville), Denis Sassou Nguesso, a French-trained army colonel,[43] ruled as a military dictator and tropical Marxist from 1979 until 1992. Multiparty elections saw Nguesso's Parti Congolais du Travail go down in defeat to the Union Panafricaine pour la Démocratie Sociale of Pascal Lissouba, a former prime minister. Nguesso, who hailed from the Mbochi ethnic group in the country's north, was replaced by Lissouba, a southerner. Lissouba had also defeated another relentlessly ambitious politician, Brazzaville mayor Bernard Kolélas, who had founded the Mouvement Congolais pour la Démocratie et le Développement Intégral (MCDDI). Following Lissouba's dissolution of Brazzaville's parliament in November 1992, new elections were held in May 1993, the results of which sparked widespread violence. After a brief pause, vicious bouts of ethnic warfare would follow, and the Angolan army invaded the country to support Nguesso, who would succeed in ousting Lissouba in October. Like his patron dos Santos, Nguesso would soon transform himself into an enthusiastic capitalist and would continue to rule the country into the twenty-first century.

Near Mobutu's birthplace, the Central African Republic, or Centrafrique (CAR), a former French colonial territory, was also marked by widespread forced labour and often outright slavery during French colonial rule. Barthélemy Boganda, the gifted son of rural farmers and a former Catholic priest, became the CAR's first prime minister but died in a mysterious plane explosion in March 1959. He was succeeded by David Dacko, a schoolteacher who became the CAR's first president and helped usher the country to full independence from France in August 1960. Dacko governed until he was overthrown in a coup by the French-trained General Jean-Bédel Bokassa. A recipient of the Croix de Guerre who saw combat alongside French forces in

Indochina, Bokassa would go on to become one of Africa's most garish and notorious tyrants, enjoying close relations with French President Valéry Giscard d'Estaing even as he crowned himself as the CAR's 'emperor' in a lavish December 1977 ceremony. After a tenure marked by bizarre excess, Bokassa was overthrown with the connivance of his former French patrons in September 1979, and Dacko was restored for another two years before being overthrown in September 1981 by General André Kolingba. Elections 12 years later were won by Ange-Félix Patassé, who had served as a minister under both Bokassa and Dacko, and whose decade-long rule was also marked by chaos and corruption.

The vast Sudan – the largest country in Africa – had been run by the Islamist military Revolutionary Command Council for National Salvation since a 1989 military coup. In October 1993, the Council's leader, a colonel in the Sudanese military named Omar al-Bashir, proclaimed himself president. Al-Bashir's strategic alliance with Hassan al-Turabi, an Islamist intellectual who had studied in London and Paris, resulted in a government of a muscular Islamic character that began to impose sharia law on the country and banned political parties. The al-Bashir and al-Turabi duopoly would also continue to prosecute a scorched-earth war against the Sudan People's Liberation Army (SPLA) in southern Sudan near the Ugandan and Zairian borders.[44] When al-Turabi advocated curbing al-Bashir's powers, he found himself increasingly marginalised. During the mid-1990s, the al-Bashir government would also become the most important foreign backer of the Ugandan rebel group the Lord's Resistance Army (LRA).[45]

To the east of South Kivu lay Burundi, where a series of brutal Tutsi minority military regimes lorded over a miserable mass of dispossessed and disenfranchised Hutus. Prince Louis Rwagasore, the son of a Tutsi king, founded the Union pour le Progrès National in 1958, and was a unifying figure in the country's pre-independence politics until he was assassinated in October 1961 by a Greek national, the culmination of a plot of which 'it is reasonable to assume that certain Belgian functionaries actively encouraged'.[46] The country became independent the following year.

In 1966 a Tutsi army officer named Michel Micombero overthrew the monarchy and proclaimed himself president of Burundi. A thuggish character driven by his concept of realpolitik, between April and June 1972, Micombero led a government that oversaw the killing of at least 100,000 Hutu civilians. A decade later Micombero himself was overthrown by another army officer, Jean-Baptiste Bagaza, who in turn was overthrown in yet another military coup, this time led by Major Pierre Buyoya. Hutu oppositionists formed the clandestine Parti pour la Libération du Peuple Hutu (PALIPEHUTU), which would grow into the Forces Nationales de Libération (FNL) rebel group. PALIPEHUTU activists attacked army installations in 1990, leading to blanket reprisals against Hutus by the army.[47]

Buyoya allowed democratic elections to take place in 1993, elections in which the Hutu-aligned Front pour la Démocratie au Burundi (FRODEBU) won a majority in the country's parliament. Melchior Ndadaye, a Hutu, became the country's president, only a week after a coup attempt by a mutinous Tutsi army officer had been put down. The détente was short-lived, however, and on 21 October, soldiers from Burundi's Tutsi-dominated army killed Ndadaye along with the president and vice-president of the National Assembly. Ndadaye was succeeded by FRODEBU's Cyprien Ntaryamira, also a Hutu, but Burundi had already toppled over into the civil war that would ravage the country for much of the next decade. A subsequent United Nations panel characterised the attacks against the Tutsi in Burundi by vengeful Hutu during October 1993 as 'acts of genocide',[48] and tit-for-tat violence in the coming years would drive nearly a million Hutu refugees to Tanzania, Zaire and Rwanda.

Perhaps the most stable of the lot at its core, despite also being riven by war, Uganda had been headed by Yoweri Museveni since January 1986, his National Resistance Army having driven dictator Milton Obote from power six months earlier.

Although a semblance of a functioning state existed in the southern half of the country, upon taking power, Museveni launched a brutal search-and-destroy mission against former government soldiers throughout northern Uganda. Although Obote himself was a Lango, the Acholi – an ethnic group that spills across the borders of Uganda and Sudan – had been particularly heavily represented in his government's army. Some Acholi mobilised to defend themselves, first under the banner of the Uganda People's Democratic Army (largely made up of former soldiers) and then the Holy Spirit Movement, directed by Alice Auma, an Acholi who claimed to be acting on guidance from the spirit Lakwena. Holy Spirit Movement combatants succeeded in reaching Jinja, just 80 kilometres from the capital Kampala, before being decimated by Museveni's forces in November 1987.

And then there was Rwanda.

Significantly, in both his drive to oust Obote and the Bush War against regime remnants that followed, Ugandan President Museveni's forces had been aided by vast numbers of Tutsi exiles from Rwanda and a not insubstantial contingent of child soldiers (the latter referred to throughout central Africa by the Swahili word *kadogo*). Among the Rwandans backing Museveni were Paul Kagame, who served as the Ugandan president's head of military intelligence, and Fred Rwigema, who would become chief of staff of the Ugandan army and minister of defence.[49] The pair had been the prime movers behind the formation of the Rwandan Patriotic Front (RPF), a rebel movement that invaded Rwanda from Uganda in October 1990 and sought to drive its Hutu dictator Juvénal Habyarimana from power.

Tiny Rwanda had been ruled by various Tutsi monarchies since some time in the fifteenth century, although initially, as in Burundi, the division between Hutu and Tutsi was not as stark as it was presented to be (and later became), and Rwanda's vaunted royal armies contained many Hutu soldiers.[50] Like the rest of Africa, though, Rwanda could not escape the gaze of the European colonisers for long, and by 1890 it was part of Deutsch-Ostafrika (German East Africa) along with Burundi and Tanganyika (present-day Tanzania). The monarch Yuhi V collaborated with the German government to strengthen his own kingship, and shrewdly saw the Europeans as an arrow to place in his quiver.[51]

The Germans had a light, almost theoretical, presence in Rwanda from 1897 until 1916, and as late as 1914 there were only 96 Europeans living in the entire country.[52] Following the Belgian military conquest of 1916, under Belgian supervision the Tutsi monarchy seized traditional Hutu landholdings, thus significantly impoverishing a population whose main mode of existence was subsistence farming.[53] Unlike his relationship with Berlin, Yuhi V's relations with Brussels were dismal, and Belgian hostility eventually culminated in a Belgian-engineered palace coup that put Yuhi V's son, the nearly 7-foot tall and wisp-thin Mutara III, in his place. Mutara obligingly converted to Catholicism but was viewed as so dominated by his foreign masters that Rwandans derisively referred to him as *Mwami w'abazungu* (King of the Whites).[54] He would act as a figurehead for Belgian rule of the country until he died of an undetermined ailment en route back from Burundi in July 1959. To this day, many Rwandans still believe he was murdered as part of a colonial plot.[55]

A January 1961 revolt toppled the monarchy and would eventually bring the Hutu politician Grégoire Kayibanda and his Parti du Mouvement de l'Emancipation Hutu (Parmehutu) to power following independence in July 1962. Concluding that the Tutsi were not sufficiently co-operative for their designs, the Belgians simply switched their allegiance to the newly ascendant Hutus, and began replacing Tutsi officials with Hutu ones in a breathtaking display of political cynicism and expediency. A Hutu elite seized power from a Tutsi elite, leaving the vast majority of

Rwandans – both Tutsi and Hutu – still disenfranchised from any sort of representative political system.

When a December 1963 Tutsi invasion from Burundi failed, an estimated 10,000 Tutsis were slain in the government-sanctioned collective punishment that followed, including virtually every Tutsi politician who had remained in Rwanda after independence.[56] Kayibanda presided over another pogrom against the Tutsi in an effort to reinvigorate his waning power in May–June 1973.

In July 1973, growing tensions between Kayibanda's clique of southerners and Hutus from Rwanda's north led to Kayibanda's overthrow by Juvénal Habyarimana, the Hutu chief of staff of the Forces Armées Rwandaises (FAR). Habyarimana, who enjoyed a conspicuously close relationship with Mobutu, established the Hutu-supremacist Mouvement Révolutionaire National pour le Développement (MRND) as the country's sole legal political party. Kayibanda was subsequently to die in prison in 1976 after likely being starved to death by his jailers. The regime would prove to be a durable one, with Habyarimana and his supporters ruling over Tutsi and Hutu peasants alike in a kind of fascism with a monarchical flair. Much like Mobutu, Habyarimana was 'elected' by farcical margins in 1983 and 1988 elections.

Despite all of this, Rwanda was a darling of donors and foreign non-governmental organisations in the late 1980s, few glimpsing the catastrophe that lay ahead. The most significant circle of power eventually coalesced around the president's wife, Agathe Kanziga (known as Madame Agathe), in what became known as *le clan de Madame* and, eventually, the *akazu* (little house). As the 1980s drew to a close, the president himself was more and more in the grip of the *akazu*, and, at the same time, Rwanda was rocked by a series of high-profile political murders.

On 1 October 1990, Fred Rwigema and the RPF launched their invasion of Rwanda, and, in response, nearly 350 Tutsi civilians were massacred in Rwanda's Mutara region.[57] After first taking the FAR by surprise, the RPF suffered major reversals, including the killing of Rwigema in circumstances that remain in dispute to this day. Upon Paul Kagame's arrival from Fort Leavenworth, Kansas, where he had been receiving military training, the RPF opted to regroup and lay low for two months on the chilly slopes of the Virunga mountains. French troops deployed on the ground in Rwanda to defend the Habyarimana regime.

In April 1992, a coalition government was formed with the prime minister's seat going to Dismas Nsengiyaremye of the Mouvement Démocratique Républicain (MDR), the country's largest opposition party. In July 1992, the RPF and the Habyarimana government signed a ceasefire agreement that was to pave the way for future power-sharing between the president's MRND and its adversaries.

As in Zaire, by this point Rwanda's body politic was frighteningly dysfunctional. Beyond the RPF, much of the so-called 'opposition' within Rwanda itself – representing various strains of the extremist Coalition pour la Défense de la République (CDR) party, the *impuzamugambi* militia, and the *akazu* itself – referred to themselves by the incongruous (in a Francophone, Kinyarwanda-speaking country) name Hutu Power. The party structure, so critical in the doling out of cabinet positions, had broken down almost completely amid claims and counterclaims of leadership, leaving the intricately arranged cabinet almost irrelevant.

Habyarimana attempted to survive by playing each side off against the others. In late January 1993, more than 300 Tutsi and Hutu oppositionists were killed in MRND- and CDR-organised massacres in north-western Rwanda.[58] Following the killings, the RPF broke the ceasefire and fought their way to within 30 kilometres of Kigali before stopping. Despite the killings, French Minister of External Co-operation Marcel Debarge flew to Kigali to voice full-throated backing for the regime and French policy towards Habyarimana continued to be 'total, uncritical and unconditional support'.[59] An extremist radio station affiliated with the CDR, Radio Télévision Libre des Mille Collines (RTLM), began broadcasting in July 1993. That same month, the moderate MDR politician Agathe Uwilingiyimana became prime minister.

Having been backed into a corner, Habyarimana signed the Arusha Accords on 4 August 1993. The document reiterated the terms of the July 1992 ceasefire calling for power-sharing, reorganisation of the armed forces and a return of refugees. After Arusha, Habyarimana delayed and double-dealed, seeking to avoid implementation of the accords, but he was now viewed as a traitor and, even worse, as useless by the extremist elements he had long fostered.

After Arusha, despite a comprehensive arms embargo imposed on the Habyarimana regime and the RPF, the government of French President François Mitterrand continued to supply Kigali with weapons.[60] The existence of Hutu Power death squads became a matter of public record after it was revealed in an October 1992 press conference in Brussels by the Belgian Senator Willy Kuijpers and the academic Filip Reyntjens, with many of the participants (including Habyarimana's brothers-in-law and FAR Colonel Théoneste Bagosora) even named.

The murder of Burundi's Hutu President Melchior Ndadaye in October 1993 had a profoundly negative effect on the political atmosphere in Rwanda, and by the time the United Nations Assistance Mission for Rwanda (UNAMIR) began deploying in the country that autumn – headed by Canadian General Roméo Dallaire – the mood was one of intense foreboding, a feeling reinforced when CDR-linked riots rocked Kigali in February 1994.

This was the landscape that Mobutu surveyed when he looked around Africa as 1994 dawned. Given his longevity and mastery of the political game, he could perhaps be forgiven for believing that he could play for ever. He had been gambling at stakes this high his entire political life, after all. Mobutu had held such a series of winning hands and had kept his many enemies off balance for so long that, despite being the consummate gambler he was, he forgot the one cardinal rule of the game: everybody loses some time.

3 | THE GREAT CONGO WARS

The First Congo War

The opening shot in the Rwandan genocide was fired by a still-unknown hand at around 8 p.m. on the evening of 6 April 1994, when a Falcon 50 jet carrying Juvénal Habyarimana and Burundi's Hutu President Cyprien Ntaryamira was hit by a surface-to-air missile and crashed in a ball of fire near Kanombe military camp at Kigali's airport.[1] From almost the moment of the plane's thudding descent to earth, Hutu Power elements in the military and the *interahamwe* and *impuzamugambi* militias began their bloody business. They were able to continue it, almost completely unmolested by the international community, for nearly 100 days, a period during which nearly 1 million Tutsis and moderate Hutus would be killed. The genocide would change the face not just of Rwanda but of Africa, setting off a continent-wide conflict that would prove even more deadly than the genocide itself.[2]

It is hard to overstate the immorality that characterised the response of Western governments during the crisis. In the case of the government of French President François Mitterrand, this meant outright collusion with the forces of genocide, both in its continued arming of extremist Hutu Power elements in violation of an arms embargo, and in the conduct of Opération Turquoise, an ostensible French peacekeeping mission that, even as it saved Tutsi lives, provided cover by which escaping *genocidaires* could flee and regroup amid their human shields.[3]

In the case of US President Bill Clinton, it meant a policy of feckless, narcissistic self-interest, as the administration in the person of officials such as US Secretary of State Warren Christopher, then US ambassador to the UN (and future Secretary of State) Madeleine Albright and National Security Council adviser Richard Clarke spearheaded efforts to remove UNAMIR troops from Rwanda,[4] refused to use US technological know-how to block *genocidaire* radio transmissions and avoided any public use of the word 'genocide' for fear that it somehow might be compelled to act. This attitude was perhaps best summed up in a September 2001 article by journalist Samantha Power for *The Atlantic* magazine, in which Power quotes Susan Rice, then working under Clarke at the National Security Council, asking during an April 1994 inter-agency teleconference 'if we use the word "genocide" and are seen as doing nothing, what will be the effect on the November [congressional] election?'[5] On 21 April, the UN voted to reduce the UNAMIR mission by 90 per cent.

As Paul Kagame and the RPF stormed down from northern Rwanda to find fields, latrines and rivers choked with corpses, the authors of the genocide, and those under their command, fled in the opposite direction. From Rwanda, up to 800,000 people crossed into North Kivu between 14 and 17 July 1994 alone,[6] the departing *genocidaires* taking the equivalent of US$30 million to US$40 million in Rwandan francs with them.[7]

Once over the border in Zaire, Rwanda's ousted army officials reconfigured what remained of the force into two divisions, one consisting of 7,680 men and one of 10,240 men, with units of supporters numbering some 4,000.[8] After committing a genocide in front of the unresponsive gaze of the international community, the forces of Hutu Power rearmed under that same community's equally paralysed view. In the Zaire camps, former local political chiefs, most of whom took an active role in the killings, became adept at using daily food distributions as a weapon of control over the refugee community as a whole.[9]

In her memoir of her time serving as the UN High Commissioner for Refugees, Sadako Ogata confessed that 'militarisation was the major problem in the refugee camps' in Zaire, with the *genocidaire* element being particularly strong in and around Magunga camp (near Goma, North Kivu) and Panzi and Bulange camps (near Bukavu, South Kivu). The Office of the UN High Commissioner for Refugees (UNHCR) felt poorly supported by the larger UN and the international community as the militarily tinged refugee crisis exploded.[10] A June 1994 attempt to remove a well-known *genocidaire* from the Benaco refugee camp resulted in the UNHCR compound being surrounded by machete-wielding thugs.[11]

At the same time, in the Rwandan district of Rubavu, where the border city of Gisenyi was located, UNHCR investigators found that 'there was a systematic pattern of arbitrary arrests and disappearances of adult males ... suspected of being [Hutu] militia elements', as well as evidence of mass killings and of 'systematic and sustained killing and persecution of civilian Hutus by the RPF'.[12] In the face of these concerns, the UNHCR stopped supporting the voluntary return of refugees to Rwanda in September 1994, only to lift the suspension three months later. By late summer 1994, two non-governmental organisations (NGOs) – Médecins Sans Frontières (MSF, France) and the International Rescue Committee (USA) – had withdrawn from the camps in the Kivus, warning that:

> if the United Nations does not act immediately to ensure safe conditions for the return of the Rwandan refugees, it will be too late to prevent the authors of the genocide from asserting control ... [which will] inevitably lead to a flare-up of the conflict.[13]

In Rwanda itself, when the RPF finally succeeded in driving the Hutu Power forces out of power and out of the country, they named Pasteur Bizimungu, a Hutu RPF member, as president, although Paul Kagame became vice-president and minister of defence and was widely assumed to be the true power behind the new government.

As chaos swirled around him, where was the Warrior? As commanding as Mobutu's rule of Zaire appeared to be to outsiders, the reality on the ground was somewhat different. The much-vaunted Congolese army, which could seem such an oppressive fact of daily life to the Congolese, was, in fact, as one analyst observed, 'like much of the state ... a hulking, decrepit edifice'.[14] As was masterfully documented in Crawford Young and Thomas Turner's 1985 work, by the 1980s the Mobutu regime had begun a process of inexorable and probably irreversible decline, so when millions of refugees flooded into the country in 1994, the government was unable, both materially and temperamentally, to show any sort of leadership amid the crisis engulfing the region. The most Mobutu could do was evacuate his protégé Habyarimana's body to his private mausoleum in Gbadolite. Habyarimana's wife fled under French military protection to France, where she has remained ever since. As the first anniversary of the start of the genocide approached, the camps in Zaire provided a staging ground for the reorganised FAR and *interahamwe* to launch attacks into Rwanda with the eventual aim of toppling the Kigali government and returning to power.

In the absence of any genuine diplomatic leadership on the issue, one of the great questions posed by post-genocide Rwanda was how the new RPF government and the country's new Rwandan Patriotic Army (RPA) would address the problem of tens of thousands of women and children interspersed among the *genocidaires* in the sprawling camps within Rwanda itself. Kigali gave a stark answer at a camp of over 80,000 people in the town of Kibeho in southern Rwanda in April 1995.

After surprising UNAMIR with an announcement that the camp would be closed – an announcement that gave the mission time to do no more than put a small team of Australian medics on the ground to support Zambian peacekeepers stationed there – the RPA surrounded Kibeho. Between 16 and 22 April, the Australians heard sustained automatic weapons fire as the RPA set about emptying internally displaced persons (IDPs) out of the camp, killing many in the process.[15] RPA soldiers blocked access to the wounded, but, of those the medics were able to see and treat, 'every single casualty had been shot or attacked with machetes'.[16] The killing was most intense on 22 April, when the RPA opened fire on masses of trapped refugees amidst a driving rain.

Seth Sendashonga, a Hutu who had joined the RPF in 1982 and was serving as minister of the interior, visited Kibeho on 19 April and, after returning to Kigali and briefing Kagame and Bizimungu, was denied entry back into the Kibeho area.[17] The Kigali government blamed the killings on *interahamwe* elements and announced that the closing of the camp was in fact a process of 'repatriation' rather than a war crime. Although a complete death toll may never be known, some analysts looking at the data have concluded that at least 20,000 people were killed or disappeared as a result of the operation.[18]

Kibeho, as ghastly as it was, was not a cross-border war of pillage and extermination. But it was a shadow of what was to come.

It is hard to think of a figure in modern African history save Nelson Mandela who was the object of more hope than Paul Kagame, the darling of Western governments and aid organisations who nevertheless became a uniquely destructive force in the history of central Africa. Leading a rebel army that swept into Rwanda and stopped the genocide, Kagame made a compelling figure. In contrast to the ossifying, corrupt Mobutu, Kagame was stern, disciplined, ascetic. At the time, many welcomed him as a breath of fresh air in Africa's often depressing political landscape, his rhetoric of political reconciliation belying the fact that he led a minority politico-military movement that was committed to seizing and retaining power in Rwanda at virtually any price. Time would reveal that he could be every bit as ruthless of Mobutu or Habyarimana had been, although largely away from the glare of the press and with a far greater flair for public relations than either man had ever displayed.

But for years the outside world heard none of this. Kagame was praised effusively by American journalists such as Philip Gourevitch and Stephen Kinzer, the latter writing a hagiographic biography of Kagame.[19] He was a new man, we were told, for a new chapter in the history of Africa. And since July 1994, the Kigali government had been stating plainly that if the international community would not act to disarm the *genocidaires* and empty the camps, the Rwandans would.

In mid-1996, the Rwandan government arranged a meeting in Kigali between the heads of several of Zaire's opposition movements. There was André Kisase Ngandu, an ageing rebel leader from the Rwenzori Mountains who led the Conseil National de la Résistance pour la Démocratie (CNRD). There was an architect from North Kivu, Déogratias Bugera, who led the Alliance Democratique des Peuples (ADP). There was a young former RPF sergeant, Anselme Masasu Nindaga, a native of Bukavu and the offspring of a Mushi father and a Rwandan Tutsi mother. And there was the PRP's Laurent Kabila.[20] Of the groups, only the PRP and the CNRD had military capabilities.[21] After some discussion, it was decided that the groups would merge under the umbrella of a single rebel movement, the Alliance des Forces Démocratiques pour la Libération du Congo-Zaïre (AFDL), and act as the tip of the spear of a Rwandan invasion of Zaire to begin the coming autumn.

To oversee the invasion of Zaire, the Rwandans selected the RPA's James Kabarebe, a Tutsi born in 1959 who had been commissioned into the Ugandan army in 1989. Kabarebe's family had fled from Rwanda to Uganda in the year of his birth, and he remembered being chased in 1982 along with thousands of other Rwandan immigrants by the military of Ugandan dictator Milton Obote to the marshland between Uganda and Rwanda. From his family's hiding place, he could hear a Rwandan Hutu soldier taunt the huddled, wretched mass through a megaphone that 'even God' did not want them and that they should throw themselves into the river.[22] Over the years, Kabarebe had proven himself a skilled military commander and, as such, made a logical choice as the eyes and ears of Kigali on the ground. Kabarebe was later described bluntly by a US embassy official in Kinshasa as the most powerful commander in Congo during the war.[23]

Relations between the rebel leaders and their foreign patrons were cordial, to the extent that Laurent Kabila, who was often addressed by the Swahili honorific title *Mzee*, and his son Joseph stayed for a time at Kabarebe's Kigali home as the invasion was being planned.[24] Later, there would be much speculation as to whether Joseph was Congolese at all, or in fact Rwandan.

Conditions on the ground within Zaire itself were favourable to such an undertaking. In the years immediately preceding 1994, the Banyarwanda of North Kivu made up about half the population of 3 million in the province, and consisted of about four times as many Hutu as Tutsi. In South Kivu, the Banyamulenge numbered around 200,000. The arrival of the ex-FAR and *interahamwe* after the genocide totally disrupted the cold peace that had existed between ethnic groups there. With an ailing Mobutu casting his lot in with the *genocidaires* in the camps, the situation for the Banyamulenge, in particular, had grown ever more precarious.

In September 1996, the Centre Hospitalier Universitaire Vaudois in Lausanne, Switzerland announced that Mobutu had been operated on there and was suffering from prostate cancer. As Mobutu convalesced, during the drenching rainy season, Rwandan troops and elements of the newly minted AFDL crossed into Zaire, eventually to be joined by rebels from Katanga flown into the area from Angola. Fighting continued throughout September and grew in intensity in October.

Early on the morning of 6 October, the hospital in Lemera, South Kivu, was attacked, allegedly by Banyamulenge militia. Eyewitnesses recounted the killing of at least 38 people and the looting of the hospital premises.[25] On 7 October, Lwasi Ngabo Lwabanji, deputy governor of South Kivu, ordered all Banyamulenge to leave Zaire within a week. For several hours the next day, Zairian troops went on a looting rampage in Uvira.[26] Following a tour of the Kivus, Zairian General Eluki Monga Aundu declared that a 'state of war' existed in South Kivu and that the country was facing aggression by the Banyamulenge operating with the support of Kigali.[27]

As Goma and Bukavu fell and the RPA/AFDL forces fanned out to the surrounding camps, atrocities began almost immediately. Between September and November, the RPA/AFDL forces 'attacked and destroyed all the Rwandan and Burundian Hutu refugee camps set up around the towns of Uvira, Bukavu and Goma'. Although many thousands of refugees fled back to Rwanda, many more – several hundred thousand – fled towards the territories of Walikale in North Kivu and Shabunda in South Kivu.[28]

Others never had the chance to flee. Over the night of 25–26 October, RPA/AFDL soldiers bombarded the camp at Kibumba with heavy weapons, killing an unknown number of refugees and sending around 194,000 people fleeing towards Mugunga. On 31 October, the RPA/AFDL are alleged to have killed several hundred refugees at Kahindo and Katale. Between November 1996 and January 1997, civilians and a local NGO, the Équipe d'Urgence de la Biodiversité, buried a total of 4,006 bodies in and around Kibumba camp alone.[29] During the month of October 1996, in Goma and in the camps surrounding the town, the UNHCR made arrangements for the burial of more than 6,800 people. Eyewitnesses stated that the AFDL had used a front loader to dispose of bodies from the camps before granting the UN access.[30] In flight, the ex-FAR and *interahamwe* behaved no more humanely than the invading forces and on 6 November attacked a convoy of trucks near Burungu, killing several hundred Congolese civilians.[31]

Washington had given the green light to Kigali in November, when US Defence Secretary William Perry cited the 'return' of 500,000 refugees to Rwanda as the reason for which any US contribution to a proposed Canadian-led multinational force proposed for central Africa would number fewer than 1,000 troops.[32] The force, tentatively named Operation Assurance, never got off the ground.

On 17 December, Mobutu finally returned to Zaire from Switzerland, six weeks after the rebellion had begun. Now gravely ill, he raised his silver-topped cane to greet the crowd that awaited him at Kinshasa's airport and denounced 'the enemies of our country [who] have chosen when I was sick to put a sword in my back'.[33]

Across the vast country he still ostensibly ruled, however, his words had little effect. As the RPA/AFDL forces advanced, tens of thousands of people fled north-west towards the Kahuzi-Biega National Park, one of the last refuges of the eastern lowland gorilla and an untamed swathe of primary tropical forest spreading out from two massive extinct volcanoes. As if materialising from the jungle mist, in mid-December 1996 at least 120,000 refugees suddenly resurfaced and formed makeshift camps at Tingi-Tingi and Amisi, about 140 miles south-east of Kisangani and almost 400 miles from their point of departure. By the time the AFDL reached Tingi-Tingi in late February 1997, many refugees fled towards Ubundu, while a contingent of ex-FAR, *interahamwe* and civilians broke off from the main group and headed towards Opala. The majority of refugees, estimated to be some 85,000 at this point, trudged along a path cut through the forest by a jungle railway line towards Kisangani. On 25 March, the hardiest souls found their way forward blocked by the AFDL 7 kilometres south of Kisangani. The refugees were herded into temporary encampments where their situation was described as 'catastrophic'. One of the camps, Kasese (in fact made up of two adjoining camps), was believed to hold between 40,000 and 50,000 people alone.

Between 21 and 23 April, the AFDL attacked the camps.

When the UNHCR was finally allowed to enter, they found, to their alarm, that the camps were completely empty, even though a substantial number of the refugees had been treated by international relief organisations and were too sick even to walk. All told, from Kasese and its environs, some 85,000 people had simply vanished. A week later, several thousand refugees began filtering out of the bush in the most pitiful state. The AFDL blocked humanitarian access to them.[34]

In the Bukavu–Shabunda region, the AFDL used the presence of international organisations to lure refugees out of hiding in the forests, at which point they were killed. An 'ideological seminar' was held in Shabunda in March, whereupon local residents were given a deadline to stop assisting refugees, after which point anyone found to be doing so would be executed by the AFDL.[35] Witnesses told of how RPA soldiers fighting alongside the AFDL in and around Shabunda gouged out their victims' eyes and disembowelled pregnant women. Although some of the refugees were armed, survivors insisted that many of the rest were unarmed Rwandans, including women and children. The killing was said to be particularly fierce as the Rwandans overtook several thousand refugees at a dilapidated bridge over the Ulindi River. There, witnesses said, the killing went on for three days.[36] An MSF team approaching Shabunda in early 1997 surprised an AFDL contingent with shovels on the roadside and observed what they took to be evidence of freshly dug mass graves.[37]

By the time a group of refugees reached Mbandaka, on the Congo River, they had been stalked for over 1,000 miles through some of the most unforgiving rainforest on earth. On 13 May, at least 800 refugees were massacred by AFDL soldiers, while tens of thousands of unarmed civilians, mostly Rwandan refugees, went missing.[38] It is believed that at least 1,300 refugees were killed by AFDL and Rwandan troops during the siege of the Mbandaka camp.[39] By July 1997, at least 213,000 refugees overall were unaccounted for.[40]

UN investigators would later conclude that:

the apparently systematic nature of the massacres ... suggests that the numerous deaths cannot be attributed to the hazards of war or seen as equating to collateral damage. The majority of the victims were children, women, elderly people and the sick, who were often undernourished and posed no threat to the attacking forces.

The killing, the investigators said, was 'systematic, methodical and premeditated'.[41]

The slaughter went on under the impassive gaze of the international community, with the Clinton administration remaining taciturn. According to those who observed Washington's reasoning at the time first-hand, 'American officials had written off the Hutu as a pariah population and no one had time for questions about their fate'.[42] For those who would ask too many questions, grave dangers awaited. In April 1997, south of Kisangani, AFDL-allied troops threatened to kill a high-level diplomatic delegation seeking to investigate reports of massacres in the area.[43]

There were also changes afoot within the rebel ranks. On 8 January, André Kisase Ngandu, the leader of the CNRD faction of the AFDL, was killed in mysterious circumstances. According to some sources, he was slain by RPA loyalists suspicious of his closeness to Uganda.[44] With his death, Laurent Kabila became the undisputed leader of the rebellion. The young former RPF sergeant, Anselme Masasu, had become the de facto commander of the *kadogo* (child soldiers) in the AFDL, and kept in close communication with James Kabarebe to that end.

Mobutu, who had again returned to Europe for cancer treatment, decided that Kisangani would be his line in the sand, and recruited Serbian and Romanian mercenaries and smuggled weapons and ammunition into the east of the country in DC-3s meant to deliver humanitarian aid.[45] Nevertheless, Kisangani was captured on 3 March 1997, with Kabila arriving in town three weeks later on the same day that Mobutu returned to Zaire from Europe. Town after town fell into rebel hands, including the diamond centre of Mbuji-Mayi and Lubumbashi, the nation's second largest city and a mining centre. In an effort to split the opposition, Mobutu again appointed Étienne Tshisekedi – who had met with him in France in November 1996[46] – as prime minister. Tshisekedi quit a week later.

Showing more leadership than the rest of the international community combined, in an effort to stem the violence South African President Nelson Mandela arranged a meeting between Mobutu and Kabila – the only time the two men ever met – aboard the South African naval ship *Outeniqua* off Pointe-Noire in the Republic of Congo on 3 and 4 May. Kabila, sensing that victory was within his grasp, saw no need to compromise. On 17 May, Mobutu fled the country to die in exile in Morocco the following September.

Under cover of darkness, Kabila arrived in Kinshasa for the first time since the 1960s. One wonders how much the sprawling, chaotic, riverine metropolis had changed since the days of his youth. Even before his arrival in the capital, Kabila wasted little time seizing the reins of power, renaming Zaire as the République Démocratique du Congo and, with unfortunate irony, suspending the activities of all political parties the same day. Kabila assumed the right to rule by decree until a new constitution was adopted, and he was sworn in as Congo's president at a ceremony attended by most of his main benefactors, including Paul Kagame, Yoweri Museveni and José Eduardo dos Santos.

Surprising everyone except perhaps himself, Kabila would rapidly outrun the governments that had consecrated his power grab and set up an altogether different kind of system to the one they had envisioned. After the fall of Mobutu, the world at large generally tuned out to what was happening in Congo, and was only awoken with a start by a disastrous joint press conference in Kinshasa with US Secretary of State Madeleine Albright and

Kabila in December 1997. Albright said that the United States had asked Kabila to honour promises of democratic reforms and free elections, after which Kabila, with an intensity verging on hysteria, defended his decision to imprison critical journalists and opposition politicians.[47]

Speaking to an early December 1997 meeting of the Organisation of African Unity in Addis Ababa, Albright, whose itinerary for her trip also included Uganda and Rwanda, praised 'Africa's best new leaders' who had brought 'a new spirit of hope and accomplishment to their countries'.[48]

One wonders if the ghosts of Tingi-Tingi, Mbandaka and Shabunda could hear her in their unquiet graves.

The Second Congo War

The relationship between the Kabila government and the international community was abusive and dysfunctional almost from the start. As Kabila blocked any serious investigation into the massacres, foreign powers either withheld or delayed aid, with the World Bank demanding that the cash-strapped new government pay interest on the US$14 billion debt racked up during the Mobutu era. In terms of domestic policy, Kabila viewed Kinshasa's deal-cutting, unarmed opposition as little more than sell-outs and collaborators totally unworthy of inheriting the AFDL's victory. Instead, Kabila brought in his own people, many of them, like him, from the diaspora and a fair proportion of them with roots in Katanga.

Mwenze Kongolo, a 37-year-old former bail officer from Philadelphia, was appointed minister of the interior. Célestin Lwangi, born in Katanga but a long-time exile in Belgium, became minister of justice. Bizima Karaha, a young Banyamulenge physician from South Kivu who had studied and lived in South Africa, became minister of foreign affairs. All told, 7 of 13 portfolios went to AFDL members, with two to the UDPS (the positions of minister of agriculture and minister of the civil service, insulting positions for the country's largest opposition movement) and the rest to other political groupings. All those invited to join the government were told they must do so as individuals rather than as members of political parties. Kabila's minister of information, Raphael Ghenda, crystallised the AFDL's view of its right to power when he said that: 'We [the AFDL] liberated the Congo from the dictator and its regime ... No other force succeeded in doing this.'[49] To many Congolese who had suffered under Mobutu's rule for decades, this consolidation of power was unsettling.

Yet at this critical juncture Étienne Tshisekedi's demand for the prime minister's position was viewed by some as 'very destructive' and founded on 'a sense of entitlement based on the CNS, a process that had run out of steam'. Tshisekedi simply 'didn't have a huge political base on behalf of which he was speaking, and he made things more difficult, giving Kabila a useful fig leaf to reject dialogue'.[50]

The Rwandan presence in the new government was difficult to ignore; even the captain of Kabila's presidential guard was a Rwandan. James Kabarebe, the RPA officer who had overseen the invasion, was viewed as the acting chief of staff of the newly constituted Forces Armées Congolaises (FAC), as opposed to the FAC's public leader, the former *kadogo* commander Anselme Masasu Nindaga. The marginalisation of Masasu, in particular, would prove significant: upon arrival in the capital after marching across Congo with the AFDL, the *kadogo* found they were 'orphans in Kinshasa'.[51]

The issue of the Rwandan presence was also fraught with irony, because, despite the tens of thousands of civilians that Kabila's forces and their Rwandan allies had slaughtered, by 1997 a new Hutu rebel group had coalesced around the former FAR power structure. By May 1997, the Armée pour la Libération du Rwanda (ALiR) had become a presence in north-western Rwanda, where it promptly began committing atrocities in the time-honed fashion of Hutu Power, killing government officials, doctors, nurses and schoolchildren.[52] Abandoned by the international community and fearful of attacks by the Rwandans and by government forces, by mid-1997 some communities in eastern and central Congo (especially in Kabila's former stamping ground of South Kivu) formed self-defence forces called Mai-Mai, some of which collaborated with rebel groups in the area such as Burundi's Hutu militias.[53] Isolated in Kinshasa, the AFDL government allowed tensions in the eastern provinces to continue, sometimes overtly repressing the efforts of the population there to come to formal understandings between themselves.[54]

Kept on a tight leash by the Rwandans, Kabila chafed at his lack of room to manoeuvre. He was a man who had emerged into the light of the late 1990s as if cryogenically frozen, ideologically and intellectually, in the anti-imperialist struggles of the 1960s. Therefore, the presence of foreigners – no matter how much they had aided his cause – at the heart of his government, together with the fact that many Congolese viewed him as little more than Kigali's puppet, must have been a bitter pill to swallow. The sense of disconnect between the ruled and the rulers, back from their long sojourns abroad, was significant enough that by late 1997 a popular satirical comedy, *Diaspora Mania*, was ridiculing the expatriate ministers and their governing of the 'new' Congo.[55]

Kabila was at his core a nationalist, and as he sought to distance himself from Rwanda, it was the combatants of the ex-FAR and *interahamwe* who offered their fighting capabilities to his government in exchange for protection from the forces of Kigali. In November 1997, Kabila threw *kadogo* commander Anselme Masasu in jail. Initially sentenced to 20 years in prison for allegedly being in contact with enemies of the state (an obvious reference to James Kabarebe), Masasu was released after serving 15 months, a time during which many of the *kadogo* voiced their displeasure and a rebellion within their ranks appeared to be in the offing.

In late April 1998, the UN announced that it was withdrawing the investigators it had sent to probe the RPA/AFDL massacres, citing a 'total absence of cooperation' from the Kabila government.[56] The east of the country seethed, with fighting breaking out between local Mai-Mai and the FAC. In the midst of all this, US President Bill Clinton visited Rwanda in March 1998, the fourth anniversary of the genocide and the third anniversary of the massacre in Kibeho. After meeting with President Bizimungu and Vice-President Kagame, Clinton told a press conference at Kigali's airport that 'the international community, together with nations in Africa, must bear its share of responsibility for this tragedy', and that, although 'we cannot change the past ... we can and must do everything in our power to help you build a future without fear, and full of hope'.[57]

One of the potential architects of that future met his end less than two months later when Seth Sendashonga, the moderate Hutu who had served as minister of the interior and who had attempted to stop the killings at Kibeho, was killed in Nairobi along with his driver. A previous attempt had been made to assassinate Sendashonga by Rwandan agents in February 1996[58] and in exile he had continued to be scathingly critical of both the leadership of the Hutus and the new government under Kagame. Sendashonga had launched the Forces de Résistance pour la Démocratie in April 1997, and had begun exploring the possibility of launching an armed insurrection while seeking, in vain, Washington's backing for this venture. Several men were arrested on suspicion of involvement with the killing, but none was convicted. The slain politician's widow accused Kigali of being behind the killing, specifically pointing the finger of blame at acting Rwandan ambassador to Kenya Alphonse Mbayire. Mbayire later returned to Rwanda and was killed there by unidentified gunmen in February 2001.

Perhaps with an eye to solidifying his own grip on the security services, Kabila sent his 26-year-old son, Joseph, already an FAC officer, to China for further military training in mid-1998. When he returned, Joseph Kabila was promoted to the rank of general. Then, after returning from a trip to Cuba, on the evening of 27 July, Laurent Kabila delivered a late-night address to the nation in which he thanked the Rwandans for their service to the country and ordered all Rwandan troops out of Congo.

The Rwandan response was not long in coming. A rebellion erupted among Banyamulenge in the armed forces in the Kivus, and soon both Bukavu and Goma were seized, with Kisangani and Kindu following shortly afterwards. In one of the most spectacular and highly publicised events of the war, RPA contingents in Goma seized three civilian aircraft, loaded them with 500 Rwandan soldiers and headed for the Kitona airbase in Bas-Congo province far to the west of Kinshasa, 1,500 kilometres away from Goma.[59] It was an audacious plan and typical of the kind of bold strategic thinking of James Kabarebe, who oversaw the mission. In the following days, additional flights brought the number of invaders at Kitona to nearly 3,500, and by 13 August the invaders had captured Boma, Buama and the real prize, the Bas-Congo capital of Matadi, where rebel forces shut down the Inga dams' turbines, cutting off power to Kinshasa.

The Rwandans had overreached, however, and within a week Angolan troops were pouring into Congolese territory. By September, the Rwandans made a dash across the Angolan border to a remote municipal airport in Maquela do Zombo (a one-time UNITA stronghold), which they held against ferocious Angolan assault for nearly two months, ferrying the remnants of their contingent back home.

After the attacks commenced, Kabila promptly fled with much of the government to Lubumbashi, a move that could hardly have made the Congolese any more confident in the durability of his regime. On 8 August, he met with Rwandan President Bizimungu and other regional leaders in Zimbabwe, but any agreement remained out of reach. If anything, after the meeting, the violence accelerated, and soon 120 people were dying each day in North and South Kivu.[60] On 18 August, Kabila met with Dos Santos and Namibian President Sam Nujoma in Luanda, thereby solidifying an important element of his defence strategy. The Rwandans were proved unwise to provoke Dos Santos, one of the continent's wiliest political survivors. Thus reassured, Kabila returned to Kinshasa.

In the immediate aftermath of the rebellion, the Kabila government's rhetoric became positively genocidal and reminiscent of that heard in Rwanda four years earlier, referring to all Tutsis as 'viruses', 'mosquitoes' and 'garbage' to be eliminated.[61] On a 12 August radio broadcast on government-run Radio-Télévision Nationale Congolaise (RTNC), a Congolese army officer called on the Congolese 'to take revenge' on the Rwandans in their country and to 'massacre them without mercy'.[62] Across the Atlantic, despite the fact that the United States had actively supported the Rwandan-helmed invasion of Congo two years earlier, US State Department spokesman James Rubin told reporters, without apparent irony, that the US didn't 'believe that governments should be intervening in the affairs of their neighbors'.[63]

There were other considerations as well. Militarily strong but resource starved, Rwanda had to find a way to pay for the war, and a way to bankroll Kagame's grandiose plans for national renewal. Congo, rich with minerals and militarily weak, proved a tantalising prize. Given such sensitive issues, it was perhaps not surprising that, despite having a functioning parliament, decisions relating to Kigali's manoeuvring in Congo were little discussed beyond a small circle around the executive branch, and, even as early as 1998, some within the Rwandan government believed that Rwanda's involvement in Congo had nothing to do with security, but rather was about 'something else'. Congo 'was an issue that was handled by Kagame, his military and his intelligence services ... It was managed by Kagame and the people he chose.'[64]

Uganda, sensing an opportunity to expand its own regional footprint, pursue the various Ugandan rebel factions operating out of Congo and pressure Sudan, and lured by the promise of mineral riches for its officer class, soon followed suit. The UPDF began fanning out through Orientale province, using its allies in the SPLA to lay siege to such towns as Dungu in Haut-Uélé.[65]

The as-yet-unnamed rebels captured Beni in North Kivu on 10 August. Six days later, the RCD announced both its existence and that one Ernest Wamba dia Wamba would serve as its president.

An academic originally hailing from Bas-Congo and a member of the Bakongo ethnic group, Wamba dia Wamba held a degree from Western Michigan University and had taught in the United States and Tanzania.[66] A strange choice, perhaps, to become the figurehead for a Rwandan-dominated rebel movement in eastern Congo, but the choice becomes less obscure when one realises that Wamba was initially selected as president of the RCD at a meeting in Kigali two weeks after military operations had already begun. Also present at that first meeting were former UNESCO official Zahidi Ngoma as well as other assorted diplomatic and academic activists, opportunists and agitators to give a sheen of credibility to Kigali's naked land grab. Once formed, the RCD political leadership ensconced itself in a former Mobutu residence in Goma.

In his management of the RCD, we begin to see flashes of the Paul Kagame who would appear later, when his political personality more fully defined itself as president of Rwanda, a role he would assume in less than two years. A brilliant military strategist, Kagame was also skilled at appealing to the vanity and fear of those he wanted to control, as he did with the RCD leadership. Kagame demanded discipline, austerity and sacrifice, but many of the individuals scooped up to form the RCD's public face appeared interested in little other than self-enrichment.

Kagame – and to a lesser extent Museveni – understood how to play the international press. Kagame matter-of-factly told one journalist that the Rwandan government 'used communication and information warfare better than anyone'.[67] It was this gift for publicity that would enable him to invade and occupy a neighbouring country, setting off a conflict that would burn in fits and starts for the next 15 years, while still remaining the toast of foreign donors and governments as a 'new' breed of African leader diligently rebuilding his country from the ashes of genocide.

The reality of the new Rwanda on the ground in eastern Congo was something altogether different, as attested to on 20 August 1998, when RCD forces killed at least 47 civilians in Kizimia near Fizi.[68] Kizimia, however, was a mere prelude to the many massacres that would take place during the Second Congo War. One of the earliest and most shocking, and certainly the one that left the deepest impression on the Congolese, was the mass killing of villagers that took place in Kasika in South Kivu in August 1998.

The trouble began when RCD and RPA soldiers were fired upon by local Mai-Mai commanded by a renegade chief, although no one was injured. Passing back through the town several days later, the soldiers were fired upon again; this time three of their number died, including a well-known commander.[69] The RCD then shot and hacked to death the village chief, a priest, nuns and many women and children, dismembering and defiling the corpses in ghastly ways. At least 856 people were slain in and around the village.[70] Most of the women were raped before they were butchered, and the corpses of numerous infants were thrown into latrines.[71]

The guns of Kisangani

The alliance of convenience between Rwanda and Uganda showed serious fissures almost from the beginning. Although both countries had invaded Congo with a view to their own internal security, they had starkly different ideas about what that entailed, with the Rwandans having a far more expansionist mindset than Kampala.

In early November 1998, yet another rebel group appeared on

the scene, one that would be based in Mobutu's former stronghold of Gbadolite in Équateur province. Jean-Pierre Bemba, the man at the helm of the Mouvement pour la Liberation du Congo (MLC), was the son of a Portuguese-Congolese businessman who had been a confidant of Mobutu's. Bemba's father had educated his son mostly in Belgium, and upon his graduation from university, the younger Bemba took an ever more prominent role in his father's businesses in Zaire, later starting a successful mobile phone company. While Bemba *fils* was the MLC's political face, military command of the rebel group was delegated to a former head of Mobutu's personal guard, Colonel Dieudonné Amuli, with Mobutu's former prime minister Lunda Bululu joining later. The movement was largely sponsored by Uganda, and, unlike the ever shifting web of alliances of other Congolese rebel groups, the MLC had a top-down management style with Bemba at its head that would remain largely intact for the duration of the war.

In the east, the days of the massacre had returned. Between 30 December 1998 and 2 January 1999, RCD troops, Rwandan soldiers and members of the army of Burundi's Tutsi dictator Pierre Buyoya killed more than 800 people in villages throughout the Fizi region of South Kivu. The attackers told their victims that the massacre was in retaliation for the locals' suspected support of Mai-Mai militias.[72]

By early 1999, the national armies of Rwanda and Uganda and their respective RCD and MLC apprentices stood arrayed against the Kinshasa government. On its side, Kinshasa could boast the FAC, the Mai-Mai, the remnants of the former Rwandan army and the *interahamwe* and the national armies of Angola, Zimbabwe and Namibia. Other regional politico-military groupings (such as Chad and Sudan) flitted in and out of the picture like visions in a nightmare.

The linchpin of the new rebellion would prove to be Kisangani, the somnolent city on the Congo River where brush exploded on all sides when one ventured a few metres outside the town.

An agreement was arrived at between the Rwandans and the Ugandans whereby the RCD – largely a Rwandan creation despite Ernest Wamba dia Wamba's close links with Kampala – would operate south of Kisangani, while the Kampala-aligned MLC would operate to the north. Kisangani itself would boast a duopoly of power between the two. The only people missing from this splendid arrangement, of course, were the Congolese themselves. The Rwandans even created a centralised structure to oversee the procurement and export of minerals seized from Congo, referred to as the Congo Desk, in which virtually the entire top command of the Rwandan military was involved.[73] The Ugandans were less organised, but Major General James Kazini, a UPDF commander who had directed troops in the northern Ugandan city of Gulu before coming to Congo, was in many ways the definitive symbol of Uganda's role in the illicit procurement.

As the RPA and the UPDF eyed one another warily over the division of the spoils, the Congolese population continued to suffer the wrath of the invaders. Another terrible massacre occurred in July 1999 in the village of Mazembe in northern Katanga when a vehicle transporting RCD/RPA soldiers was blown up by a mine. In response, the aggrieved soldiers locked villagers in huts that they then set on fire. This time, 48 people, including at least ten children, were killed.[74] Also in July, Bemba's MLC finally succeeded in taking Gbadolite and shortly thereafter had much of Équateur province in its grasp. Unlike the RCD troops, who were viewed as little more than pawns of Kigali, Bemba and the MLC, despite their connections with Uganda, were able to secure a measure of popularity among the Bangala people. Like all of Congo's warlords, however, Bemba was prone to overambition, and a mid-1999 MLC attempt to seize Mbuji-Mayi ended in defeat in the face of a fierce defence by Zimbabwean troops.

With things growing ever more tense within the Kampala- and Kigali-aligned groupings of the RCD, Wamba dia Wamba arrived in Kisangani in May 1999, effectively ceding leadership of the

Goma-based faction of the RCD to Katanga native Émile Ilunga. After Wamba's departure, Ilunga's faction would become known as the RCD-Goma (RCD-G). Upon his arrival in Kisangani, Wamba was put under the protection of Ugandan soldiers and began holding rallies urging dialogue with Kinshasa, much to Kigali's horror. He announced the formation of a new movement, the RCD-Kisangani (RCD-K).

Following negotiations conducted under the aegis of Zambian President Frederick Chiluba and others, a ceasefire agreement was signed in the Zambian capital of Lusaka on 10 July 1999 between the six countries involved in the conflict (Democratic Republic of Congo, Angola, Namibia, Zimbabwe, Rwanda and Uganda), but not by many of the rebel factions and militias. The agreement had almost no effect on the violence in the Kivus, and was subsequently ignored in every particular by all parties.

In such a cauldron of mistrust, the inevitable happened. On 7 August 1999, the UPDF and the RPA turned their guns on one another in Kisangani, and the fighting raged for more than a week. Bodies lay decomposing in the torpid humidity of the riverside city as Pasteur Bizimungu flew to Kampala to meet with Yoweri Museveni.[75] By mid-September, Ugandan commander James Kazini was removed from Kisangani.[76]

Finally realising the potential for a continent-wide war, on 30 September the UN Security Council passed Resolution 1279 mandating the creation of the Mission de l'Organisation des Nations Unies en République Démocratique du Congo (MONUC). It would be the first UN peacekeeping mission in the country since 1964, and it was announced that Tunisian diplomat Kamel Morjane would act as Special Representative of the UN Secretary-General, a position he assumed in November 1999. MONUC's mandate would eventually come to include: monitoring and implementing the ceasefire agreement; investigating any violations of it; contributing to the successful completion of the electoral process; and, significantly, ensuring 'the protection of civilians, including humanitarian personnel, under imminent threat of physical violence'.[77]

In late 1999 and early 2000, as the conflict grew to affect areas of the country that had previously been relatively peaceful, Laurent Kabila began arming Mai-Mai in his home area of Katanga to assist in the government's fight against the RCD. During and after this period, the north of Katanga became heavily permeated with militias originally created to stop the Rwandan advance. Katanga governor Aimé Ngoy Mukena helped create the groups, along with such Kabila loyalists as Minister of Justice Mwenze Kongolo and Brigadier General John Numbi, then commander of the Fourth Military Region and, like Kabila, a Luba. Groups such as the Forces d'Auto-Défense Populaires and Moyo Wa Chuma (Hearts of Steel) under the command of at least 19 warlords in Katanga's northern and central territories had somewhere between 5,000 and 8,000 armed men.[78] Some of these militias would grow out of the Union des Fédéralistes et des Républicains Indépendants (UFERI), a political movement founded in August 1990 by Mobutu's former prime minister Jean Nguza Karl-i-Bond but taken over in May 1994 by Gabriel Kyungu wa Kumwanza. John Numbi, who would play an important role in subsequent Congo governments, had a particularly long history of stoking ethnic venom as an organiser for UFERI's youth wing, the Jeunesses de l'Union des Fédéralistes et des Républicains Independents (JUFERI).

With Mai-Mai proliferating throughout Katanga and the Kivus, by 2000 the RCD itself had splintered into several competing movements. Émile Ilunga's RCD-G had remained based in Goma and tied to Rwanda, but later that year Ilunga was to be replaced by Adolphe Onusumba. After the defeat of Uganda in the Kisangani fighting, Ernest Wamba dia Wamba's RCD-K had decamped from Kisangani to Bunia. There, with Ugandan connivance, the Nande businessman Mbusa Nyamwisi would seize control of much of the remaining forces and rename them the RCD-Mouvement de Libération (RCD-ML). This faction would further break down when dissenters followed former RCD-G politico Roger Lumbala to form the Rassemblement Congolais pour la Démocratie-National (RCD-N). Wamba himself would become an increasingly pathetic figure, at one point even attempting to go into business with the notorious international confidence man Van Arthur Brink, aka Gilbert Allen Ziegler, who was residing in Kampala at the time.[79] In Équateur, Jean-Pierre Bemba's MLC remained relatively unchallenged and would eventually attempt to expand eastward. The former *interahamwe* continued to operate throughout the east of the country, along with other rebel movements from Uganda and Burundi.

On 24 February 2000, a year and a half after the conflict had begun, the UN Security Council passed Resolution 1291, approving the deployment of 5,537 peacekeepers to monitor the implementation of the totally disregarded July 1999 ceasefire. By the end of the year, there would be a handful of troops deployed across the country's massive expanse who could do little more than report on the violations of the Lusaka accords.

They had plenty of material to work with. The Rwandan and Ugandan armies blazed away at one another again in Kisangani in May and June 2000. During the latter confrontation, the Ugandans commenced with a furious assault of heavy artillery, as Ugandan and Rwandan soldiers stormed through densely populated neighbourhoods, gutting entire districts and destroying hundreds of homes. During almost a week of fighting, at least 1,200 civilians were killed.[80] Following the Kisangani clashes, the UN passed Resolution 1304, which called for the withdrawal of all foreign forces from the Congolese territory without specifying any deadline.

Although the second Rwandan invasion of Congo had begun amid concerns for Rwanda's own security, by 2001 it had turned into something else entirely – namely a way for a poor, landlocked country dragging itself back from the abyss to bankroll its reconstruction and enrich its officer class with another country's relatively easily accessible minerals. A 2002 UN report concluded, despite protestations to the contrary, that 'the rationale for Rwanda's presence is to increase the numbers of Rwandans in the eastern Democratic Republic of the Congo and to encourage those settled there to act in unison to support its exercise of economic control'.[81]

The true level of Rwandan duplicity was demonstrated by, among other things, a May 2000 letter from RCD-G Vice-President Jean-Pierre Ondekane that found its way into the hands of UN investigators. In the letter, Ondekane urges RCD-G soldiers to maintain good relations 'with our *interahamwe* and Mai-Mai brothers', and 'if necessary ... let them exploit the subsoil for their survival'.[82]

Entrances and exits

In Rwanda itself, things were also changing. Since taking power following the genocide, Paul Kagame had slowly and methodically been putting in place the apparatus of an authoritarian state, first by creating the office of vice-president for himself, then by creating a Forum of Political Parties – an RPF-led body with the power to remove any member of parliament at any time – and finally by marginalising his political opposition. In January 2000, the highly popular Tutsi former president of Rwanda's parliament, Joseph Sebarenzi, fled the country after being forced out of office and apprised of a plot to assassinate him.[83] Following Sebarenzi's flight, in March 2000 an assistant to President Pasteur Bizimungu was killed by a trio of men in military uniforms. During the preceding year, Bizimungu's relationship with Kagame had cooled off tremendously and he resigned the presidency, which Kagame then assumed. He has held the office ever since. Bizimungu would attempt to launch the opposition Party for Democratic Renewal, known in Kinyarwanda as Ubuyanja; this was quickly banned by the Kagame government and Bizimungu was placed under house arrest. Another Ubuyanja official, Gratien Munyarubuga, was murdered in December 2000.[84]

As the war concluded its second year, Kabila, desperately searching for a source of hard currency, granted a monopoly on diamond sales from Congo to the Israeli businessman Dan Gertler. One of Israel's wealthiest tycoons and in part financier of several Israeli settlements in the occupied West Bank, Gertler, who was only 27 at the time, was the grandson of Israel Diamond Exchange founder Moshe Schnitzer. Lavishing such an opportunity on the young Israeli in exchange for US$20 million per year might have seemed like good business sense until one realised that diamond exports from the Congo were actually valued at around US$600 million at the time. Such a move could not help but earn Kabila the enmity of Congo's long-standing community of Lebanese diamond traders. Thereafter, Kabila apparently believed – perhaps correctly – that some of the country's Lebanese tycoons were plotting a coup against him.[85]

Unlike Kagame, Kabila could not be bothered to maintain even the facade of democracy, and, at the beginning of September 2000, he reshuffled his cabinet, appointing, among others, former Mobutu public relations man Dominique Sakombi as minister of communications. Sakombi would aid Kabila in setting up an ever more bellicose cult of personality during the remainder of his presidency.

Along with grandiosity came paranoia. Former *kadogo* commander Anselme Masasu, agitating against the Kabila regime since his release from prison, was finally re-arrested in October 2000 along with dozens of other soldiers. A month later, during fierce fighting there, Masasu was taken to the Katanga town of Pweto. North of this small community on Lake Mweru near the Zambian border, fighters from Rwanda and Burundi on one side and those from Zimbabwe and Hutu combatants on the other faced off in one of the few examples of trench warfare to occur in recent memory. Following the battle, Masasu was executed on 27 November 2000, which set off rioting among the *kadogo* in the capital.

Perhaps it could have gone on for ever – the ageing crypto-nationalist Kabila and his allies versus the media-savvy but authoritarian Kagame and Museveni in some strange African version of Europe's Thirty Years' War. Fate, however, and a mysterious hand moving behind the scenes, thought otherwise. On 16 January 2001, Laurent Kabila was shot several times while conferring with his economic adviser, Emile Mota. The gunman, a young former child soldier from eastern Congo named Rashidi Kasereka, was himself then killed by the president's aide-de-camp, Eddy Kapend. Several conspirators waiting outside the presidential residence with a car in the event of an unlikely escape fled as the gunfire erupted.[86] The dead or dying president was then flown to Zimbabwe, as perhaps was appropriate for a man who owed his existence as long as it lasted to his patchwork of foreign patrons. Kabila's death was finally announced by government spokesman Dominique Sakombi at around 8 p.m. on the evening of 18 January. *Mzee* Kabila, the man whose journey had taken him from Katanga to Kinshasa to the Kivus to Tanzania to Rwanda and back again to Kinshasa, was dead.

In the aftermath of Kabila's murder, security forces summarily executed a number of people, including at least 11 Lebanese citizens whom they blamed for involvement in the killing. Eddy Kapend was later convicted – in what many observers viewed as a gross miscarriage of justice – of having plotted to assassinate his boss and sentenced to death. Kapend received his sentence bravely, and television cameras showed his fellow soldiers stripping the colonel's bars from his uniform and ripping off his hat as he stood before the sentencing judge.[87]

4 | ENTER HIS FATHER'S HOUSE

Only 29 years old at the time of his father's assassination, Joseph Kabila found himself at the helm of a nation nearly destroyed by decades of corrupt mismanagement and half a decade of nearly continuous war. Although some characterised the younger Kabila as mere window-dressing for a Luanda-affiliated Congolese government, and although he was dismissed by some – particularly *Kinois* – as *Petit Joseph* (Little Joseph) and by the foreign press as Silent Joe for his reticent manner, after he was sworn in as president on 25 January 2001, he would soon prove himself a much more adroit politician than his father.

After addressing the nation on 22 January, Kabila took off on a whirlwind tour of world capitals, meeting French President Jacques Chirac in Paris on 31 January, flying to Washington to attend a prayer breakfast with US President George W. Bush and Paul Kagame on 1 February, addressing the UN Security Council on 2 February and then flying back across the Atlantic to meet with Belgian Prime Minister Guy Verhofstadt a day later. At the time, suitably impressed, Washington looked at the younger Kabila and saw someone they rather liked, in the words of one American diplomat 'a bright young guy ... [who] had that dynamic leadership potential ... [we] saw years ago in Mobutu',[1] a perhaps unwittingly telling analogy.

In a move that helped reinforce the image of Kabila as a leader with the support of the international community, in late March 2001 the newly created MONUC deployed its first contingents in the east, first in rebel-held areas and then in government-controlled zones. For nearly two years, the mission would be led by the veteran Cameroonian diplomat Amos Namanga Ngongi.

The young president's inner circle was an interesting assemblage of personalities, once again heavily slanted towards his father's home province of Katanga. Katanga-native Augustin Katumba Mwanke had been appointed governor of that province by Laurent Kabila in April 1998 and became perhaps the closest adviser to Kabila *fils* on economic matters. To son as to father, he would prove himself invaluable. John Numbi, a former policeman and partisan of the Luba-supremacist UFERI party, became Kabila's feared iron fist in the security sector. Katanga-born and Bukavu-raised Samba Kaputo had been deputy chief of staff to Laurent Kabila and became a special adviser on security matters to his son. Vital Kamerhe, a former UDPS partisan from South Kivu who had served Laurent Kabila in a variety of roles, would become Kabila's main interlocutor in the peace process and, eventually, his rival. Although Kabila took office with a formal cabinet (which he then promptly fired on 5 April), these were the individuals who wielded real power within the new regime.

As the young president took office, the power of Congo's neighbours to openly (as opposed to covertly) wage war within its borders was also being challenged. In March, Yoweri Museveni won another term as Uganda's president, competing against former UPDF colonel and physician Kizza Besigye in a ballot marked by fraud and intimidation.[2] For many, the shine of Uganda's latest strongman, so long a favourite of the Western media, had begun to wear off.

In the east, the war continued; and in Ituri it only got worse. Uganda remained a major player in the region, as did Antipas Mbusa Nyamwisi, who had renamed the military wing of his RCD-ML the Armée Populaire Congolaise (APC). Tit-for-tat killings between Hema and Lendu ethnic groups erupted with alarming regularity and, on 26 April, six staff members of the International Committee of the Red Cross were killed in an attack that was believed to have been carried out by Hema militias and Ugandan soldiers.[3] In July 2001, Bemba's MLC expanded eastwards from Équateur into Ituri itself in an attempt to merge the MLC with other rebel groups, especially the Hema-supremacist UPC, which had been created by Thomas Lubanga that same month.

But as the year drew to a close, almost all outside combatants in the fray were exhausted. The killing of Angolan UNITA rebel leader Jonas Savimbi in February 2002 removed an important linchpin in Angola's involvement in the conflict, which had always been largely strategic rather than commercial.

Against this backdrop, talks began in February 2002 at the apartheid-era resort of Sun City, South Africa. Quite apart from the feckless blandishments (and often outright collusion) of the United States, France and Britain, South Africa had hewn a steady course of diplomacy throughout the Congo conflict, first under Nelson Mandela and then under his successor, Thabo Mbeki, and so holding negotiations with its borders was a logical choice. After much chaos and many threats, the representative of Bemba's MLC, to general surprise, signed a power-sharing agreement with Kinshasa, a move that, given the MLC's attached-at-the-hip relationship with Kampala, was rather significant. The RCD-G contingent, on the other hand, made common cause with Kabila enemy Étienne Tshisekedi's UDPS to try and block the agreement. The latter two groups proved badly out of step with sentiment on the continent and elsewhere, however, which was strongly in favour of ending the long war.

As Kabila and his retinue solidified their own power, Kinshasa's erstwhile Hutu allies were also growing more formidable. The Rwandan Hutu guerrillas of the ALiR were further demoralised by the July 2001 capture of one of their leaders, former FAR colonel Peter Habimana, by the Rwandan army,[4] and by the end of the year the ALiR had largely been subsumed into new group, the Forces Démocratiques de Libération du Rwanda (FDLR).

Founded in May 2000 in Lubumbashi,[5] the FDLR was ostensibly divided into (often overlapping) political and armed wings, with the latter called the Forces Combattantes Abacunguzi (FOCA). Directed by General Sylvestre Mudacumura, among the most extremist elements in a group of extremists, the FOCA was suffused with a quasi religious element of belief that God 'gave' Rwanda to the Hutus and thus it should be taken back by them. An exiled economist who was living in Germany during the genocide, Ignace Murwanashyaka co-ordinated the FDLR's political leadership in Europe and Africa, serving as the group's president. Straton Musoni, who had lived in the Stuttgart region since 1986, served as Murwanashyaka's deputy and the FDLR's vice-president.[6]

Despite its tactics being similarly brutal to those of its Hutu Power predecessors, it might fairly be said that the FDLR had a more sophisticated 'political' agenda. This was coupled with the fact that, rather than being the ragtag *genocidaires* of years past, the FOCA was a tightly organised combat force, one of the most formidable in the country. The existence of a general directorate able to travel at will throughout Europe and between Europe and Congo, in the words of one fighter, filled the FDLR in the forests of the Kivus with 'hope'. Defecting FDLR members would subsequently speak about the esteem in which Ignace Murwanashyaka was held, and how powerful they believed him to be.[7]

If the *genocidaires* were showing no signs of slackening, neither was Kigali or its Congolese proxies. This was vividly illustrated in May 2002 when Kisangani was again a flashpoint of violence as dissident soldiers of the RCD-G mutinied against their commanders with the rallying cry that the 'Rwandans' should be thrown out of Congo. A youth group, Bana États-Unis (Children of the United States), from the Mangobo district of the city, marched through the streets in support of the rebellion as mutinous soldiers killed at least six people they believed to be Rwandan.[8]

Shortly before midday on 14 May, arriving by plane from

Goma to put down the mutiny were, among others, RCD-G commanders Gabriel Amisi (known as Tango Fort), Laurent Nkunda (a Congolese Tutsi and sometime lay preacher from the Rutshuru area of North Kivu) and Bernard Byamungu. Men under the command of Amisi, Nkunda and Byamungu committed 'a wave of killings, rapes, and looting'.[9] Victims of the killings included an 89-year-old vegetable seller. The RCD-G troops also raped several women at Simisimi, Kisangani's 'old' airport, where commanders had set up their base.[10] When it was over, Kisangani was again firmly in RCD-G hands and at least 80 civilians had been slain. Despite having 1,000 soldiers on the ground in Kisangani and authorisation as per its mandate 'to protect civilians under imminent threat of physical violence', MONUC troops did not intervene to aid the people of Kisangani as they came under attack.[11] In a move further cementing the Kigali government to its old warmongering policies in Congo, James Kabarebe, who had overseen Rwandan prosecution of both the First and Second Congo Wars, was appointed as the chief of staff for the Ministry of Defence in July 2002, a position just below that of the minister of defence.

Despite the tentative progress of the Sun City talks, as Kisangani convulsed, Ituri erupted. During the leadership struggle between Ernest Wamba dia Wamba and Mbusa Nyamwisi that occurred in 2000, Nyamwisi had rallied support from the ethnic Hema community in Ituri while Wamba appealed to the Lendu.[12] Although Nyamwisi was himself a Nande, once he had triumphed over Wamba, he also began reaching out to the Lendu, in early 2002 naming Kasai-native Jean-Pierre Molondo Lompondo as governor of Ituri in an effort to sideline Hema militia leader Thomas Lubanga. Molondo Lompondo promptly set about integrating more Lendu militiamen into Nyamwisi's armed force, the APC.

When one of Nyamwisi's bodyguards was killed in April 2002 – allegedly on Lubanga's orders – the APC skirmished with Lubanga's UPC forces, with the latter subsequently seizing part of Bunia. As negotiations continued regarding the Sun City agreements, Kabila's FAC began training the APC forces, and thereby the Lendu and Ngiti militias, to try to exert some control over the area; the FAC also gave them weapons and uniforms.[13] By mid-2002, Uganda had turned against Nyamwisi because of his links with Kinshasa and began backing Lubanga's UPC. But in an effort to stem some of the violence, both Lubanga and his deputy Bosco Ntaganda were arrested in Kampala in June 2002, with the former shipped to Kinshasa. A summer of tit-for-tat violence followed until, in August, Uganda decided to seize control of Bunia. Ironically, in the same month, Kabila's Minister for Presidential Affairs Katumba Mwanke signed an accord in Luanda with the foreign ministers of Uganda and Angola whereby Uganda would withdraw its remaining troops from Congo and the two countries (Congo and Uganda) would normalise relations.[14]

Once let out of the bottle, the genie in Ituri would not be put back in again so easily, however. Along with North Kivu, more than any other region of Congo, Ituri represented the irresponsible adventurism of Congolese politicians and Congo's neighbours in their willingness to loose the forces of hell on a defenceless population for monetary gain, and their unwillingness or inability, if they so wished, to rein those forces in.

On 26 August 2002, a Congolese government delegation to Bunia, including Minister of Human Rights Ntumba Luaba and Thomas Lubanga himself (the latter theoretically still under arrest) degenerated into a hostage situation when UPC combatants seized Luaba and his colleagues and demanded freedom for Lubanga, Bosco Ntaganda and others. Luaba was finally allowed to fly back to Kinshasa three days later after the UPC prisoners were released. After this saga, the UPC set up another rump government in Bunia with Lubanga as president and Ntaganda as assistant minister of defence.[15] The reality, however, was that

Ituri remained a patchwork of fiefdoms and battlegrounds, and on 5 September 2002, APC forces, aided by Ngiti militias, attacked at Nyakunde, methodically killing at least 1,200 Hema, Gegere and Bira civilians in little more than a week, with special attention paid to the Centre Médical Evangélique hospital. Adorned with religious fetishes, the Ngiti fighters were said to be even more ruthless than the APC, who from time to time tried to stop certain killings.[16]

When Jean-Pierre Bemba's MLC arrived at the gold-mining centre of Mongbwalu in October 2002, they dubbed their campaign to eradicate the APC as *effacer le tableau* ('erase the blackboard'). Thereafter, Bemba's soldiers were known to locals as *les effaceurs*. Joining them were troops from Roger Lumbala's RCD-N – yet another RCD splinter faction, this one largely a creation of rapacious Ugandan army officers – as well as members of the UPC and the UPDF itself. In a late November assault on Mongbwalu that saw mortars rain down on the town, at least 200 people were killed. The attack – spearheaded by Bosco Ntaganda – also included the widespread use of machetes and spears. During the siege, the Ngiti priest of Mongbwalu parish, Abbé Boniface Bwanalonga, disappeared after being seized by UPC combatants.[17] The town would change hands several more times in the course of the conflict, with another attack, this one by the FNI in May 2003, killing at least 500 people.[18]

A subsequent UN investigation would conclude that, during their time in Ituri, the MLC and the RCD-N had engaged in rape, torture, executions and cannibalism in and around Mambasa and Mangina between October and December 2002.[19,20] This conclusion was buttressed by another report that found that, during the last three months of 2002, MLC and RCD-N combatants:

> raped, killed, and cannibalized Pygmies ... [seeking] to terrorize the Pygmies into helping them as guides through the dense forest so that they could avoid travel on the main roads where they would be subject to attack.[21]

As Mongbwalu groaned under the assault, several Ngiti militias unified in November 2002 to form the Beni-based FRPI, which was closely linked to the FNI. The Mambasa-born Germain Katanga would emerge as the FRPI's driving force, and would be in command as the FRPI decimated the village of Bogoro in the attack described in the opening pages of this book.

As Ituri burned, to the south the Mai-Mai fighters continued to make their presence felt. Over the night of 24–25 September, as the RCD-G left Shabunda, Mai-Mai fighters flooded into the area.[22] A November 2002 dispute between Mai-Mai under the command of Mukalay Jean 'Deux Metres' and government forces in Ankoro in northern Katanga resulted in the deaths of at least 100 civilians.[23]

At the eleventh hour of the year, on 17 December, the warring parties in Congo finally signed the Global and All-Inclusive Agreement in Pretoria, which on paper marked the end of the Second Congo War and outlined plans for a transitional government. Kabila would continue as president, but now with four vice-presidents. These would be the RCD-G's Azarias Ruberwa (a Banyamulenge from South Kivu); the MLC's Jean-Pierre Bemba; former RCD official Arthur Z'ahidi Ngoma; and former Laurent Kabila foreign minister Abdoulaye Yerodia Ndombasi, known for his blood-curdling rhetoric against Tutsis in the wake of the 1998 uprising. The Senate was to consist of 120 senators, with the Kabila government getting 22 seats, 22 to the RCD-G, 22 to the MLC, 22 to civil society, four to Mai-Mai groups, and so on. The MPs (in the lower house of parliament) and ministerial posts were similarly divided.

The RCD and the MLC became political parties. With the aid of Vital Kamerhe, Kabila formed the Parti du Peuple pour la Reconstruction et la Démocratie (PPRD). Kabila would be sworn in under the new constitution as transitional president for two years. The FAC would eventually become the Forces Armées de la République Démocratique du Congo (FARDC) and members of various factions were integrated into its ranks. Also out of the Pretoria agreements was formed the Comité International d'Accompagnement de la Transition (CIAT), a body to oversee the transition and composed of the five permanent members of the UN Security Council (China, USA, France, UK, Russia) as well as South Africa, Angola, Belgium, Canada, Gabon, Zambia, the African Union, the European Union (EU) and MONUC itself.

By the end of 2002, the uniformed armies of Rwanda (which had been renamed the Rwanda Defence Force or RDF in May of that year), Angola, Namibia and Zimbabwe had completed their withdrawal from Congo. On the ground, as they departed, the Rwandans left military proxies that they had spent years cultivating.

But the fires of conflict would not burn out quite so fast. By early 2003, the sands under the opportunistic allegiances in Ituri were shifting yet again, as the UPC began to move away from Uganda and started working with the RCD-G, the first contacts having been broached by James Kabarebe in June 2002.[24] As the UPC fell into the sphere of influence of Rwanda, which supplied it with military training and weapons,[25] the Ugandans turned to Floribert Njabu, who had created the Lendu-centric political movement the FNI. Thomas Lubanga would later dismiss the FNI as 'a bunch of independent, unorganised groups under the leadership of no one', but they were to prove a serious challenge to the UPC.[26] A former officer in the Mobutu-era FAZ, Mathieu Ngudjolo Chui would become one of the FNI's (and later FRPI's) senior commanders. By the end of the year, in yet another rearranging of the chessboard, the UPC itself would split apart, with one side led by Lubanga – who at this point was being held in the gilded cage of Kinshasa's Grand Hotel by the transitional government – and the other led by Kisembo Bahemuka. With Lubanga detained in Kinshasa, Bosco Ntaganda became the most powerful figure in the Lubanga faction of the UPC. By this point he had earned himself the sobriquet *Le Terminateur* (The Terminator) from the people of Ituri, an all-too-telling name.

In Ituri, the Pretoria agreement had no effect at all. The combined forces of the UPDF and the FNI steamrolled towards the mining town of Kilo on 10 March 2003, with the latter arriving first and attacking en masse. By the time UPDF troops arrived, the FNI had killed over 100 people they suspected of belonging to the Nyali ethnic group, who were viewed as sympathetic to the Hema.[27] On 7 April, attackers descended on the mostly Hema village of Drodro and its neighbouring communities, killing at least 966 people with firearms and machetes.[28] Only days after the UPDF completed its withdrawal from Bunia, FNI fighters murdered two unarmed UN observers who were stationed in Mongbwalu.[29] Speaking to the Ituri Pacification Commission, Brigadier General Kale Kayihura of the UPDF even went as far as asking those assembled to forgive the atrocities committed by Ugandan troops.

He had reason to beg forgiveness. According to an exhaustive subsequent investigation, Uganda 'failed in its obligation under international humanitarian law to protect the civilian population' and stimulated 'new political parties and militia groups to form', deepening the conflict in Ituri which Uganda then used 'as a pretext to remain in the resource-rich area, exploiting its minerals and commerce'.[30]

Despite Kigali's new-found love for the Lendu, support among Congo's Tutsi community for Rwanda's plan for the east of the country was by no means uniform. A rebellion launched in early 2002 and led by Commandant Patrick Masunzu, a Banyamulenge RCD-G officer who opposed Rwanda's expansionist plans, met with ruthless reprisals from Kigali,[31] with heavy fighting occurring throughout early 2003 around Uvira and in the Hauts-Plateaux region of South Kivu.[32]

For some of the other combatants, it was a time for tying up loose ends. In a decision that would have fateful consequences,

Jean-Pierre Bemba's MLC had ventured north into the Central African Republic in October 2002 to back the faltering government of Ange-Félix Patassé against an insurgency launched by his former chief of staff, François Bozizé. Roaming the country for five months alongside Patassé's forces and fighters sent by Libyan dictator Muammar Gaddafi, Bemba's men were nevertheless unable to prevent the capture of Bangui by Bozizé's men while Patassé was out of the country. A later human rights report would conclude that, while in the Central African Republic, the MLC had engaged in a campaign of rape that was 'systematic and widespread' and that, in Bangui in particular:

> the rapes perpetrated by MLC combatants were partly
> intended to punish the women for alleged assistance to the
> Bozizé-led combatants ... [And] to humiliate the men and
> demonstrate their powerlessness to protect their women and
> families.[33]

Bozizé promptly declared himself president, which he remained until his overthrow in March 2013. As the MLC troops trudged back to Congo and their leaders made haste to Kinshasa, it all simply appeared like a depressing subplot in Bemba's attempts to now re-cast himself as a statesman. And it did seem that way. At the time.

At roughly the same time as the transitional government was being established in April 2003, MONUC's strength in Congo was almost 9,000 soldiers. With Amos Namanga Ngongi departing in June 2003, leadership of MONUC passed to US diplomat William Lacy Swing, who had served as US ambassador in Kinshasa from 1998 until 2001 and had also done ambassadorial stints in the Republic of the Congo, Liberia, Nigeria, South Africa and Haiti. With Swing's arrival, MONUC began to pay more attention to the violence that continued to roil the country's east, particularly Ituri. In November, the UN Secretary-General listed 12 parties to the Congo conflict that used children in violation of international law, including the RCD-G, the RCD-K/RCD-ML, the FNI and FRPI, the Mai-Mai militias, the FDLR and the Congolese army itself.[34] Children were said to make up at least 40 per cent of the members of some armed groups, with at least 30,000 boys and girls being involved.[35]

In Rwanda, in August 2003, Paul Kagame was elected president in a ballot that saw him take 95 per cent of the vote, with EU observers saying the vote was 'not entirely free and fair' but nevertheless 'an important step in the democratic process'.[36] In his victory speech Kagame called his election 'a victory for all Rwandans' and 'a victory which contradicts the prophets of doom'.[37] Pasteur Bizimungu, the country's first post-genocide president and one of the highest-ranking Hutu members of the RPF, had been sentenced to 15 years in prison the previous June.

On 5 September, Mai-Mai leader David Padiri Bulenda was inaugurated into the FARDC and passed command of his group to Marcel Munga, formerly one of his chief advisers, who spoke warmly of the spirit of 'reconciliation' and 'integration' that was informing the process.[38] Munga also stated that, as 'the soldiers that belonged to the RCD are being integrated into the national army ... the forces of the [Mai-Mai] and RCD-Goma now form one entity'. Munga also said that the Mai-Mai 'had no child soldiers', while qualifying in the same breath that 'if there are any, it is a bare minimum, maybe ten at most'.[39] In early October 2003, Padiri Bulenda's Mai-Mai militia also signed a ceasefire agreement with the RCD-G in Shabunda.[40]

As the transitional government finally began gathering steam in 2004, an ethics and anti-corruption commission (La Commission de l'Éthique et de la Lutte contre la Corruption) finally began functioning, a year after its creation. Tasked with investigating corrupt activities, the body was largely paralysed due to the necessity of bloating its staff with members of various political factions.[41] Later in the year, in an obvious sop to Kabila's allies in the east, a new law on nationality gave citizenship to Hutus whose families had been present in Congo before independence, as well as the right to land ownership and the right to involvement in the political process. The Hutus thus moved deeper into the government camp and further away from the Tutsis, despite their shared Rwandaphone heritage.

Over the next few months, with the president and his vice-presidents residing in the capital some 3,500 kilometres away, the fraught nature of actually implementing the Pretoria accords in the east would become clear.

In Bukavu on 26 May 2004, a clash between forces loyal to former RCD-G commander Colonel Jules Mutebutsi, who had been suspended from the national army in February, and forces of the pro-Kinshasa Tenth Military Region under the command of General Félix Mbuza Mabe resulted in the death of at least one of Mabe's men. This set in motion a series of ghastly, ethnically based attacks where soldiers of the Tenth Military Region killed at least 15 civilians, most or all of them Banyamulenge. Government soldiers also invaded the compound of an international humanitarian organisation in Bukavu where they raped one female aid worker and shot another, also stealing money and telephones.

En route to Bukavu to support Mutebutsi, the forces of Brigadier General Laurent Nkunda, who oversaw many of the atrocities in Kisangani in May 2002, victimised villages such as Minova and Babamba. After seizing Bukavu, Nkunda's men went 'house-to-house raping and looting', with their victims including a mother and her three-year-old daughter, and five other three-year-olds. Some witnesses claimed that the Rwandan military was present during the rebel assault on the town, and the residents were able to identify commanders from the previous Rwandan occupation as well as vehicles, weapons and uniforms used by the Rwandan army.[42] As in Kisangani nearly two years earlier, during the fighting in Bukavu MONUC did little to aid civilians under immediate threat of their lives, and 'different [MONUC] contingents reportedly consulted with their capitals before deciding whether they would obey the orders of their UN force commanders'.[43] Following a negotiated end to the fighting, Nkunda withdrew with his forces (consisting of several thousand men) to the forests around Masisi.

As efforts to integrate the various armed factions were under way, the east remained a recalcitrant holdout. Eugène Serufuli Ngayabaseka, a Rwandaphone Hutu and former member of the RCD-G, served as governor of North Kivu from July 2000 until 2007; during the transition he maintained a 3,000-strong (predominantly Hutu) protective militia and a 'financial co-ordinator' whose authority on the ground exceeded that of the minister of finance.[44] As Serufuli brandished his private army, the Tutsi and Hutu problem continued to grind away, with the government doing little to undermine the strength of Hutu extremists operating within its borders.

In mid-2004, a splinter group of the FDLR known as the Rastas began making its first appearances in South Kivu, centred first around Bunyakiri. They quickly established themselves as enthusiastic perpetrators of the wanton violence that the population of the province had endured for many years. Not to be outdone, on the night of 13 August 2004, Burundian FNL Hutu rebels attacked a refugee camp at the Gatumba transit centre on the Congolese border, killing 152 (mostly Banyamulenge) refugees who had sought shelter there. Brigadier General Germain Niyoyankana of the Burundian army would state that the Congolese army itself was also involved.[45] By late 2004, more than 20,000 people had fled Kanyabayonga to escape clashes between Congolese government forces and those of Captain Kabakuli Kennedy, who claimed he was fighting to defend the Banyamulenge.[46] A meeting point of main roads in North Kivu, Kanyabayonga had been a hotly contested prize among various rebel groups in the area.

On 22 December, yet more fighting broke out when Rwandan Hutu militia members attacked Congolese soldiers in the villages of Kalengera and Rhana. The fighting lasted several days, killing at least five Hutu fighters and wounding six Congolese.[47] MONUC Brigadier General Jan Isberg, the commander of peacekeepers in North and South Kivu, confessed to a reporter that the UN mission was 'not equipped' for what was taking place in his zone of command, and that 'we don't have the manpower to deal with an army cracking'.[48] Barely a week earlier, MONUC forces exchanged fire with an unknown armed group again trying to enter Bukavu.[49]

Fighting also continued among unintegrated militia members, regular army and Nkunda's deserters. In October 2004, clashes between Mai-Mai and RCD-G forces near Bishange in South Kivu displaced at least 11,000 people.[50] By late December, towns in the Lubero region of North Kivu were virtually empty as villagers fled fighting between the Congolese army and the deserters.[51] The effect of the continued battles on the population was horrendous, as in the town of Kpandroma, about 50 miles north-east of Bunia, which saw an average of one rape case reported every day between July and mid-December 2004.[52] Following a late-December meeting with Congo's Senate President Pierre Marini Bodho, the mutineers demanded that the transitional government withdraw its forces from eastern Congo.[53]

By the time Congo greeted 2005, the FNI and the UPC had fought five battles in the struggle to control the Ituri gold-mining town of Mongbwalu. The transitional government offered the UPC's Bosco Ntaganda the post of general in the new army, an overture Ntaganda refused. The FRPI's Germain Katanga – whose forces had killed over 200 people during the 2003 raid on Bogoro – assented, and joined the new national army at the rank of general. Such deal-making naturally made the Congolese wonder exactly what kind of 'peace' their leaders had in mind.

Peace proved a difficult adjustment for the former Ituri militia leaders. On 25 February, a MONUC convoy travelling near Bunia was attacked by FNI gunmen and nine Bangladeshi peacekeepers were killed. In response to this affront – a rather idiotic and self-destructive move given the now generalised rhetoric of 'reconciliation' among the political actors who possessed the most potent firepower – Kinshasa sent an additional 3,000 troops into Ituri while the FNI's leader Floribert Ndjabu was arrested in the capital, as was the FRPI's Germain Katanga.[54] In Ituri itself, the FRPI fell largely into the hands of Matata Wanaloki aka Cobra Matata. For good measure, the Kabila government also detained the UPC's Thomas Lubanga, first housing him in the salubrious surroundings of Kinshasa's Grand Hotel and then, feeling less generous, in Kinshasa's fetid central prison.[55] Although it would prove delicate, the situation in Ituri, if not exactly calm, gradually settled into something less spectacularly violent than before. At the time, given the very real sacrifice the Bangladeshi peacekeepers had made, it was thought in bad taste to ask why, when it moved so swiftly to facilitate arrests after the killing of nine of its own, the UN was not similarly moved to action in the face of the massive loss of civilian lives in Kisangani, Bakavu or Ituri itself.

If the situation in Ituri was somewhat calmer, however, the situation elsewhere in the country remained explosive.

At one point in Katanga, Pasteur Daniel Ngoy Mulunda, a 'spiritual adviser' to Kabila, promised to hand out bicycles to local Mai-Mai combatants who disarmed. But when the promised bicycles did not appear, Mai-Mai who had turned in their weapons ran amok in an April 2005 rampage near Katala that claimed at least seven lives and forced some 4,000 to flee.[56] The previous month, also in Katanga, during an attack on Nkong, at least nine women were murdered and their bodies mutilated when Mai-Mai attacked Congolese troops.[57]

Although in March 2005 the FDLR leadership released a statement after peace talks in Rome saying that the group 'condemned the genocide committed in Rwanda and its authors', and that the FDLR was opting 'to transform their armed struggle into a political one',[58] the reality on the ground was considerably different.

On 9 July, in the village of Kabingu near South Kivu's Kahuzi-Biega National Park, at least 30 fighters from the FDLR-splinter group Rastas attacked civilians, killing at least 50 – including at least 17 children – locking many in their homes which were then set alight.[59] On 10 October, South Kivu villages were again attacked by a machete-wielding group of Rastas that claimed the lives of 24 people, including six children. Thousands of villagers fled the attack to the town of Walungu.[60]

Throughout the worst of the crisis, the approach of the government of US President George W. Bush, preoccupied with military operations in Iraq and Afghanistan, was one of indifference and neglect. By June 2005, the seemingly endless violence in Congo had stirred a bipartisan body of US senators (a group not known for its moral courage) to publish an open letter to the Bush administration pleading for a 'high-level engagement' in Congo similar to the administration's sustained attention in dealing with the civil war in Sudan.[61] At the time, the US ambassador to Congo was Roger A. Meece, who would serve from August 2004 until August 2007 and was an Africa veteran.

Given the circumstances under which it was conducted, there were remarkably few incidents of violence when the long-promised referendum on the country's new constitution was held over the weekend of 18–19 December 2005. The vote was held under the aegis of Congo's new independent electoral body, the Commission Électorale Nationale Indépendante (CENI), which was provided with technical and logistical assistance by MONUC. All in all, the two (CENI and MONUC) managed an extraordinary feat to hold such a potentially explosive vote over such a wide expanse, the first of its kind in Congo since 1965.[62] When all the votes were finally cast, the referendum had had a participation level of 62 per cent, and the new fundamental law, as it was called, had been approved by 84 per cent of the valid votes.[63] With their vote, the Congolese devolved greater autonomy from Kinshasa to the provinces (although in truth the state's presence was already more theoretical than actual much of the time), lowered the minimum age for presidential candidates from 35 to 30 (in an obvious sop to Kabila) and paved the way for presidential and parliamentary elections to be held in March of the following year.[64] It was understood that both Kabila and Bemba would be running for the top job. Unwisely, Étienne Tshisekedi and the UDPS, scornful of the entire process, had called for voters to boycott registering for the referendum, leaving the ageing leader as something of the odd man out in the new political order.[65]

It was during the electoral contest that was to come – and its aftermath – that the Congolese were to take a leap of faith by participating in an electoral process when elections had been a farce in the past; by believing that, given the chance, their politicians and the international community would work together to improve their lives; and also by trusting in the retiring, still youthful president who had somehow stepped out of his father's shadow to cobble together a peace deal, however imperfect and disingenuous, with hated rivals. Before long, the Congolese would see the true face of their young president, and when they did, it was a face that was not so unfamiliar after all.

5 | ONE HUNDRED PER CENT CONGOLESE

As 2006 dawned, Congo found itself torn by its expectation for the elections that loomed on the horizon and fear for developments, once more, in the east. During late January 2006, Laurent Nkunda's forces battered the FARDC from pillar to post, with the latter frequently bailed out at the last minute by MONUC forces, but not before tens of thousands of civilians were forced to flee their homes.[1] In the first weeks of 2006, a quadruple increase in rape cases was recorded in the Kanyabayonga–Kayna axis in North Kivu's Lubero territory, directly related to the Nkunda rebellion.[2] By early February 2006, tens of thousands of people fleeing fighting in the Kibirizi area north-west of Rutshuru, many of whom had endured terrible abuses, had arrived at Kanyabayonga, Kayna and Kirumba, with many others still hiding in the bush.[3] By March 2006, Nkunda's forces began forcibly recruiting child soldiers.[4]

Conducting elections in a country as vast as Congo with so many infrastructure-related hurdles to overcome would have proven a challenge in any event, but as conflict continued to rage in the east and south, it proved to be doubly difficult.

The electoral campaign was not exactly designed to inspire confidence in the politicians among the Congolese people, either. With sniggering references to Kabila's murky origins, Bemba's campaign portrayed his opponent as a foreign interloper and himself as 'one hundred per cent Congolese', while Kabila's camp depicted Bemba as a treacherous war criminal and probable cannibal, a reference to the MLC's atrocities in Ituri. While RTNC was solidly pro-Kabila, Bemba's Canal Congo Télévision

(CCTV) and Radio Liberté Kinshasa (RALIK) pumped out non-stop MLC propaganda. Even more worrisome, as the electoral campaign commenced, Kabila still had between 10,000 and 15,000 Republican Guard soldiers under his direct control and not integrated into the army, while Bemba's personal guard was thought to number around 1,000, half of them in Kinshasa. Both men had extensive political networks, with Bemba's MLC strongest in the capital and in his native Équateur, while Kabila's PPRD, led by Bukavu local boy Vital Kamerhe as its secretary-general, was strongest in the country's east. Despite being headed by a native son, the PPRD's campaign did little to de-escalate the situation in the Kivus, and at a rally in Goma in May 2006, the vice-president representing the government, Abdoulaye Yerodia (who had served as Laurent Kabila's foreign minister from 1999 until 2000), roared at Congo's Tutsi population, saying that:

> we will tell them to leave our territory ... If you don't want
> to go back from where you came from, we will put sticks into
> your backsides to make sure you go back.[5]

Also seeking the top job were a variety of individuals, each of whom represented, in their own way, the currents of political life in the country over the previous four decades. The 81-year-old Antoine Gizenga, who had served as Lumumba's deputy prime minister before the latter's murder, ran as the presidential candidate of the Parti Lumumbiste Unifié (PALU). Mobutu Sese Seko's son, Nzanga Mobutu, announced that he was forming an apparently unironically named Union des Démocrates Mobutistes (UDEMO) and would run as the party's presidential candidate. Former rebel Azarias Ruberwa declared that he would be running under the banner of the RCD. The Ituri warlord Antipas Mbusa Nyamwisi would stand as the candidate for the political party Forces du Renouveau, which had grown directly out of his own RCD faction. Étienne Tshisekedi announced that he was refusing to register for the presidential ballot and a UDPS spokesman said that the party would 'block the elections, peace-fully', claiming that a 'second-class democracy' was being foisted on the Congolese. The UDPS subsequently announced that it would boycott the poll in its entirety – and it did just that.[6] By this point Tshisekedi, long viewed as Congo's most senior democratic militant, was well on his way to becoming that most unfortunate of historical figures: a one-time political icon who was utterly overtaken by events and thus missed his moment to lead. Likewise, the UDPS was increasingly viewed as, rather than a mass movement, a political organ committed – ineffectually – to bringing Tshisekedi to power, not 'democracy' per se.

Tshisekedi, however, did have a point. Although, upon taking power, the younger Kabila had desires to disband Katanga Mai-Mai factions such as the Forces d'Auto-Défense Populaires and Moyo wa Chuma and integrate them into the national army, he was straitjacketed by his advisers, some of whom had vested interests in retaining the groups, and his suggestions were largely ignored.[7]

Although it did not garner as much international attention as the open warfare raging in the Kivus, by late 2005 and early 2006 the humanitarian and security situation in central and northern Katanga had drastically deteriorated following an FARDC push against formerly loyal Mai-Mai groups such as that led by Gédéon Kyungu Mutanga in the area. A MONUC report characterised the operation as 'ill-prepared and badly conducted by ill-equipped, unpaid and largely unfed soldiers who live on the back of the local population'.[8] By early February 2006, at least 165,000 people had been displaced in the region and at least 33 civilians killed by the FARDC and 31 by the Mai-Mai, with villagers simultaneously victimised and accused of being hostile collaborators by both sides. The 63rd Brigade of the FARDC – notorious for its atrocities against civilians – killed and 'disappeared' villagers if they were suspected of being Mai-Mai collaborators, while the Mai-Mai (in Katanga largely shut out of the political process following the end of hostilities) targeted and executed traditional chiefs they accused of working with the FARDC.[9] The FARDC manoeuvres did land a major fish, however, when Gédéon Kyungu Mutanga himself was captured in March 2006.

As elections loomed, the Union Nationale des Démocrates Fédéralistes du Congo (UNAFEC), something of a Luba supremacist party that had grown out of Gabriel Kyungu wa Kumwanza's UFERI (closely affiliated with Kabila security adviser John Numbi), recruited youth groups in Katanga to campaign for Kabila, with its youth wing, the Jeunesse de l'Union des Nationalistes Fédéralistes du Congo (JUNAFEC), being particularly active.[10] UNAFEC militants attacked both UDPS supporters and members of the Solidarité Katangaise organisation.[11] Claiming that a 'secession' was afoot, several of Numbi's rivals in Katanga (including André Tshombe, son of Moïse Tshombe) had been arrested as far back as April 2005.

Amidst all the politicking, Kabila found time to marry Marie Olive Lembe di Sita, with whom he already had a five-year-old daughter, Sifa, on 17 June 2006. Dan Gertler, the Israeli diamond merchant, was among the guests at the wedding.

As the election drew ever closer, fears of violence and fraud touched the heart of the Congolese capital, as they would do again in the future. In a 21 July statement, Congo's Catholic bishops said that necessary conditions to have a free and fair poll did not exist in the country, while the country's National Episcopal Conference denounced 'double-dealing' and 'cheating' in the process, both obviously referring to Kabila.[12] Following a huge 27 July 2006 pro-Bemba rally at the Stade Tata Raphaël in Kinshasa, the candidate's supporters ran amok, looting a media building and a church, killing at least six people and raping at least one woman.[13]

When the first round of elections were held on 30 July, the Congolese, despite the intimidation, threats, decades of miserable poverty and warfare and the denial of their democratic rights since 1960, responded massively, with an overwhelming show of support for the electoral process as 9,700 candidates vied for 500 National Assembly seats.[14] By 13 August, results from 65 of Congo's 169 constituencies showed Kabila with nearly 48 per cent of the vote and Bemba, his nearest rival, with around 18 per cent.[15] The elderly Lumumbaist Antoine Gizenga was also running strongly, particularly in his stronghold of Bandundu. The east and south were solidly pro-Kabila, while the west (including Kinshasa) and north were pro-Bemba.

On Sunday 20 August, following sporadic exchanges of gunfire between Kabila and Bemba loyalists throughout Kinshasa during the day, the CENI's president Apollinaire Malu announced that Kabila had won 44.81 per cent of the votes to Jean-Pierre Bemba's 20.03 per cent in the 30 July elections. Antoine Gizenga had placed third with 13.06 per cent of the votes. A run-off was provisionally set for 29 October.[16]

On the same day the need for a run-off election was expected to be announced, Bemba was due at CCTV to give an address, but before he arrived some of his bodyguards exchanged fire there with the Republican Guard (Garde Républicaine) and police. Bemba did not give his speech and the results were announced a short time later. The following day, Kabila's forces moved armoured personnel carriers and tanks mounted with howitzers into central Kinshasa.[17]

Early in the day on 21 August, members of the CIAT arrived at Bemba's home to discuss the violence. Shortly after the meeting began, the residence came under fire from a variety of armed Kabila loyalists present in the area. A flurry of calls between Kabila, Bemba, UN Secretary-General Kofi Annan and the trapped diplomats ensued, as MONUC forces and a small EU armed contingent moved into the vicinity of Bemba's home. The diplomats were eventually extracted successfully. On their way, international forces had noted a company of Republican Guard, with three armoured personnel carriers (including one with a 90 millimetre mounted gun) and two howitzer guns waiting on the Boulevard du 30 Juin near Bemba's home. During the fighting, Bemba's personal helicopter, located only 300 metres from his residence, was destroyed.[18] As fighting continued sporadically for the next two days, at least 23 people died and 43 were wounded.[19]

Although the international community seemed content to adhere to the fiction that, in this instance, both sides were equally at fault, according to those present at the time, Kabila's troops were indisputably the aggressors and used overwhelming force, even though Bemba's guards also killed civilians.[20] Fearing assassination, neither man would campaign personally during the second round of the elections, preferring to allow friendly media outlets and their surrogates to spread the message for them. Bemba's media outlets were sporadically shut down, however, and Kabila's message remained the dominant one. Over the next 20 months, the Republican Guard would be responsible for the summary execution or disappearance of at least 125 people.[21]

Congo's new parliament, comprising the Senate and the National Assembly, was sworn in on 22 September. Adroitly, Kabila and his advisers had consumed several parties, including Antoine Gizenga's PALU and Pierre Lumbi's Mouvement Social pour le Renouveau (MSR), into a pro-government coalition, the Alliance pour la Majorité Présidentielle (AMP). Politically as well as militarily, Bemba appeared to have been significantly outflanked. The parliament boasted not a single representative from the UDPS after the party's boycott of the ballot. In late October 2006, Nzanga Mobutu, who had responded favourably to Kabila's overtures, was seized by Bemba's soldiers as he campaigned in Bemba's stronghold of Gbadolite, following a gun battle at a radio station that killed at least four people. Mobutu was eventually released to the UN and taken away in a MONUC tank.[22]

The day of voting – 29 October – passed relatively calmly, with the African Union commending 'the smooth conduct of the second round of the presidential election'.[23] Former Canadian Prime Minister Joe Clark, who served as the head of the observation team for the Carter Center, also praised the vote, saying that, although attempted manipulation was 'very serious in a few cases, [it] appears at this point to be isolated and unlikely to affect the overall success of the vote'.[24]

When the final results were eventually released on 15 November, Kabila had 58 per cent of the vote to Bemba's 42 per cent.[25] A statement by the MLC the previous evening accused Kabila of manipulating the electoral result and that it was Bemba, not Kabila, who had won more than 50 per cent. Although foreign observers noted some irregularities, the consensus appeared to be that none was of a magnitude to substantially alter the outcome and that Kabila had won the ballot more or less legitimately.[26] On the evening of the announcement, Kabila addressed his countrymen and beseeched them to 'remain united and to live in fraternity and tolerance'.[27]

As Congo's Supreme Court reviewed Bemba's complaints on 21 November, pro-Bemba protesters fired on police in front of the court, sparking a gun battle that lasted for nearly an hour and which resulted in the burning of part of the building and several vehicles. MONUC troops evacuated several Supreme Court justices, Bemba's lawyers and CENI officials.[28] Six days later, the Supreme Court reaffirmed Kabila's victory.

Kinshasa held its breath for further violence, but, on 28 November, Bemba, who would go on to serve as a senator in Congo's parliament, accepted Kabila's victory in a public statement, saying that, although he stood by his complaints, he would lead a 'strong republican opposition in the interests of the nation'.[29]

Congo was indeed a nation in need of unity of purpose, as, during 25–26 November, Laurent Nkunda's rebel army, over the previous summer re-dubbed the Congrès National pour la Défense du Peuple (CNDP), shelled Sake near Goma in North Kivu without warning, an attack in which 25 civilians died either from the shelling itself or from subsequent indiscriminate weapons fire between Nkunda's troops and the FARDC.[30] In the United States, a bill sponsored by senators Barack Obama and Hillary Clinton, officially called Senate Bill 2125 but which would become known as the 'Democratic Republic of the Congo Relief, Security, and Democracy Promotion Act of 2006', was signed into law by US President George W. Bush. The bill sought to 'hold accountable individuals who illegally exploit the country's natural resources' and to 'hold accountable individuals, entities, and countries working to destabilize the country'. Significantly, it also authorised the Secretary of State:

> to withhold assistance made available ... other than humanitarian, peacekeeping, and counterterrorism assistance, for a foreign country if the Secretary determines that the government of the foreign country is taking actions to destabilize the Democratic Republic of the Congo.[31]

In Congo, at the end of the year, John Numbi, by this time head of the Congolese air force, began negotiations with Nkunda in Goma, which were then moved to Kigali; James Kabarebe, at the time chief of staff of the Rwandan army, also participated. In early January 2007, an agreement was hammered out by which Nkunda's troops would be integrated with Congolese army troops present in North Kivu, troops who would then be deployed locally and sent into operations against the FDLR. There was some discussion that Nkunda might leave Congo, possibly for a year or two of further 'military training', possibly in South Africa.[32] Peace seemed to be at hand, an impression reinforced when the government hailed the signing of a disarmament deal with the FRPI's Cobra Matata, whom FARDC General Vainqueur Mayala characterised as the 'last of the militia chiefs', outside the disarmament and demobilisation framework for Ituri.[33] At the time, Matata was believed to have around 1,000 men (some of whom in fact were just boys) under arms.

In Kabila's new government, announced on 5 February 2007, Antoine Gizenga's PALU would receive four cabinet posts including the ministries of mines and justice, while Gizenga himself would become prime minister. Nzanga Mobutu and Mbusa Nyamwisi would take over as agriculture minister and minister of foreign affairs respectively.[34] The minister of infrastructure position went to another former Kabila rival, Pierre Lumbi.

The 'strong republican opposition' that Jean-Pierre Bemba spoke of in his concession speech was, however, the last thing that Kabila and those around him wanted, as the events of March 2007 would demonstrate.

Emboldened by the lack of international reaction to the violence perpetrated by government forces in Kinshasa in August 2006, Kabila was handed an ideal pretext to further neutralise his opponent by Bemba's refusal to put his personal guard under the command of the national army in exchange for the protection of 12 police officers. This was perhaps understandable, given the events of the previous year; however, the fact that Bemba's guards – around 500 men in all – behaved as little more than an ill-disciplined, predatory rabble somewhat undermined his argument. Matters accelerated considerably when Bemba gave a television interview on 14 March during which he described the government's decision to cede territory to Angola as 'treason', decried the regime's corruption and referred to it as a 'dictatorship for money'.

On 21 March, the government cut off the ability of Bemba's CCTV and RALIK stations to broadcast over its transmitters. The following day a terrifying battle between government and Bemba-allied forces erupted along the Boulevard de 30 Juin in the heart of the Gombe diplomatic quarter, setting off street fighting that raged in the capital for three days. In densely populated urban areas, each side attacked the other with machine guns and rocket-propelled grenades, with the Republican Guard employing T-55 tanks and mortars.[35] The Groupe Spécial de la Sécurité

Présidentielle (GSSP) also took part in the fighting. Government forces looted CCTV on 23 March, and also killed a number of Bemba supporters who had gathered there with their families for protection.[36]

The UN would later conclude that over 300 people were killed in the violence, most by the Republican Guard, which had also engaged in summary executions.[37] At Camp Tshatshi, Republican Guard soldiers are thought to have killed at least 100 people in the ensuing days.[38] Many civilians died, the Nigerian ambassador was gravely wounded, and the Greek, Spanish and Nigerian embassies were all damaged significantly. Bemba and his family fled to the South African embassy, as many of his militiamen and their families escaped across the river to Brazzaville.

It was finally too much. Kabila had won, and in using overwhelming force, he had finally brought to heel his most potent enemy. After more than two weeks of negotiations between foreign diplomats advocating on Bemba's behalf and Kabila himself, Bemba left Kinshasa on 11 April and flew to his villa in the Portuguese city of Faro. Out of Congo but, as it would happen, not out of the headlines.

6 | GLITTERING DEMONS

The two Congo wars and subsequent violent struggles for power were indeed a holocaust, but they were also an armed robbery of epic proportions, a robbery in which Congolese officials, their neighbours in Africa and the international community were all complicit. As the citizens of this land, endowed with unsurpassed natural gifts, fled in terror across its great expanse, those very resources poured across its border, making enormous fortunes for a handful of people.

As Jean-Pierre Bemba was exiting the country, Martin Kabwelulu, the PALU politician serving as minister of mines, announced in April 2007 that Congo would be reviewing all the existing mining contracts between private companies and the state. Kabwelulu's announcement followed the findings of a special parliamentary commission, chaired by Christophe Lutundula. The commission had completed a 271-page report in June 2005 (this was not made public until February 2006) which found that many contracts signed during the war were either illegal or of little value. The Lutundula Commission, as it was known, also concluded that Kinshasa's political elite intervened 'in the shadows ... using their influence and giving inappropriate orders to the negotiators or signatories' of contracts.[1] However, the Kabwelulu-mandated body charged with investigating the contracts was composed, in its entirety, of representatives of various government ministries (such as the presidency, the prime minister, the ministries of mines and finance) and government civil servants, with not a single civil society figure among its number. In the discussion about how their natural resources would benefit them, the Congolese people appeared to have been shut out once again.

The natural blessings bestowed on Congo almost exhaust superlatives, with its national territory containing more than 1,100 different mineral substances.[2] The country has the largest known diamond resources in the world in terms of carats – approximately 150 million, accounting for 25 per cent of the total known reserves – the majority of which are found in Kasaï Occidental and Kasaï Oriental.[3] The province of Katanga alone has 34 per cent of the cobalt and 10 per cent of the copper reserves in the world.[4] In Congo as a whole one finds 64 per cent of the world's known coltan reserves, mostly in the two Kivus and in Maniema province, which borders both North and South Kivu immediately to its east. The most important ore from which tin is extracted, cassiterite, is found in extensive deposits around Walikale and Masisi in North Kivu, Kamituga in South Kivu and Kalima in Maniema. The largest and richest cassiterite mine, found in Bisie near Walikale, also contains coltan. New environmental regulations at the turn of the millennium saw a more aggressive need for tin as it became a favoured replacement for lead in various products. The province of Orientale, particularly its Ituri region, is studded with vast deposits of gold.

As a nation, Congo should stride across the continent as an economic and political powerhouse; however, for the first half of the twentieth century the country was little more than an open cupboard of baubles to be looted by the Belgians, and for the second half as a personal, seemingly bottomless bank account for its kleptocratic rulers.

The country to which Joseph Kabila got himself elected president in 2006, and over which he began asserting control in 2007, was a place where economic exchange had been conducted from behind the barrel of a gun since 1885. As a Goma-based NGO wrote in late 2005:

> the entire history ... of the rules governing (Congo's) economy
> is one of unaccountable, short-lived and arbitrary laws
> succeeding one another, co-existing in contradiction to one
> another, applied selectively and capriciously and at the same
> time masquerading as immutable, eternal and incontrovertible
> truths.[5]

Setting the mould for those who would come after, of course, was Belgium's King Leopold, who, once he had established the Congo Free State, proceeded to terrorise Congo's various ethnic groups into submission as his proxies helped him drain the country of rubber and ivory.

After the Belgian colonial period, under Mobutu Sese Seko the state of affairs became not so much one where the system was corrupt but rather one where corruption *was* the system. Following the creation of the mining enterprise Gécamines out of the Union Minière du Haut Katanga, the dictator and his cronies gobbled up much of the profit. This continued until, as mismanagement beset the company, Mobutu re-allowed foreign investors to operate Gécamines' state-owned mines, again at little benefit to the Congolese people. During the 1960s and 1970s, Zaire was the world's leading producer of cobalt and copper, but the bottom fell out of the cobalt market in 1978, a development that hit the Zairian economy hard. The Kilo-Moto mines in Ituri were directly exploited by the state until the 1980s,[6] whereas Sominki, the former dominant mining concern in the Kivus, was largely out of business by 1985. After Mobutu legalised artisanal mining in the Kivus in 1983, for the next decade small-scale miners operated there in a primitive but somewhat sedate environment, a situation that would change after the Rwandan invasion of the east in 1996. Although Kengo Wa Dondo, Mobutu's prime minister, had started the process of privatisation of the state's mines on Mobutu's behalf in 1995, the move was halted by the rebellion and Mobutu's eventual overthrow.

During Laurent Kabila's four years in office, the government's attempts to regulate extractive industries were a wild melange of expedience and grand design.

In mid-1997, Kabila set up something called the Office des Biens Mal Acquis, the chief task of which appeared to be redistributing the assets of Mobutu's cronies among Kabila's cronies.[7] The Service d'Assistance et d'Encadrement du Small Scale Mining was set up by the government in 1999 to help organise and exercise oversight over artisanal and small-scale mining, but it was not until 2003 that the body was incorporated into the Ministry of Mines. During the course of the Second Congo War, a UN investigation found that, in government-controlled zones, those who profited most handsomely from the country's mineral resources included National Security Minister Mwenze Kongolo (who was deeply involved as a shareholder and deal-broker for various diamond and cobalt ventures); adviser to both Kabila *père* and *fils* Augustin Katumba Mwanke; and Minister of Planning and Reconstruction Denis Kalume.[8] Although Article 27 of Congo's mining law specifies that civil servants, members of the armed forces, police and security services, judicial authorities and employees of parastatal companies involved in mining operations are ineligible to hold mineral rights, government officials are – extraordinarily – exempt from restrictions on owning shares in mining enterprises.[9]

Once Joseph Kabila succeeded in gaining the presidency through the ballot, and succeeded in driving his most potent political rival out of the country by the bullet, the question remained: who was making money from Congo anyway?

The short answer was that, when it came to those with guns or those with connections to those with guns, almost everybody was. The October 2002 final report of the UN Panel of Experts found that the criminal networks linked to the exploitation of minerals in Congo consisted 'of a small core of political and military elites and business persons'.[10] The huge prize in Congo is, and has been, the control of transportation routes, the commercial

flows of everything that goes in and out of the country. Despite
a popular perception to the contrary, that is what the Rwandans
and Ugandans were seeking to take over. They didn't particularly
care who did the actual mining.

The armies

First to benefit from Congo's war were the armed groups
themselves, chiefly the Rwandan army – formerly the RPA but
since May 2002 known as the Rwanda Defence Force (RDF).
It would prove one of the great, bitter ironies of recent African
history that the Kigali government, in particular, paid for its war
against Congo and its people by looting the very same nation
it was attacking.

Shortly after it seized power in Goma in 1998, the Rwanda-
backed RCD 'government' began requiring every mining operation
in North Kivu to pay a US$15,000 fee for a 12-month licence, after
which an 8 per cent tax on the total value of exports was imposed
on the licensees.[11] The RCD-G then founded the Société Nationale
d'Exportation in Kigali in March 1999 in order to aid the transfer
of coltan from Congo to Rwanda.[12] The explosive growth of the
electronics industry as the millennium drew to a close led global
consumption of coltan to increase 38 per cent year on year by
2000, and by November of that year coltan was fetching a record
US$164 per kilo. Before 2000, Congo did not even place in the
published statistics of world tantalum (coltan) production. In that
year, it leapt into second place with 130 tonnes, more than one-
seventh of total world production, surpassed only by Australia.[13]
In November 2000, the RCD-G and its minders in Kigali formed
the Société Minière des Grands Lacs (SOMIGL), which was
granted a monopoly on all coltan exports from territories held by
the RCD-G (as should be apparent by now, Congolese rebels are
great fans of monopolies). Under the auspices of Nestor Kiyimbi,
the RCD-G 'minister' in charge of mining, some proceeds from
SOMIGL went directly to fund the RCD-G.[14]

Mineral smuggling and control of outposts were managed by the Rwandan army's Congo desk in Kigali, and revenues and expenditure 'kept strictly separate from Rwanda's national budget'.[15] Between late 1999 and late 2000, the Rwandan army was thought to have gained revenues from coltan exploitation in eastern Congo in the region of US$20 million a month.[16] By 2002, up to 70 per cent of the coltan exported from eastern Congo was under the direct supervision of the RDF, often later exported by aircraft to Kigali or Cyangugu airstrips. The Rwandans also made use of the criminal network of arms dealer Viktor Bout, whose planes helped transport coltan and cassiterite, as well as troops and equipment.[17]

In 2003, Rwanda produced 283 tonnes of cassiterite but exported 1,458 tonnes.[18] Although by the middle of the decade the value of cassiterite leaving eastern Congo via Rwanda was being assessed at US$1 million a month, independent observers estimated that the trade in fact measured at least US$46 million per year and sustained the meagre livelihoods of several hundred thousand artisanal miners in the Kivus.[19] In 2004, Kigali's Régie d'Exploitation et de Développement des Mines alone produced 205 tonnes of cassiterite, compared with 168 tonnes the year before.[20]

By 2003, there was an entente cordiale between the Mai-Mai militias and the RCD-G that gave the Mai-Mai control of the Bisie mine in Walikale and the RCD-G control of the town of Mubi, thereby allowing both groups to extract taxes at key points.[21] At the turn of the millennium, as if by royal fiat, the Rwandans also named a succession of questionable businessmen – Aziz Nassour, Philippe Surowicz, Hamad Khali – as rulers of the diamond concession in Kisangani.[22]

Although not as extensive in scope or duration, Uganda's military, the UPDF, also benefited from its involvement in Congo. The UN Panel of Experts estimated that between 1998 and 2000, about 1,800 trucks loaded with cassiterite, timber and coffee headed out of Congo via Uganda bound for Mombasa and Dar es Salaam and, eventually, Europe.[23] By August 1998, the UPDF had seized Durba in Orientale province and with it gold mines at Agbarabo and Gorumbwa, as well as in Durba itself. The Ugandans began mining activities shortly thereafter and continued until late 1999, when the Gorumbwa mine collapsed and reportedly killed at least 100 miners.[24]

During the Second Congo War, in Virunga National Park, the UPDF also 'organized and facilitated the exploitation of timber within the park'[25] while coltan was 'exploited extensively in Orientale Province by various armed groups under the protection of UPDF'.[26] According to former RCD members who spoke to the UN commission, as early as September 1998, Ugandan President Yoweri Museveni's brother, General Salim Saleh, was talking openly about creating a company to export natural resources from eastern Congo, and UPDF Major General James Kazini had already commenced commercial activities in zones under his command.[27] Although it was evidently under significant pressure from the Museveni government,[28] the Porter Commission, a body created by Uganda's Ministry of Foreign Affairs and charged with investigating allegations of illegal exploitation of natural resources during Uganda's presence in Congo, nevertheless also came up with some interesting material regarding Kazini's involvement. After a number of delays, Kazini himself was hauled before investigators in Kampala, and, in something of a kangaroo court atmosphere, asked why he had disobeyed Museveni's orders while in the county. He responded that he was 'only being flexible'.[29]

Although it often escaped the scrutiny accorded to other actors in Congo's misery, there is evidence that the government of Zimbabwe's President Robert Mugabe and his ruling ZANU-PF party also used their support of the Kinshasa regime as a vehicle for personal enrichment. During the Second Congo War, the Katanga copper belt remained under Kinshasa's control, with Zimbabwe, whose troops were mostly stationed there and in Kasai, enjoying the status of a preferred partner for mining concessions. Zimbabwe's Speaker of the Parliament and former National Security Minister Emmerson Mnangagwa was described in the UN report as:

> the key strategist for the Zimbabwean branch of the elite network ... [and] part of the inner circle of [Zimbabwe Defence Forces] diamond traders who have turned Harare into a significant illicit diamond-trading centre.[30]

A separate, late 2001, report concluded that 'Zimbabwe's continued military presence [in Congo allows] companies controlled by key Harare officials to continue to maximize economic gains'.[31] Between 1999 and 2002, the Congo–Zimbabwe military–business nexus saw:

> at least US$5 billion of assets from the state mining sector [transferred] to private companies under its control ... with no compensation or benefit for the state treasury of the Democratic Republic of the Congo.[32]

Congo's minister of planning and reconstruction, General Denis Kalume Numbi, was a stakeholder in both the Sengamines diamond concern in Kasai and in Cosleg, the joint venture created out of the Kinshasa-based Comiex-Congo and Osleg, a company controlled by the Zimbabwean military.[33]

Nor was the UN itself immune to the lure of the glittering demons. An internal UN investigation found that there was 'significant evidence to suggest there was a familiarity' between MONUC peacekeepers and foreigners suspected of illegally trafficking diamonds and gold who arrived in Mongbwalu to buy gold in late 2005. Witnesses reported peacekeepers and the businessmen meeting at the Mongbwalu airfield and the men being driving through the town in UN vehicles. The report concluded that the MONUC soldiers' denials were 'false' and that peacekeepers had in fact 'provided transport, meals and security' to the foreign visitors. The report subsequently concluded that the peacekeepers had 'misused their authority by providing logistical support and security to private business interests engaged in the illegal trafficking of unwrought gold in eastern DRC'.[34]

The businessmen

Beyond the official armies, there was also the network of operators and private business concerns.

The Belgian-Congolese businessman George Arthur Forrest was born in Lubumbashi in 1940, the son of Malta Forrest, founder of the Entreprise Générale Malta Forrest (EGMF), a company that had its roots in transportation but eventually expanded to mining. In 1988, the younger Forrest took full control of the company, then creating the George Forrest International Group (GFI) in 1995. Beginning in 1994, Forrest, conveniently enough, also 'owned 100 per cent of New Lachaussée in Belgium, which is a leading manufacturer of cartridge casings, grenades, light weapons and cannon launchers'.[35] In a stark conflict of interest, Forrest served as chairman of Gécamines from November 1999 to August 2001, appointed to the position by Laurent Kabila at the same time as his private companies were negotiating new contracts with the government designed to exploit Gécamines' assets for personal gain.[36] Forrest was identified as 'among the businessmen' in the networks set up to exploit natural resources in Congo, networks that, by the UN's own estimation, were 'often highly criminalized'. The report recommended that Forrest be put under a travel ban and financial restrictions.[37]

By 2004, the Groupe George Forrest was, along with OMG (an immense US mining firm) and Gécamines, running the Scories du Terril de Lubumbashi, a copper/cobalt tailings and smelter project located near the Katangan capital. In mid-2004, despite seven years of nearly constant war, Congo remained the second largest supplier of copper in Africa,[38] and between 2001 and 2006 the price of copper quadrupled.[39] The GFI's profits were doing so well, in fact, that in August 2009 the company would launch a US$585 million bid to take over the Canadian Forsys Metals Corporation. The deal, however, collapsed amid US fears that once Forrest controlled a Forsys uranium deposit in Namibia, the company might seek to supply Iran with nuclear fuel. These concerns were expressed in US diplomatic cables to its embassy in Ottawa that cited the GFI's ongoing discussions with senior Iranian officials that 'may be related to Iran's efforts to acquire additional uranium ore'.[40] The company said that the allegations repeated in the cables 'were and are false, baseless'.[41]

Billy Rautenbach, a white Zimbabwean businessman with close ties to Robert Mugabe, was appointed Managing Director of Gécamines by Laurent Kabila in November 1998 (he was replaced by George Forrest in the position a year later). Two weeks before Laurent Kabila was assassinated in 2001, Rautenbach, John Bredenkamp (a former captain of the 1985 Rhodesian rugby team turned billionaire businessman) and Mugabe confidant Emmerson Mnangagwa met with Kabila to discuss the Kambove/Kakanda copper/cobalt Gécamines concession.

Although Rautenbach stated that the Zimbabwean government never had an interest in or benefit from his activities in Congo,[42] in 2001 Rautenbach's company Ridgepointe International was granted mining rights to Gécamines' concessions at the Shinkolobwe mine in Katanga, which was, in its previous life, the source of the uranium used in the bombs that the US dropped on Hiroshima and Nagasaki in 1945. The mine was flooded in 1956 by the Belgian government, and was kept under guard by Mobutu until 1997. By late 2004, estimates of the numbers of artisanal miners working at Shinkolobwe ranged from 7,000 to over 13,000, with very little oversight. In July 2004, part of the mine collapsed on to a group of artisanal miners working there, killing at least nine people.[43] A UN team sent to investigate the collapse was subsequently denied access.[44] By March 2007, two men – including Fortunat Lumu, Congo's top nuclear official

– were arrested and charged with being part of a clandestine uranium network, only to be freed a few days later.[45]

As for Rautenbach's partner, John Bredenkamp had a 'history of clandestine military procurement' and, during the Second Congo War, was a major investor in the Aviation Consultancy Services Company through which he desired to 'actively [seek] business using high-level political contacts'.[46] By mid-2004, he controlled Tremalt Limited, the majority owner of the Kababankola Mining Company, a joint venture company with Gécamines whose profits were split between the Congo government (34 per cent), the Zimbabwean government (34 per cent) and Tremalt itself (32 per cent).

Both Bredenkamp and Rautenbach would subsequently be blacklisted by the EU for 'strong ties to the Government of Zimbabwe, including through support to senior regime officials during Zimbabwe's intervention in DRC'.[47] The sanctions included the freezing of assets and travel bans.[48] The bans were lifted in February 2012.

The cowboys arrive

Even as multinational conflict receded while 2007 staggered along, however, particular geographic regions in Congo posed their own specific kinds of thorny issues.

After Kabila consolidated his power, visitors to Ituri – the font of such wealth for the UPDF – could find sights such as 1,500 artisanal miners stooping ankle deep in chocolate-coloured water, labouring under the shadow of the abandoned OKIMO mining laboratory in Mongbwalu. Many of the prospectors had previously worked at OKIMO's shuttered Adidi mine, a time during which, even under Mobutu's corrupt regime, OKIMO had bankrolled both the local hospital and the technical institute. The miners now worked the site from eight in the morning until four in the afternoon, and, when they did find gold, they would pay the mine 'supervisors' (men who gave them the right to work there) 30 per cent of whatever they found, then selling their gold for around

US$30 per gram, roughly equivalent to the world market price at the time.[49] By mid-2006, between 700,000 and 1 million people were working in Congo's mining industry, the vast majority as artisanal miners.[50] As was the case in Mongbwalu, throughout Congo artisanal miners would sell the ore they discovered to Congolese *négociants* (middlemen) who would then sell this ore to Congolese or foreign trading houses.

OKIMO had once been a massive presence in the region, employing around 1,700 people in and around Mongbwalu. Then, Ghana's Ashanti Goldfields purchased an interest in a gold-mining concession that had previously existed as a joint venture between OKIMO and Mining Development International. In 2003, Ashanti Goldfields merged with South Africa's AngloGold to create AngloGold Ashanti, one of the largest mining companies in the world. The concession was now known as Concession 40, and encompassed a vast swathe of 2,000 square kilometres around Mongbwalu. The Congolese government was still the official owner, but eventually Concession 40 came under the management of AngloGold Ashanti's local subsidiary, AngloGold Kilo (AGK), which began exploration of the site in 2005.

Exactly how AngloGold Ashanti came to control the goldfields was the subject of intense speculation. A 2005 report from the New York-based advocacy group Human Rights Watch quoted an unnamed former employee of the company stating that Jean-Pierre Bemba had directed AGK to negotiate with the FNI Lendu militia – whose May 2003 attack on Mongbwalu had killed at least 500 people – as a means to begin exploratory mining. The report also cited a US$8,000 payment that AngloGold Ashanti admitted making to the FNI in January 2005, as well as claims made by an AGK consultant in Mongbwalu and FNI Commander Iribi Pitchou that senior FNI officials used a four-wheel-drive vehicle belonging to the company to traverse Ituri's decaying roads, and travelled on planes hired by the company to such cities as Beni in North Kivu and the Ugandan capital of Kampala.[51]

In a June 2005 response to the allegations, AngloGold Ashanti wrote that:

> yielding to any form of extortion by an armed militia or anyone else is contrary to the company's principles and values ... That there was a breach of this principle in this instance, in that company employees yielded to the militia group FNI's act of extortion, is regretted.

The statement continued by saying that 'AngloGold Ashanti does not and will not support militia or any other groups whose actions constitute an assault on efforts to achieve peace and democracy'.[52]

Speaking after Kabila took office to local residents such as Jean-Paul Lonema, a community organiser working for the local branch of the Catholic organisation Caritas, one would hear that AGK's 'decisions [were] taken without consulting the population ... the population doesn't know anything about the documents AGK signed with the government, they don't know their contents'.[53]

AngloGold Ashanti, however, saw things a bit differently, admitting that, although there 'clearly' was 'a big gap between the expectation of the population after a war period, after the total absence of the state, and the presence of a new company', when compared with OKIMO, 'the budget constraints are very huge'.[54]

Although Congo's Ministry of Mines put AngloGold Ashanti's start-up capital at US$18 million, the company's yearly budget for social development on the Mongbwalu projects in 2008 was just US$150,000.[55]

AngloGold Ashanti was by no means unique in occupying a moral grey area with its operations in Congo. The Australian company Anvil Mining was the first major mining company to invest in Congo following the official cessation of hostilities in 2002, mainly in Katanga. It would become the nation's leading copper producer, with its operations including the Dikulushi copper and silver mine near Kilwa on the shores of Lake Mweru, and the Kinsevere open pit mine in the province's southern reaches. Perhaps not surprisingly, the company had a conspicuously close relationship with Kabila's economic adviser Katumba Mwanke, who served as Katanga governor from 1998 to 2001, when he became director of Anvil Mining Congo, Anvil's local subsidiary, a position in which he served until 2004.[56]

During the Congo wars, and afterwards, mining in Katanga was a wild, unpredictable enterprise. The restructuring of the parastatal Gécamines in the province was recounted by one Congolese NGO as a process of uncontrolled liberalisation characterised by a 'complete lack of protection for the inhabitants of mines, pollution of drinking water [and] radioactive contamination'.[57] One investigation in mid-2004 found that the only government agency represented at the mines in Katanga was the Agence Nationale de Renseignements (ANR), that is, the state intelligence service. A year and a half later, the Police des Mines, which was the branch of the Police Nationale Congolaise (PNC) tasked with overseeing the mines, and the Ministry of Mines itself had joined the ANR in demanding payment at the entrance and exit to the mines from the desperately poor miners.[58] Death threats against members of groups such as the Association Africaine de Défense des Droits de l'Homme and the Ligue Contre la Corruption et la Fraude for their outspoken criticism of corruption in Katanga's mining industry became routine.

Early on the morning of 14 October 2004, a previously unknown rebel movement calling itself the Mouvement Révolutionnaire de Libération du Katanga, led by Alain Kazadi Mukalayi, attacked and captured Kilwa, the site of Anvil's mine. Once in the town, Kazadi announced to startled locals that he was acting with the approval of President Kabila. Kazadi and his men held a rally, recruited more soldiers, distributed money to locals and sacked government offices.[59] Two days later, government troops led by Colonel Adémar Ilunga counterattacked, driving the invaders from the town, rounding up locals they accused of being collaborators and, according to most accounts, killing at least 100 people. A quartet of human rights organisations later charged that Anvil had provided logistical support to the army during the siege, with company cars transporting the bodies of those killed in summary executions as well as stolen goods looted by soldiers.[60] Troops from the FARDC's 62nd Infantry Brigade travelled to Kilwa aboard Anvil Mining trucks from their base in Pweto, a distance of 135 kilometres,[61] and three of the company's drivers were behind the wheel of Anvil Mining vehicles used during the raid, according to a subsequent MONUC investigation. On the day following the FARDC attack, Augustin Katumba Mwanke appealed to those who had fled to Nshimba island to return home.[62]

Although there was great debate as to whether or not Kazadi had been set up for murky internal political reasons, by June 2007 a Katanga military court convicted Colonel Adémar Ilunga and another defendant of murder, but gave minimal sentences or acquitted outright the other FARDC defendants in the case, also acquitting three expatriate Anvil Mining employees. The court concluded that no massacre had taken place, and that the deaths had simply been an accidental consequence of the battle. The lawyers for the victims were unable to travel from Kilwa to Lubumbashi, thus depriving those most affected of their representation.[63] Titinga Frédéric Pacéré, the UN's independent expert on human rights in Congo, called the trial a 'sham'.[64]

By February 2007, Moïse Katumbi Chapwe, a millionaire businessman who had helped fund Kabila's electoral campaign and was the owner of the highly successful TP Mazembe football club, became Katanga's governor. The son of a Sephardic Jew who had fled the Greek island of Rhodes (then under Italian occupation) and a Congolese woman, Katumbi, despite his great wealth, was a charismatic populist often met by chants of *prezo* (president) when he appeared in public. Not surprisingly, given

Congo's post-war landscape, a large portion of Katumbi's wealth came from the Mining Company Katanga (MCK), which had benefited from the privatisation of Gécamines' mineral deposits at three separate locations in the province: Kinsevere, Tshifufia and Nambulwa. At the latter location, a deal was hammered out giving the MCK an 80 per cent share.[65] Katumbi's background was not without its complications, however, and nearly two years after he had assumed office in Lubumbashi, it was revealed that his brother, Raphael Soriano (aka Katebe Katoto), a former 'vice-president' in the RCD who had relocated to Belgium, was in fact one of the major funders of Laurent Nkunda's CNDP.[66]

Enter the People's Republic

As the Kabila regime solidified, the People's Republic of China would also play an increasingly important role in Congo's economic life. China had been providing troops and military observers to MONUC since 2003, and in September 2007 a memo of understanding was singed in Beijing between China and Congo, with a more detailed agreement signed in April 2008 by the Kabila government and two Chinese companies: China Railway Group Limited (China Railways) and Sinohydro Corporation. Although the sole Congolese government signatory of the September 2007 and April 2008 agreements was Minister of Infrastructure Pierre Lumbi, those familiar with the deal said that Kabila's financial adviser Augustin Katumba Mwanke, who had his finger in many pies, had in fact played the decisive role during negotiations.[67]

The April 2008 version of the Congo–China agreement promised the Chinese parties involved an interest rate of 19 per cent, but did not specify how this rate would be calculated. It was likewise silent on environmental and social issues. Although over 2,000 kilometres of railway track were scheduled to be upgraded and an additional 1,800 kilometres built, the agreement's stabilisation clause – which linked the deal to the legislation in effect when it was signed – demanded that all new laws and regulations that unfavourably affected China would not be applied.[68] The deal promised China up to 10 million tonnes of copper and hundreds of thousands of tonnes of cobalt from Katanga's mines. It was the crowning glory of China's new muscular assertiveness in Africa, which in 2008 saw it cap a decade of tenfold increase in trade with Africa worth US$107 billion, thus outstripping the US as Africa's largest trading partner.[69] Chinese imports from Congo alone expanded from only US$1 million in 2000 to US$1.6 billion in 2008, thus making China Congo's largest export market.[70]

The war in the east

With the end of direct active hostilities between the region's governments, it simply would not do to have truckloads of minerals disappearing across Congo's borders with the equivalent of a foreign nation's flag draped around them. Few had proven as adept at adapting to these new realities as the FDLR, which, as such, had no nation's flag other than that of Hutu Power. In the past, FDLR fighters had arrived in Bunyakiri in South Kivu on their way to North Kivu with stacks of dollars and diamonds so extensive that diamond traders from as far as Bukavu and Goma arrived in the hamlet. Paying for vegetables and livestock, the FDLR used US$100 bills, suggesting access to foreign elements with hard currency.[71] By mid-2004, the FDLR was controlling at least seven major cassiterite mines, and by mid-2007 they had around 7,000 men under arms in North and South Kivu, representing a large and aggressive politico-military force throughout much of the region and one that had perhaps the greatest and most negative impact on local communities.[72] They maintained training centres, including a military school at Matembe, along the Masisi–Walikale border region,[73] and those who visited them in the field found that, nearly 15 years after the Rwandan genocide, they 'lived and breathed' the idea of returning to Rwanda and taking power once more.[74]

The FDLR had diversified its sources of financing by early 2008 to include: control of mineral deposits such as cassiterite in the Shabunda region of South Kivu and in the Walikale region of North Kivu; the levying of taxes at roadblocks and markets in areas under its control; the sale of a range of agricultural goods, including cannabis, at local markets; the poaching of hippopotamus for both meat and ivory along Lake Albert; and simple robbery and looting of civilian individuals and homes.[75] The group also exported marijuana grown around the Uvira region to Burundi, and enjoyed generally positive relations with the FARDC for a time.[76]

As the FDLR busied itself in South Kivu, the mixing that was to take place between Laurent Nkunda's CNDP and the FARDC as per the February 2007 peace agreement was not going at all according to plan. During 2007, Nkunda's forces continued to receive additional weapons via the border areas of Bunagana (Uganda) and Runyoni (Rwanda),[77] and CNDP forces likewise continued to victimise civilians. On 9 March, two Kinyarwanda-speaking soldiers of Bravo brigade – a 'mixed' brigade but one where many soldiers still maintained ultimate loyalty to Nkunda – entered the residence of Abbé Richard Bemeriki, priest of the Jomba parish church in Rutshuru, and fatally shot him in the arm and stomach. The following day, soldiers of the Bravo brigade entered the Rutshuru territory town of Buramba after being the subject of a failed ambush and killed at least 15 civilians whom they accused of co-operating with the FDLR. The same group then killed ten more people in the villages of Kiseguru and Katwiguru.[78]

One could also have fairly wondered about the exact nature of the army into which the CNDP was integrating. A March 2007 human rights assessment painted a dispiriting picture of the murder, rape and extortion being inflicted on the Congolese population by the FARDC and PNC.[79] Even after the transition, 'the lack of discipline of the FARDC [remained] the cause of tremendous human suffering', particularly in the Kivus.[80] MONUC concluded that, during the first six months of 2007, 54 per cent of all sexual violence cases were committed by the FARDC.[81]

In South Kivu, the situation remained terrible. For the first six months of 2007, the number of reported rapes stood at 2,133.[82] Between 2005 and 2007, only 287 cases – less than 1 per cent – led to the filing of a criminal complaint.[83] In Bukavu's Panzi hospital, visits by a total of 4,311 sexual violence survivors would be recorded between November 2007 and April 2009.[84] During the night of 26–27 May 2007, a group from the FDLR-affiliated Rastas militia descended on the South Kivu villages of Nyalubuze, Muhungu and Chihamba, killing at least 17 people, including women and children, with machetes and axes.[85] The FDLR received new support when several more or less sympathetic Hutu, Hunde and Nande militias merged to form the Coalition des Patriotes Résistants Congolais (PARECO) in March 2007.[86] PARECO fighters would fight side by side with the FDLR for much of the next year.

Government security forces in South Kivu continued to commit violence against civilians with almost total impunity. To give further credence to the general impression of the lack of accountability for anyone in a uniform, in June 2007, Serge Maheshe, a respected journalist with Radio Okapi, the nationwide radio network that had been created by MONUC and the Swiss Fondation Hirondelle, was gunned down while leaving a friend's home in Bukavu.[87] Maheshe was the third journalist to be murdered in a 17-month period in Congo; his death followed those of Bapuwa Mwamba, slain when intruders burst into his Kinshasa home in July 2005,[88] and Franck Kangundu of the independent daily *La Référence Plus*, also killed at his home along with his wife in November 2005.[89] In August 2007, in what was derided by local human rights and press freedom advocates as a travesty of justice, a Bukavu military court sentenced four civilians to death in connection with Maheshe's murder, among them two of the reporter's closest friends who also happened to be the only eyewitnesses to the killing. Two navy servicemen – who had been arrested and had been considered the main suspects – were acquitted.[90]

By August 2007, Laurent Nkunda had cannily diverted enough resources away from the integration process to rearm, and gave the order for thousands of CNDP soldiers to desert their FARDC units. Clashes between the two forces began anew. This again started to fan poisonous anti-Tutsi sentiment and, in early August 2007, hundreds rioted in the Katanga town of Moba and attacked MONUC vehicles in reaction to a (false) rumour that MONUC was going to be resettling Tutsi refugees there.[91] During the final months of 2007, the FARDC continued to move reinforcements into North Kivu, with a December 2007 US embassy cable calling the FARDC military build-up over the preceding months 'unprecedented'.[92] This did not, however, keep the CNDP from capturing a significant number of weapons from raids on military compounds in December 2007.

In early January 2008, a 'peace conference' was convened in Goma. Organised under the auspices of National Assembly speaker Vital Kamerhe, the conference was marked by walkouts and threats of walkouts by Nkunda's delegation.[93] At one point Nkunda's representative Kambasu Ngeze vowed that the CNDP would fight the Kabila government and the FDLR 'with neither remorse nor regret' if Kabila did not rid the country of the 'forces of genocide'.[94] On 15 January, Kabila flew to Goma, saying that he wanted to 'personally involve' himself 'in the search for a solution'.[95] Alan Doss, the British diplomat who had taken over as head of MONUC in October 2007, also attended, despite the fact that the CNDP included in its top ranks the Ituri warlord Bosco Ntaganda as its military commander. A sealed arrest warrant for war crimes had been issued against Ntaganda by the ICC in 2005 (it would be unsealed in April 2008).[96] Nkunda himself had been indicted by the Congolese government following the

2002 killings in Kisangani. When the participants signed an 'acts of engagement' document, MONUC hailed the conference as a 'success', an optimism that would soon prove premature.[97]

Despite the pause in hostilities, the reality on the ground was somewhat more complicated, as I discovered during a February 2008 visit to North Kivu. In a mist-shrouded valley between the Mount Nyiragongo volcano and a pair of its dormant cousins looming in Rwanda, nearly 3,000 souls waited in limbo at the Kibumba camp. Amidst a sprawling collection of grass and banana-leaf huts covered with thin sheets of tarpaulin, shoeless children played, some with distended bellies and reddish hair that suggested severe malnutrition.[98] In early February, some 1,000-plus villagers had trekked through the mountains from surrounding villages to camp on the weed-choked gravel of a schoolyard in Rutshuru, fleeing fighting between the FARDC and CNDP.[99] Between January and mid-February, the sexual violence programme at the MSF hospital in Rutshuru recorded 129 cases of sexual assault with the victims ranging in age from 11 to 80 years old.[100]

In Goma, however, against the pastoral landscapes of the Hotel Karibu, Nkunda's spokesman, the attorney Muiti Muhindo, warned visiting journalists that 'the situation of exclusion and racial discrimination in this province, saying that some are more Congolese than others, continues', and that while Congo needed 'a commission of genuine national reconciliation, on the contrary the government is moving arms from Kisangani towards Walikale, from Bunia towards Beni. They are preparing for war.'[101] The Congolese forces said otherwise, however, with General Vainqueur Mayala, overall commander of the FARDC in the North Kivu region, saying that 'we are observing the ceasefire'.[102]

The Congolese state – theoretically, at least – belonged to people like those in the camps ringing towns such as Goma, Rutshuru and Masisi, and not to the assorted politicians, businessmen, opportunists, arrivistes and others who stood above its broken and bleeding form with a chequebook in one hand and a scalpel in the other, waiting to carve it up.

One figure stands out, and gives an idea of the conditions under which the Congolese were living as those remains were feasted upon. A June 2008 survey by the International Rescue Committee concluded that there had been 5.4 million excess deaths in Congo between August 1998 and April 2007, with an estimated 2.1 million of those deaths having occurred after the formal end of war in 2002. Some critics of the survey pointed to the fact that it also concluded that less than 10 per cent of the excess deaths were directly due to violence (with the rest attributed to preventable and treatable conditions such as malaria, diarrhoea and pneumonia); however, the cause of their premature exit from this life likely mattered little to those sacrificed on the altar of the will to power of their own politicians and the unabashed greed of their neighbours and other foreign forces, political and economic.[103]

Trust was not there. How could it be, when the two sides had spent so long trying to kill one another? The stumbling block, it appeared, was not ideology or levels of brutality – since both sides had little of the first and no distaste whatsoever for the second – but rather that, like Laurent Kabila before him, Laurent Nkunda made the mistake of seeing himself as a historical figure rather than as merely the quisling of great powers. This self-image would make him – for very different reasons – ever less palatable to both the Rwandans and the Congolese, and so by mid-2008, Kigali was already homing in on a suitable replacement.

7 | THREATS FROM WITHIN AND WITHOUT

As 2008 dawned, despite the continuing instability in the east, the Kabila government was solidifying into something altogether different from the collection of disparate interests it had been at its advent some seven years earlier. On 14 February, Congo's minister of foreign affairs, Antipas Mbusa Nyamwisi – the former Ituri warlord having been transformed into an international statesman – and UN Development Programme (UNDP) representative Ross Mountain signed a US$390 million five-year governance programme in Kinshasa.[1]

One day early that year, when the sun baked Kinshasa to a high of 39 degrees Celsius (102 degrees Fahrenheit) according to the old digital display towering above Boulevard de 30 Juin, a fierce wind blew sand, dust and rubbish into my face as I got out of a taxi at the entrance to the presidential compound near the Banque Nationale. I was greeted by about half a dozen members of the Republican Guard – recognisable by their red berets – lazing on chairs under a shade tree, their automatic rifles resting over their laps or hanging from straps around their shoulders.

I chatted with them as I approached, identifying myself, and one young man volunteered to walk me to my meeting. We strolled down a long, nearly deserted thoroughfare and passed the grand mausoleum that Joseph Kabila had built for his slain father. Five huge hands made out of stone held up the roof of a pavilion under which the remains of Kabila *père* resided. Funeral wreaths ringed marble stands bearing such messages as '*Nous ne t'oublierons jamais*' ('We will never forget you') and '*Que ton âme repose en paix*' ('May your soul rest in peace'). Lowered into a depression in the marble, the former leader's casket rested there, guarded by a bust of a lion, while two other lions guarded the entrance. '*Ne jamais trahir le Congo*', the legend read. 'Never betray the Congo'.

Once inside the compound, I found myself speaking to Kudura Kasongo, who, during the Mobutu era, had worked as an anchor at the state-owned La Voix Zaïre television channel and at that time was serving as Kabila's chief spokesman.[2] Amiable and relaxed as we chatted while sitting on a sofa in his office, Kasongo reflected the confidence of a regime becoming more at ease with itself.

'I think the situation here is improving more and more,' Kasongo told me. 'And human rights also include access to such things as food and healthcare. It depends on the capacity of the local government to manage these things. It's not excellent, but it's improving.'

That local capacity, as Kasongo referred to it, was about to be faced with yet another challenge, as was the reach of the state. The way in which Kasongo's boss responded to it would indicate much about what the Congolese could expect in the future.

Searching for a lost empire

For an ethnic group whose realm once stretched across the borders of four nations and that ranked as the dominant coastal power in central Africa, the influence of the Bakongo people had significantly diminished in the decades following independence. Although the ABAKO party of Congo's first president, Joseph Kasa-Vubu, himself Bakongo, was one of the main forces that pushed the country towards its independence from Belgium, Kasa-Vubu was seen as more than an ethnic leader. Despite Bakongo intellectual Ernest Wamba dia Wamba's stint as the titular head of the RCD in the late 1990s – a movement that never addressed the situation in western Congo in any significant way – Bakongo leaders would take some time after Mobutu's 1997 overthrow to orient themselves politically, but the same was not true for the Bakongo among Congo's neighbours.

In next-door Angola, the Bakongo make up the third largest ethnic group in the country. During Angola's war of independence, the União das Populações de Angola spearheaded a Bakongoist movement in Angola's north-west. Uprooted in the hundreds of thousands by the colonial response to the rebellion, many Bakongo fled to Congo. A sizeable number eventually returned to Angola, particularly Luanda, during the 1980s.[3] Some have even asserted that Holden Roberto's anti-colonial Frente Nacional de Libertação de Angola was also 'essentially a Bakongo movement'.[4]

Across the Congo River in the Republic of Congo, former Brazzaville mayor and prime minister Bernard Kolélas's MCDDI party was widely seen as being Bakongo-centric in its struggle against the 'northern' (Mbochi) dictatorship of Denis Sassou Nguesso during that country's 1997 civil war. This was despite the fact that Kolélas' Ninja militia and Sassou's Cobra militia had previously battled together against the Cocoyes of Pascal Lissouba during the 1993–94 armed conflict. By 1997, the unity, such as it was, between Kolélas and Sassou had ruptured violently, and the Ninjas, led by Frédéric Bintsamou (aka Pastor Ntumi), a guitar-strumming Protestant clergyman, battled fiercely with government forces, with the Angolan government and UNITA rebels intervening to support their respective sides. This idiosyncratic brand of militarism, mysticism and political ambition was characteristic of a strong strain in some Bakongo political thinking, and one with which the other Congo was very familiar.

That spirit was exemplified by historical figures such as Dona Beatriz, born of noble Kongo parentage under the name Kimpa Vita in what is today Angola. She began receiving visions of a spiritual and religious nature while ill with a fever in August 1704, visions that included those of the spirit of Saint Anthony.[5] During this time, the Kingdom of Kongo was in the grip of a seemingly endless civil war between the royal courts of Kinlaza and Kimpanzu. Claiming to be possessed by Saint Anthony's spirit, Beatriz preached in favour of the unification of Kongo under one ruler. She was captured and burned as a heretic by a rival king in 1706.

For a period of six months in 1921, a Bakongo spiritual leader named Simon Kimbangu began travelling around the region, allegedly healing the sick and performing miracles. Despite having been ordained as a Baptist, Kimbangu was soon praised by people as an *ngunza* (prophet) and was said to even be able to raise the dead. Fearful of the separatist and mystic overtones of his movement, the colonial government tried and failed to capture Kimbangu, who finally turned himself in to the Belgian authorities. With their characteristic questionable mercy, the Belgians lashed him 120 times before sending him to serve out his life imprisonment on the other side of Congo, where he died in 1951.[6] The unorthodox church that Kimbangu founded – the Église de Jésus Christ sur la Terre par son Envoyé Spécial Simon Kimbangu – still has many adherents in Congo today.

Following Kimbangu, the most prominent proponent of the Bakongo brand was certainly Joseph Kasa-Vubu. Since Kasa-Vubu's death in 1969, no figure in Congo's political landscape had succeeded in uniting the Bakongo in a similar way until a scientist with grand visions for the future of the Bakongo people arose from the firmament of the country's wars. His name was Ne Muanda Nsemi and his movement was the Bundu dia Kongo (Kingdom of Kongo or BDK). In a wide-ranging interview with the Kinshasa daily *Le Potentiel* published in May 2006, just before he won a seat in the National Assembly with one of the largest electoral majorities in the country, Ne Muanda Nsemi referred to the modern Congolese state as 'a multinational country created by the colonial dictatorship', then detailed what he called a long list of Bakongo prophets, to which he declined to add himself, preferring the title of 'master of Kongo wisdom'.[7]

Claiming that he first started having 'visions' during his third year at the University of Lovanium in Kinshasa, where he was studying physics and chemistry, he said that the visions had grown more intense after the death of Kasa-Vubu in March 1969. By July of that year he was seeing a 'giant', 4 metres (13 feet) in height, who told him that, as one *nganga* (leader) had been removed, another must take his place, and now it was Muanda Nsemi's turn. Muanda Nsemi said that he 'resisted' the call for 17 years, preferring to focus on science. The visions continued, however, while Muanda Nsemi was working as a professor at an Adventist university in Bas-Congo and later as the chief of the bacteriology laboratory at Mama Yemo Hospital in the capital. He finally founded the BDK as a cultural organisation in 1986.[8]

In the interview, Muanda Nsemi referred to the BDK as a 'three-sided crystal' consisting of religion, science and politics. Tellingly, he also darkly suggested that those ruling Congo were 'people who are not from the people' (an obvious reference to Kabila) and that the country was in danger of being plunged into 'a new crisis of legitimacy'.

Since Joseph Kabila had come to power, Kinshasa's relations with Bas-Congo in general and the BDK in particular had been fraught. On 22 July 2002, cities and towns throughout the province witnessed mass demonstrations as the BDK called for independence. The day's events ended in bloodshed, with at least a dozen dead and several wounded after the intervention of the security forces. Following the killings, Catholic clergy bemoaned the fact that 'even in the pacified territories, life can be sacrificed with great lightness'.[9]

As Congo waded deeper into the waters of its experiment with democracy, the situation would grow ever more volatile.

In the October 2006 elections, Jean-Pierre Bemba's MLC coalition had won 16 of the 29 provincial assembly seats allotted to Bas-Congo. When Leonard Fuka Nzola ran as the MLC's candidate for Bas-Congo governor, Ne Muanda Nsemi stood for the position of vice-governor as his running mate. However, when the provincial assembly (responsible for electing the governor and vice-governor) voted in January 2007, Fuka Nzola and

Muanda Nsemi lost, and two candidates close to Kabila, Simon Mbatshi Batshia and Deo Gratias Nkusu Kunzi-Bikawa, were elected. Extraordinarily, Kabila's advisers publicly acknowledged that legislators had been bribed to vote for the pro-government candidates.[10] Despite court challenges, the results of the corrupted elections stayed in place.

In protest, Ne Muanda Nsemi called for a general strike on 1 February. The day before the strike, at least 50 police officers raided Muanda Nsemi's home in Matadi, at which point BDK members began to pelt police with rocks, sparking a response that saw police shoot and stab at least 15 BDK members to death and injure 18. The BDK killed at least one police officer.[11] BDK members and government authorities also clashed in Boma, Muanda Tshela and Songololo. On 14 February, an emotional ceremony was held in Matadi to bury members of the sect who had died.[12]

The following day, BDK members beat nine police officers and two civilians to death in Muanda and Boma, and raided a police station. The FARDC responded by killing at least 23 people, including two children, none of whom had been involved in the disturbances. A subsequent UN investigation would conclude that at least 105 people had been killed and over 100 injured in the violence.[13]

Things quietened down, but only briefly, as in some parts of Bas-Congo the BDK had effectively replaced the state, often enforcing its will with great violence. The BDK's feared enforcers – known as *makesa* – began to act as something of an unofficial police force, handing out punishments that included floggings for infractions such as adultery. BDK places of worship, called *zikua*, began to proliferate.[14]

Throughout early 2008, the BDK's acts grew increasingly brazen and the government's response ever more brutal. On 5 January, four BDK partisans, a policeman and a bystander were killed as BDK members in Bas-Congo's Seke-Banza territory protested against the arrest of two of their number.[15] On 24–25 February, the BDK burned two men alive in two separate incidents in Kinkenge and Bethelemi after accusing them of sorcery. A local delegation sent to investigate the incidents was briefly taken hostage. A 26 February meeting between Ne Muanda Nsemi and three Roman Catholic bishops concluded with a common statement of mutual respect and commitment to non-violence but failed to defuse the situation. On 1 March, the BDK kidnapped and killed an off-duty FARDC officer.[16]

By this point, Kabila and his advisers had decided that they had had more than enough, and that the BDK, within easy reach of Kinshasa, unlike the rebels in the faraway Kivus, needed to be taught a lesson. In late January 2008, Kabila met with Minister of the Interior Denis Kalume and John Numbi, who had been appointed to head the PNC as its inspector general the previous June. It was decided to send some 600 police officers to Bas-Congo in a highly militarised operation that included members of the so-called Simba Battalion, made up of former soldiers from Kabila's ancestral region of Katanga.

When the Reuters journalist Joe Bavier and I arrived in the Belvedere neighbourhood of Matadi shortly after government forces had attacked the BDK compound there, on a broad hillside high above the meandering flow of the Mpozo River we found a handful of policemen guarding a ruin. The Congolese flag fluttered weakly over scattered bricks and broken crockery lying in mute witness to the government's commitment to stamp out the group. En route from Kinshasa, at one country crossroads we saw two lorries each containing about 30 armed FARDC soldiers, many of the troops equipped with Uzis, some with their bayonets fixed as if preparing for close-quarters combat. But in Belvedere that day, the sound was not of gunfire but of a hymn from a revivalist church floating up the hillside.

'It wasn't a conflict, it was an attack by the police,' a local man told us as he and his family stood in front of their home, which had been pockmarked by large-calibre bullet holes the size of a small child's head. He said the siege had lasted for nearly an hour.[17]

'The police stole our television, our table, even a handbag from the bedroom,' said his neighbour, pointing to more bullet holes where the projectiles had threaded their way through his family's fragile tin roof.[18]

A local PNC commander spoke to us amid the ruins of the compound and displayed what he claimed were poisoned arrows used to attack the police. 'Here are their arms, their fetishes, you can see them here,' he told us.

An emergency co-ordinator with the humanitarian aid organisation Médecins Sans Frontières in Matadi said that many BDK members had 'fled to the bush'.[19]

They would find no respite there, as soldiers began moving through the countryside with a ferocious singleness of purpose. Travelling in a convoy of 25 to 30 marked pick-up trucks along with several FARDC trucks driven by uniformed soldiers, armed with AK-47s and explosive 40 millimetre grenades, the security personnel were probably under the command of PNC Provincial Inspector General Chalwe Raus and Raus's deputy, Colonel Vumi, as they cut their way through Bas-Congo.

Some of the worst excesses took place in the village of Lufuku, north of Matadi. On 1 March, as word of the impending arrival of the police convoy spread through the area, BDK adherents from surrounding villages gathered there as non-BDK villagers fled. After hearing sustained gunfire and seeing flames rise from the village, those who had left began to return. At least 36 BDK followers had been killed by the security forces, including some who had been injured and then summarily executed. A day later, the bodies were taken by a police truck and dumped in the Luwala River, rendering the water unusable by local residents. As in other cases, the police looted shops and burned down structures, including 20 houses. Five days after the killings, Vice-Governor

Deo Nkusu and PNC Provincial Inspector General Raus visited Lufuku, offering villagers around US$60 worth of Congolese francs to cover damages and advising them that they 'must not pray in the BDK church any longer'.[20]

On 3 March in Sumbi, at least 34 BDK followers were killed, as well as an unaffiliated seven-year-old girl, Astride Nsoki Bwandi.[21] On 4 March in Mbata Siala, at least 16 people, all BDK members, were killed, including two minors.[22]

Following the violence, on 21 March the Kabila government revoked the BDK's authorisation to operate as a social and cultural organisation, in effect making the movement illegal. Beginning on 27 March, the parliament debated bitterly for three days about the events in Bas-Congo with opposition member Gilbert Kiakwama stating that the Kabila government needed to 'stop hiding behind the need to restore state authority in an area where that authority had been non-existent'.[23] When Kiakwama subsequently attempted to hold public meetings in Bas-Congo, they were violently disrupted by Kabila partisans. The only trials to come out of the 2008 violence were of BDK members, several of whom were sentenced to death.

Shortly after the fighting, Joe Bavier and I drove over rutted dirt roads towards the village of Luozi in the territory of the same name. A town associated in the popular imagination with crocodiles following the publication of Zamenga Batukezanga's sorcery-themed novel *Un croco à Luozi* in 1979, the territory of Luozi lies sandwiched between the Congo River to the south and a section of the southern border of the Republic of Congo to the north, a physical isolation that only enhances its historical and cultural separation from central government.[24]

Just beyond the outskirts of Matadi, the sense of the enveloping countryside was immediate, as birdsong, the sound of brush rustling in the wind and insects buzzing filled our ears. Train tracks, ghostly and unused, occasionally sprung into view as we drove. On a red earthen road heading towards the Congo River, we drove through sun-blasted villages of wooden tin-roofed shacks, and passed by a melancholy cemetery with faded headstones under mournful trees. Under a luminous blue sky speckled with white clouds, the road eventually became absolutely devoid of people, with a thick grass called *sobe* on either side.

We took a ride on a rickety ferry from Kibemba across the Congo River – very muddy and broad at this point – and reached Luozi in the late afternoon.

Once in the town, a doctor at the local Hôpital Général de Référence told us that at least eight bodies were deposited there after the fighting. Two victims – one BDK, one civilian – were still convalescing from gunshot wounds sustained during the upheaval. One of them, a man shot twice in the buttocks, lay amid the sickening smell of disinfectant.

In the BDK church – the *zikua* – dozens of spent shell casings littered the floor of the building as well as the earth around it, while several nearby homes had obviously been torched and looted. Above the door of the ruined *zikua*, words had been scrawled by an unknown hand. '*Pas d'autres,*' it read in French. '*C'est inutile.*'

'Not again. It's useless.'

Following the massacres in Bas-Congo in February 2007, Belgium signed a €195 million co-operation agreement with the Kabila government.[25] For its part, the World Bank saw fit to pledge US$1.4 billion.[26] As Kabila's security forces mercilessly cut down Bemba supporters and civilians alike in March 2007, the French government, in the person of Ministre Déléguée à la Coopération Brigitte Girardin, signed a €235 million partnership agreement with Kabila in Kinshasa.[27] Despite a subsequent MONUC investigation, which concluded that at least 100 people, and possibly more, lost their lives during the government's assaults, in April 2008 the UN fully exempted the FARDC from an arms embargo imposed on rebel groups in the country.[28]

The ghost of Joseph Kony

As Ne Muanda Nsemi and the BDK were learning the heavy price to be paid for failing to bow to Kinshasa, on the other side of the country a force that Muanda Nsemi would no doubt have also characterised as 'not from the people' was beginning to impact the lives of the residents of the northern province of Haut-Uélé in new and terrible ways.

The roots of the Ugandan rebel group the LRA lay in Uganda's own long struggle to free itself from tyranny. As the dictator Milton Obote sought to retain power in the early 1980s, his government's Uganda National Liberation Army (UNLA) responded to the insurgency of the Yoweri Museveni-led National Resistance Army (NRA) by killing large numbers of Bagandan and Banyarwandan civilians. At the time, the UNLA was so dominated by the Acholi, a Luo ethnic group that spills across the border between northern Uganda and southern Sudan, that it was often referred to simply as 'the Acholi', even though Obote himself was a Lango.[29] An army coup d'état eventually ousted Obote and put General Tito Okello, an ethnic Acholi, in the presidency for six chaotic months until he was overthrown by Museveni. Museveni then became president and has remained so via elections – some legitimate and some deeply flawed – ever since.

When the NRA finally defeated the UNLA remnants in March 1986 (with the aid of many Rwandan Tutsi fighters), Acholi and Lango soldiers returned dispirited to their home villages in the north of Uganda. In the words of German anthropologist Heike Behrend, some of the former soldiers 'tried to live as peasants ... [but] had learned to despise the peasant way of life ... They had become internal strangers and their return caused unrest and violence.'[30] After Museveni's army solidified its control of northern Uganda, its 35th Battalion – which included members of a mostly Bagandan insurgent force with links to those who had suffered greatly under Obote – arrived in the territory. Locals noted that with their arrival, the 'professional' conduct of the NRA became interspersed with beatings, looting and worse.[31] In this context, disaffected former soldiers from Obote's army launched the Uganda People's Democratic Army (UPDA) in August 1986. The UPDA was more or less an orthodox guerrilla force that set out a clear political programme and demands. It was also doomed to failure in the face of a brutal counter-insurgency programme launched from Kampala.

As the UPDA's campaign began to falter, a far more millenarian force began to emerge. It was called the Holy Spirit Movement, and its armed wing dubbed the Holy Spirit Mobile Force (HSMF). Directed by an Acholi woman named Alice Auma claiming to act on guidance from the spirit Lakwena, the Holy Spirit Movement brought a mystical belief in its own invincibility that the soldiers of the Kampala-based government at first found terrifying. HSMF devotees walked headlong into blazing gunfire while singing songs and holding stones they believed would turn into grenades. In November and December 1986, after the HSMF defeated the NRA in southern Kitgum, people, particularly youths, flooded to Auma's movement. This dynamic had shifted by January 1987, however, when hundreds of HSMF fighters were killed near Kilak Corner, and, in November 1987, the HSMF was surrounded and destroyed in the Bugembe forest outside Jinja, just 80 kilometres from the capital. Alice Auma fled to Kenya, where she later died.

By June 1988, the Museveni government and what was left of the UPDA had signed peace accords. The accords had been delicately managed by Museveni's brother, General Salim Saleh, disturbed to see the government he served massacring so many zealous but largely poorly armed citizens.[32] Alice Auma's father, Severino Likoya Kiberu, made a half-hearted attempt to lead a new insurgency following her defeat, but it appeared to many observers that peace was at hand. The real war, however, was just beginning.

A young Acholi man named Joseph Kony, who claimed to be

a cousin of Alice Auma, had joined the UPDA in early 1987.[33] Kony was born in Odek, east of Gulu, in 1961, and to call his world view unorthodox – even in the surreal and violent landscape of northern Uganda at the time – would be quite an understatement. Kony claimed to be able to channel spirits (including female spirits, during which occasions he dressed in women's clothing) including a Sudanese female chief of operations, a Chinese deputy chief who commanded an imaginary jeep battalion and two Americans, King Bruce and Jim Brickley. By 1988, Kony had formed a guerrilla movement first known as the Lord's Salvation Army, later as the United Christian Democratic Army, and finally as the Lord's Resistance Army (LRA). A March 1991 government attempt to quash the nagging insurgency, dubbed Operation North, coincided with the creation of local 'bow and arrow brigades', village militias hopelessly outgunned by the LRA.

For reasons that remain murky to this day, during Operation North the Museveni government chose not to pursue and finish off Kony's movement. Rather, Betty Bigombe, an ethnic Acholi who was serving as state minister for Northern Uganda, spearheaded the Museveni government's peace talks with the LRA in late 1993 and early 1994, meeting with Kony on several occasions, meetings during which Kony was said to have angrily denounced Acholi elders as being sympathetic to Museveni. Finally, after protracted delays, Museveni gave the LRA an ultimatum to disarm by February 1994, which was ignored, and the LRA retreated to southern Sudan. At this time, the LRA began receiving substantial assistance from the government of Sudan's President Omar al-Bashir. Al-Bashir was furious about Kampala's support of the separatist SPLA in Sudan's southern reaches and – the irony of Al-Bashir's Islamist government supporting the LRA's schismatic Christianity notwithstanding – Kony and company seemed like a useful bludgeon to use against Uganda. After linking up with Khartoum, the LRA became one of the toughest groups for the SPLA to fight, more often fighting the SPLA in order to do their sponsor's bidding and to protect their haven in south Sudan than against the UPDF. With Khartoum giving the Kony group sanctuary, weapons, uniforms and training, for most of their war against the Ugandan state the LRA would prove to be a much more effective fighting force than the Ugandan army.

Following the failure of Bigombe's peace overtures, northern Uganda in the mid-1990s became a hell for the Acholi people. In a fairly typical attack in April 1995, the LRA assaulted the northern trading centre of Atiak, defeating UPDF and Acholi militia after an intense battle and subsequently killing at least 220 civilians. It is believed that they were led by LRA commander Vincent Otti, an Atiak native.[34] The private Catholic secondary school St Mary's College in northern Apac district was subject to multiple assaults and kidnappings by the LRA. During one, the LRA abducted 152 girls, aged 13 to 16, but released 109 of them after a nun followed the departing rebels through swamps to beg for the children's freedom.[35] In January 1997, the LRA attacked villages near the border with Sudan, killing at least 312 people, many with axes and clubs, and displacing 60,000 more.[36]

By 1996, the Ugandan government had begun a policy of creating so-called 'protected villages' – crowded, squalid encampments into which Acholi civilians were herded under the armed gaze of the UPDF. According to UNHCR, during the course of the LRA conflict more than 1.8 million people were moved into such camps, where they were left vulnerable to disease and social ills, and with few ways to practise their traditional farming.[37] In some instances, the UPDF shelled villages whose residents refused to relocate.[38] Far from benefiting the Acholi, civilians in northern Uganda 'came to be caught between two fires', with the Museveni government contending that it was failing to defeat the LRA because the Acholi population was providing information to them, and the LRA convinced that its group was failing to overtake the government because civilians were providing information to Kampala's forces.[39] After the Acholi were relocated, the UPDF 'seized the opportunity to loot foodstuffs, cattle, sheets of iron and other valuables from deserted villages and rural schools'.[40] Ultimately, those in the 'protected villages' served as human shields for the UPDF, although, given the LRA's disregard for Acholi civilian lives, not very effective ones.

In March 2002, the UPDF launched Operation Iron Fist, a military offensive designed to drive the LRA out of its bases in southern Sudan. The operation was largely a failure, scattering the LRA but failing to crush then, and dramatically increasing the number of displaced people.

By 2005, the LRA's policy of targeting civilians (though not the Museveni government's draconian measures) had drawn international condemnation and that year the ICC, acting on a December 2003 request from the Museveni government, issued arrest warrants against Kony and several other senior LRA commanders for crimes against humanity and war crimes. In addition to Kony, those indicted included Vincent Otti (who in late 2007 would be killed, almost certainly on Kony's orders), LRA commander Okot Odhiambo and Dominic Ongwen. Ongwen, the commander of the LRA's Sinia Brigade, presented a particularly thorny issue for prosecutors as he himself had been kidnapped at the age of ten before becoming a senior LRA commander, making him both perpetrator and victim.[41]

After the Al-Bashir government and the SPLA signed a peace agreement in January 2005 (an agreement that would eventually lead to South Sudan's independence), the LRA realised that its days of having Sudan as a haven from which to launch attacks into Uganda were numbered. Later that year, Vincent Otti, for the first time, led a contingent of LRA fighters into the Democratic Republic of Congo. The rebels began moving about Congolese territory and were there for nearly a year before much of the outside world realised what was going on. The wake-up call came in late January 2006, when eight Guatemalan peacekeepers were killed in Garamba National Park during a four-hour gun battle with LRA fighters, allegedly as the Guatemalans sought to seize Otti.[42] At least 15 LRA combatants were also killed.[43] By April 2006, Guatemala's human rights ombudsman Sergio Morales announced that his country had 'serious doubts about the place and type of operation' in which the Guatemalan soldiers had been involved, suggesting that the soldiers may have been party to an undertaking well beyond the borders of their agreed involvement with MONUC.[44]

Beginning in July 2006, another round of negotiations began between LRA representatives and the Museveni government, this time held in Juba in South Sudan under the aegis of former SPLA rebel leader (and future vice-president of the Republic of South Sudan) Riek Machar. Before the talks, Machar is said through intermediaries to have given his old foes in the LRA three choices: they could leave South Sudan of their own accord; they could have the SPLA chase them out; or Machar and his colleagues would mediate peace talks in good faith between Museveni's and Kony's forces.[45] When the peace talks collapsed in late 2007, the LRA (which had used the interim to rearm) formally decamped to Congo and the Central African Republic. For its part, following the end of negotiations, the Museveni government launched its Peace Recovery and Development Plan, an effort to stabilise northern Uganda after years of war. By 2012, according to the UN, 98 per cent of internally displaced persons had left the camps there.

Concerned about the LRA's ability to further destabilise Congo, in September 2008 MONUC and the FARDC launched Operation Rudia, intending to surround the LRA inside Garamba National Park, cut off the group's supply lines and encourage defections from within its ranks. The operation, however, never came to fruition due to underdeployment of troops and the failure to build a tactical headquarters. In response, between September and November 2008, the LRA killed at least 167 civilians and abducted 316 children.[46] When a November 2008 deadline for Kony to sign a peace agreement passed, the UPDF, FARDC and SPLA made plans to attack Kony's forces. MONUC was not informed, and the fact that such an operation was allowed to commence with the mission's leadership being almost totally unaware of it speaks volumes about the gaping holes in MONUC's intelligence capabilities. Seventeen US military advisers provided logistics, communications and intelligence for the campaign, dubbed Operation Lightning Thunder. [47]

Lightning it was not, but it was certainly thunderous, as bad weather caused the UPDF to jettison its planned assault with MiG fighter jets on the LRA's Garamba bases for attack helicopters that could be heard clearly on approach. Although the bombardment destroyed the camps, the UPDF ground forces arrived nearly three days later and the entire top command of the LRA escaped.[48]

Revenge was not long in coming. In a series of attacks between December 2008 and January 2009, the LRA killed over 850 people, mostly in Congo but also in Sudan.[49] Between 25 and 27 December 2008 alone, in the towns of Faradje, Doruma and Gurba in the Haut-Uélé district of Congo's Orientale province, the LRA massacred 620 civilians and abducted more than 160 children. A year later the LRA would return, killing 321 and abducting another 250 people in December 2009. Many more were grotesquely mutilated but kept alive, having ears, noses and other body parts severed. A new and terrible addition to Congo's litany of armed groups had announced its presence.

The battle for North Kivu

The Goma Peace Agreement – agreed on 23 January 2008 – broke down on 28 August 2008 with the CNDP facing off against the FARDC, Mai-Mai militias and the FDLR. Speaking to the BBC in early October, Laurent Nkunda called for the Congolese to 'stand up' and fight with the CNDP until they were 'liberated' from the Kabila regime.[50] In mid-October 2008, the Congolese government claimed to have recovered Rwandan weapons, money, military insurance cards and other items from the front, which proved that Kigali's troops were actively aiding the CNDP.[51] With surpassing duplicity, Paul Kagame told one visiting journalist that his government was 'only linked with Nkunda and the CNDP just by accident of history and the fact that these are Congolese who speak Kinyarwanda, and we share borders with Congo'.[52]

By late October, the CNDP was pushing from two different directions: south towards Goma, and north towards Rutshuru. On 26 October, the CNDP seized the Rumangabo military camp – looting a significant stockpile of weapons and ammunition – and several positions in Virunga National Park. The next day the CNDP and FARDC exchanged artillery fire in the Kibumba–Kalengera region. That same day, MONUC installations and vehicles in Goma were pelted with stones by demonstrators angered at the CNDP advance. On 28 October, the FARDC pulled back to Kibumba from the surrounding camps, causing terrified people to flood towards Goma. As the CNDP stormed towards the city, tank and mortar fire rained down in support of the advance from an area of the Rwandan border not previously under CNDP control. A MONUC attack helicopter received anti-aircraft fire from the same location.[53] Laurent Nkunda, his troops gathered on Kibati hill, paused 'as if directed by a magician's hand'[54] and declared a unilateral ceasefire. By this point FARDC Regional Commander General Mayala had lost control of his troops, many of whom fled towards South Kivu, leaving MONUC all that stood between the CNDP and a takeover of the province. As they fled, the FARDC troops committed gross outrages against the population of North Kivu.

At least nine cases of arbitrary killings committed by Congolese soldiers (including that of an eight-year-old boy) were recorded in Goma during the night of 29–30 October 2008, as the FARDC stole vehicles in which to flee and looted private homes. On the same night, the Goma general hospital treated 17 cases of rape attributed to the FARDC, while in Kanyabayonga the number was closer to 45. Ironically, during the looting in some parts of the province, PARECO and Kasindien Mai-Mai fighters, often victimisers themselves, are said to have tried to protect local populations.[55] In early November 2008, Angolan troops arrived in Goma to help provide the pro-government forces with some much-needed backbone.[56]

As the fighting raged in North Kivu, Kabila had announced that he was appointing Adolphe Muzito, Antoine Gizenga's 51-year-old budget minister, as prime minister. Like Gizenga, Muzito was a PALU member, and his selection followed the spirit of the 2006 power-sharing agreement.[57] In Muzito's new cabinet, Minister of Foreign Affairs (and former RCD-K/RCD-ML rebel) Antipas Mbusa Nyamwisi received what many viewed as a demotion, being transferred to become minister of decentralisation and regional planning. Nyamwisi would subsequently vent his frustration to US embassy officials, referring to Kabila's confidants Augustin Katumba Mwanke, John Numbi and others as 'bandits' and 'robbers'.[58] Nyamwisi also voiced his fears that North Kivu's Hutu governor Eugène Serufuli Ngayabaseka (whose tenure ended in 2007) wanted to divide North Kivu into two provinces, one Nande and one Rwandaphone, and that 'Rwandaphones always bring their Hutu–Tutsi problems and issues with the indigenous population with them and it infects all political activity'.[59] Nyamwisi was replaced in his old job by former Mobutu minister and later MLC partisan Alexis Thambwe Mwamba. PALU's Martin Kabwelulu remained minister of mines.

Kabila's hand was bolstered by the neutralisation of his most potent rival. From exile in Europe, Jean-Pierre Bemba had continued to apply pressure on Congo's government, asking in an interview with one news outlet: 'Do you know many Congolese who have been attacked with tanks and bombed with mortars in their private homes?'[60] In May 2008, Bemba was arrested in Belgium pursuant to an ICC warrant against him which charged that, while the MLC was fighting in the Central African Republic, Bemba was 'criminally responsible' for 'rape as a crime against humanity', 'rape as a war crime', 'torture as a crime against humanity', 'torture as a war crime', 'committing outrages upon personal dignity' and 'pillaging a town or place'.[61] Guilty as he may have been, many in Congo were shocked and disgusted with the blatant politics of the indictment and the self-righteous grandstanding of the ICC's Chief Prosecutor Luis Moreno-Ocampo, a trait that in coming years would become even more pronounced in Moreno-Ocampo, who had at one time starred in his own reality television show in his native Argentina.

'Look at what Kabila did. He did just as bad if not worse,' a Congolese physician told me a few years later in North Kivu, which few would confuse with a Bemba stronghold. He added that, if Bemba ever ran again, he would vote for him.

By the time of the second CNDP rebellion, the collusion between Rwanda and the CNDP had become embarrassingly obvious. On 9 November, members of the UN's Group of Experts saw the CNDP's Bosco Ntaganda alight from a jeep on a 'road [that] did not lead anywhere else besides the Rwandan border'.[62] The previous April, the ICC had unsealed an arrest warrant against Ntaganda, charging him with the enlistment, conscription and active use of children during the 2002–03 era of his tenure with the UPC in Ituri.[63] Investigators found that Rwandan authorities had also been 'complicit in the recruitment of soldiers, including children, have facilitated the supply of military equipment, and have sent officers and units' from the Rwandan army into Congo in support of the CNDP.[64] Between January 2007 and October 2008, MONUC had repatriated over 150 Rwandans, including 29 children, the vast majority of whom had been recruited into the CNDP in Rwanda itself.

The CNDP was drawing its funds from a variety of sources, including taxes it extracted from control of the Bunagana border crossing with Uganda. Additionally, the Belgium-based Congolese businessman Raphael Soriano alias Katebe Katoto (brother of Katanga governor Moïse Katumbi Chapwe) was found to have transferred money to, among others, Laurent Nkunda's wife, Elisabeth Uwasse, and Goma-based Lebanese businessman Bilal Abdul Kalim Bakizi, who, according to a UN investigation, had 'been used as a conduit for external funding coming into CNDP'.[65] Funds were also raised for the rebels by Tribert Rujugiro Ayabatwa, a close adviser to Paul Kagame, founder of the government-backed Rwandan Investment Group and a North Kivu native.[66]

The brief pause in fighting around Goma did not extend to elsewhere in North Kivu. On 5 November in the town of Kiwanja, after chasing the FARDC out of the area, CNDP forces led by Bosco Ntaganda killed at least 150 people (and perhaps many more), most of whom were young men accused of being Mai-Mai members.[67] These killings occurred despite the fact that 100 MONUC peacekeepers were stationed less than a mile away. Ntaganda was videotaped in the town, strutting around, protected by gunmen and chatting on a walkie-talkie.[68] On the night of 11 November, up to 800 FARDC soldiers rampaged through Kanyabayonga and surrounding villages, looting homes and raping several residents.[69] On 14 November, the CNDP announced that it was 'at the entrance of Kanyabayonga' as the FARDC fled before its advance.[70] As Ntaganda terrorised the population of North Kivu, Nkunda himself became something of a media whore during this period, a favourite interview subject for foreign journalists who would traipse to his headquarters near Masisi, where, leaning on a cane and gazing from behind professorial glasses, he would hold forth apparently completely reasonably – but, as it happened, also completely dishonestly – about the state of affairs in eastern Congo.[71]

But forces were at work that Nkunda could not control. On 16 November, Nkunda agreed to take part in new peace talks.[72] In 'celebration' of this development, he presided over a CNDP rally in Rutshuru characterised by an atmosphere of forced revelry as music and dancing mixed with armed rebel soldiers.[73] After meeting with UN peace envoy and former Nigerian President Olusegun Obasanjo in late November, Nkunda said that the CNDP would pull back from its positions around Kanyabayonga,[74] although the reality on the ground revealed a more tangled scene of ever shifting front lines.[75] Direct negotiations between Kinshasa and Kigali started in early December 2008,[76] during which Kabila's advisers Katumba Mwanke and John Numbi once again proved instrumental.[77] During the first week of December, after meeting in Goma, Congo's Minister of Foreign Affairs Alexis Thambwe Mwamba and his Rwandan counterpart Rosemary Museminali announced that their governments had agreed on a 'plan' to disband the FDLR, although they declined to give details.[78]

The odd man out in this arrangement, of course, was Laurent Nkunda, who had begun to believe his own rhetoric that he was the protector of the Congolese (even as he was victimising them) and a force for revolution against Joseph Kabila. Having outlived his usefulness, as Congo greeted the new year, the inevitable happened; on 5 January 2009, Bosco Ntaganda announced that Nkunda had been dismissed as head of the CNDP and that he was taking control of the movement.[79]

The following week, Ntaganda met with Minister of the Interior Célestin Mbuyu Kabango and announced that the CNDP would stop fighting the Congolese government and instead work with them to fight the FDLR.[80] In addition, the CNDP was to be transformed into a political movement. A joint military operation by the FARDC and the RDF against the FDLR – something that would have been unthinkable only weeks before – began on 20 January under the name Umoja Wetu ('Our Unity' in Swahili). The operation would continue for 35 days and significantly disrupt the FDLR's operations, forcing its high command and some of its 6,000-plus fighters to flee south from Kibua to Ntoto near Walikale. This blow against the FDLR came at a terrible price, however, as the group took blanket revenge on civilian populations in its midst, and Rwandan and Congolese coalition forces killed at least 201 civilians, including 90 in the village of Ndorumo.[81]

On 23 January, after he had travelled to Gisenyi at the request of Rwandan army Chief of Staff James Kabarebe,[82] Rwandan military officials announced that they had arrested Laurent Nkunda because he had become 'a barrier' to the new co-operation between Kinshasa and Kigali.[83] The long and bloody career of one of central Africa's most quixotic rebel leaders appeared to be at an end. Nkunda would disappear into Rwandan custody and, as of early 2013, has not been interviewed and has not spoken publicly since.

By 29 January, at the same Rumangabo military barracks in North Kivu that the CNDP had twice taken over during fighting the previous year, the first CNDP fighters were integrated into the FARDC at a ceremony presided over by Minister of Defence Charles Mwando.[84] In the final peace agreement signed in Goma on 23 March, the CNDP confirmed 'the irreversible nature of its decision to cease its existence as a politico-military movement' and pledged to undertake integration into the FARDC, 'transform into a political party' and 'seek solutions to its concerns strictly through political means and in accordance with the institutional order and laws of the Republic'. For its part, the Kabila government pledged 'to respond swiftly to the CNDP's request for recognition as a political party' and both parties agreed 'with the principle of the CNDP's participation in DRC politics'.[85] It was announced that Bosco Ntaganda would become a general in the FARDC. Many members of the FDLR-affiliated PARECO Mai-Mai group also announced that they would integrate into the FARDC. However, a substantial breakaway faction led by 'General' Janvier Buingo Karairi and comprised mainly of Hunde fighters from the Masisi area re-dubbed themselves the Alliance des Patriotes pour un Congo Libre et Souverain (APCLS) and said they would not.[86]

Bosco Ntaganda. The Terminator. The Butcher of Mongbwalu. The Assassin of Kiwanja. This was the man upon whom the peace of eastern Congo was to rest. Like Mobutu before him, Joseph Kabila was nothing if not a gambler, and, surrounded by ruthless men such as John Numbi and Augustin Katumba Mwanke, he had every reason to believe that, having swallowed the very bitter pill of ceding to Rwandan influence in the east, the cards were in his favour as Congo looked towards the electoral season two years in the future. But Bosco Ntaganda and Paul Kagame, no matter how the international community looked the other way, could not help but revert to type. The peace that Ntaganda offered would prove but a brief pause in Congo's long battles with its neighbours and with itself.

8 | A FALSE PEACE

That the FDLR was still running amok was beyond dispute. Before the Umoja Wetu offensive, if one ventured to FDLR camps in South Kivu, it was not hard to find youthful soldiers who had lost their parents during the Congo wars and were filled with hatred for the Kagame government and Tutsis in general.[1] One defecting FDLR commander estimated that 75 per cent of the rebels were too young to have taken part in the genocide and only 1 per cent were *genocidaires*, although 'it is this 1 per cent that are in control'.[2] On 26 November 2008, the FDLR killed seven people and raped four women in the village of Kahunga, near Kiwanja, the scene of the CNDP's crime that same month.[3] During a February 2009 attack on the village of Kanyatsi, the FDLR gang-raped eight women and looted a number of homes, causing the population to flee.[4] All told, between late January and September 2009, the FDLR would kill at least 700 civilians in North and South Kivu.[5] But, as Umoja Wetu and the previous years had shown, the FARDC and its partners in the RDF behaved no better towards Congolese civilians. This was ignored when MONUC forces backed the FARDC as the latter launched Operation Kimia II ('Quiet' in Swahili) in March 2009, the second phase of the latter's campaign against the FDLR.

Against the advice of the UN Office of Legal Affairs, MONUC began providing logistical and operational support for the FARDC's offensive before any safeguards were in place for the protection of civilians as required by its mandate. Despite the common knowledge that Bosco Ntaganda – a wanted accused war criminal – was acting as a de facto deputy commander for Congolese forces during Kimia II, MONUC's command refused to acknowledge this, instead hiding behind transparently false Congolese government assurances that Ntaganda was not involved.[6] Given the outstanding arrest warrant against Ntaganda at the time, MONUC's support of his leadership of Kimia II – attested to by Ntaganda's regular presence at the offensive's command centre and visits to troops in the field – was illegal, as the UN's legal office explained to the MONUC chieftains in an April 2009 note.[7] The Kabila government, as a signatory to the Rome statute, was likewise under a legal obligation to hand Ntaganda over. As with Umoja Wetu, Kimia II was marked by a high degree of human rights abuses against civilians, such as the killing by the FARDC of at least 129 Rwandan Hutu refugees in Walikale territory between 27 and 29 April.[8] Finally, on 2 June, the UN Policy Committee ordered MONUC to cease participating in joint operations with the FARDC units who were at serious risk of committing human rights violations, which in the east meant virtually the entire force.

By disregarding international law and the advice of its own lawyers and supporting Kimia II, MONUC fell even further in the eyes of the Congolese it was ostensibly there to protect, and became an even more compromised player, one with both feet firmly in Kabila's camp and perceived as a supporter of 'whatever crazy thing the regime wanted to do'.[9] A month later, MONUC chief Alan Doss was still defending the mission's involvement in Kimia II, writing in an op-ed that the campaign was 'a concrete action to deal with a brutal group that has plagued the region for 15 years'. Doss went on to write that 'doing nothing in the face of systematic violence is not an option', ignoring the FARDC's extensively documented record of the same behaviour.[10]

What was the outcome of Umoja Wetu and the MONUC-backed Kimia II? According to one investigation, between January and September 2009 more than 1,400 civilians were slain in North and South Kivu, at least 700 by the FDLR and the rest by Congolese and Rwandan government-allied forces. Over the same time period in the same provinces, over 7,500 women and girls were raped and over 900,000 people forced to flee their homes.[11] If this was the 'peace' that MONUC and the Rwandan and Congolese governments were so enthusiastically celebrating, Congo's people must have wondered how, in any particular, it differed from the war that had plagued them before.

Elsewhere in the country, the picture was one of 'justice' fraught with the potential for upheaval. Mai-Mai leader 'Commander' Gédéon Kyungu Mutanga, captured three years earlier, was convicted in March 2009 by a military court in Katanga for 'war crimes, crimes against humanity, insurrection and terrorism' and sentenced to death.[12] That same month, and into early April 2009, attacks by the Front Populaire pour la Justice au Congo (FPJC) on villages in Ituri and a counterattack by the FRPI drove 30,000 people from their homes. The fighting happened despite the fact that the FPJC and the FRPI were both ostensibly Lendu in orientation.[13] The FRPI's former chieftain, Germain Katanga, still awaited trial at the ICC in The Hague. At the beginning of the year, the first of several trials stemming from the Congo wars would begin, as Bosco Ntaganda's former comrade-in-arms from the UPC, Thomas Lubanga, stood accused of conscription of child soldiers.[14] Lubanga's trial would continue fitfully for another three years.

Never one to let a good crisis go to waste as an opportunity to rid himself of potentially irritating adversaries, in April 2009 Kabila engineered the removal of his former party leader, Vital Kamerhe, from the presidency of the National Assembly. Kamerhe, so instrumental in the formation of the PPRD and in the January 2008 Goma peace conference, had strongly denounced the presence of Rwandan troops in the country and their actions during Umoja Wetu, a stance that did not fit at all with the new regional rhetoric of 'partnership'. He was replaced in his job by Kabila's former chief of staff, Évariste Boshab. In late July,

Kabila spokesman Lambert Mende announced that the government was banning broadcasts of Radio France Internationale due to the station making 'statements of a nature to demoralise the Congolese armed forces' by reporting on the fighting in the east. The decision was reversed and the French broadcaster's signal restored without explanation two weeks later.[15]

Despite the military battering it had taken, the FDLR was down but far from out. During 9 and 10 May, the group massacred more than 60 civilians in Busurungi, a time during which its German-based president Ignace Murwanashyaka contacted local FDLR commanders in Congo 14 times. The scene left behind was described as one of 'total desolation'.[16] Murwanashyaka had previously boasted on a German television programme that 'I know exactly what is going on' in Congo.[17] On 19 June, 27 FDLR fighters and five FARDC soldiers were killed when the Hutu rebels overran Congolese army positions near Nyabiondo in North Kivu, which the FARDC later retook.[18] By late July, at least 35,000 people had been displaced by fighting, which brought the total number of civilians displaced in South Kivu since January 2009 to 536,000, and the number displaced in eastern Congo as a whole to over 1.8 million.[19] Given the facts on the ground, the inaction of the European politicians in power at the time, who could have interrupted the FDLR's base of operations there, is inexplicable.

After touring the Magunga camp outside Goma for those fleeing the fighting, a visit during which she was shown a skeletal four-year-old weighing less than 15 pounds and suffering from extreme malnutrition, US Secretary of State Hillary Rodham Clinton said that the United States believed that 'there should be no impunity for the sexual and gender-based violence committed by so many, that there must be arrests and prosecutions and punishment'.[20] Congo's Minister of Foreign Affairs Alexis Thambwe Mwamba stood at her side as she spoke. Bosco Ntaganda, whose troops were ruling Goma and much of the rest of the east that the FDLR did not control, was not present. In one bright spot, during the first week of October 2009, FDLR grandee and wanted *genocidaire* Idelphonse Nizeyimana was snatched in Uganda by local police.[21]

In mid-October 2009, a coalition of 84 humanitarian and human rights groups bemoaned the fact that, since the start of the FARDC's UN-backed military offensive against the FDLR, more than 1,000 civilians had been killed, 7,000 women and girls had been raped and 900,000 people had been forced to flee their homes, 6,000 of which had also been burned down.[22] Appearing to fixate on the disarming of the FDLR regardless of the human cost, and also seeming to bow before Kigali's whims, Alan Doss told an October meeting of the UN Security Council in New York that 'reducing the pressure now would give the FDLR time to regroup and rearm ... Rwanda might also see this as a step backwards from the rapprochement that has opened up an entirely new perspective.'[23]

Simultaneously concluding a trip to Congo, the UN's special rapporteur on extrajudicial executions, Philip Alston, called the results of the military operation 'catastrophic' and concluded that 'in many areas, it is [the FARDC] themselves who pose the greatest direct risk to security ... No amount of sophisticated strategic rationalization should be permitted to obscure that fact.'[24] On 2 November, MONUC announced that it would be suspending military aid to FARDC units implicated in the deaths of civilians.[25] Speaking at the Royal United Services Institute in London on 11 November, Alan Doss told those assembled that 'any MONUC support for the FARDC is criticised as condoning such abuse ... And yet I believe that the women and the children of eastern Congo would probably suffer more should we give up and walk away from the FARDC.'[26]

On the international stage, however, the Kabila regime continued to shine. After an October 2009 visit to China by Minister of Defence Charles Mwando Simba, it was announced that the

Asian nation would be providing US$1.5 million in military aid to Congo.[27] That same month, a new mutation of the China–Congo deal specified that a US$3.2 billion Exim Bank loan for mining operations would be invested by Sicomines, the joint venture between Congo state-controlled firms and their Chinese partners.[28] Following a late October visit by Minister of Foreign Affairs Alexis Thambwe Mwamba, it was announced that India was offering Congo US$263 million in loans to build hydroelectric plants and repair its infrastructure.[29]

At the same time as India was lavishing largesse on Kabila, two villages concerned with the more immediate practicalities of fishing ponds launched a mini-war against one another in Équateur province. Villagers of Enyele and Monzaya began battling in late October 2009, soon forcing 130,000 to flee to neighbouring countries, most of them to the Republic of Congo, while another 100,000 sought refuge in other parts of Équateur.[30] By the time Minister of the Interior Célestin Mbuyu visited the town of Dongo, the area was largely deserted.[31] Armed villagers subsequently killed at least 47 policemen sent to quell the fighting, an affront to which the Kinshasa government responded in time-honoured fashion.[32] After a few months of skirmishes, Équateur's governor, Jean Claude Baende, announced the end of the conflict, stating that nothing was left of the gunmen but 'small groups of residual elements who are searching for means of survival'.[33] In response to Baende's announcement, some 100 rebels, whom many believed were linked to Jean-Pierre Bemba's MLC, landed at the port of Banika on the Congo River and fought their way into Mbandaka, seizing the airport.[34] The rebels killed at least 12 Congolese and three UN workers in addition to losing nearly two dozen of their own.[35] The Congolese NGO Association Africaine de Défense des Droits de l'Homme would later state that the FARDC killed at least 50 civilians while retaking Mbandaka in early April 2010.[36]

Meanwhile, on the opposite side of the country, refugees

flooded back into Congo when, between July and October, the Angolan government carried out an expulsion of Congolese in the country which saw at least 18,000 people pushed back across the border.[37] During the operations, UN investigators concluded that at least 600 women and girls had been raped.[38]

The month of November 2009 also saw increased developments with regard to the LRA, leaping back into the light like a vision from a nightmare, when LRA commander Charles Arop, one of those most responsible for the 2008 Christmas massacres in Congo, turned himself in to the UPDF.[39] Later the same month, LRA fighters attacked the area around Djemah in eastern Central African Republic, killing several dozen people before being ambushed by the UPDF along the Ngoangoa River, during which a number of LRA fighters were slain.[40] Despite the military pursuit of Joseph Kony and his fighters, few if any safeguards were provided to the civilian population in the zones where he operated, and between early 2009 and mid-2010, the LRA kidnapped around 700 adults and children in the Central African Republic and the Bas-Uélé district of Orientale province in northern Congo.[41]

In Uganda itself, those occupied with reading the tea leaves of the Museveni government thought that they saw signs that the old crocodile was slipping even as he paved the way for his successor. In June 2008, Yoweri Museveni's son, Muhoozi Kainerugaba, a major in the UPDF, graduated from the US Army Command and General Staff College at Fort Leavenworth, Kansas, which Paul Kagame had also attended.[42] But by September 2009, tension between the Museveni government and the Buganda ethnic group (Uganda's largest) erupted into bloodshed in Kampala, with at least 21 people slain when Museveni refused to allow the Bugandan king to travel north to the Kayunga district, allegedly due to friction with a smaller tribe.[43] Over 600 people were arrested during the disturbances.[44] Several months later, at least three people were killed by security forces when violence erupted after the burning of the 128-year-old Kasubi tombs of deceased Bugandan kings in Kampala, which many Bugandans blamed on the government.[45]

By this time, James Kazini, Museveni's old ally and once such a powerful figure in Congo, found himself adrift and alone in Kampala. Lashed by the Porter Commission and the UN for his alleged misdeeds in Ituri, and suspected by some in the Museveni government of planning to form a rebel movement based in the West Nile, Kazini made an oddly grave guest at a family wedding on the night of 9 November 2009. Taking the podium and coaching his advice to the groom with a reference to 'if I'm not there any more', Kazini was videotaped telling those assembled that 'life is a programme that has both a beginning and an end'.[46] Less than 24 hours later he would be dead, allegedly beaten to death by his much younger girlfriend, an explanation about which Ugandans across the board were sceptical.

At long last, in mid-November 2009, both Ignace Murwanashyaka and Straton Musoni, the FDLR's president and vice-president respectively, were arrested in Germany on suspicion of involvement in war crimes that occurred in Congo.[47] After their arrests, Gaston 'Rumuli' Iyamuremye replaced Murwanashyaka as president of the FDLR and assumed the position of second vice-president, and Sylvestre Mudacumura replaced Musoni as first vice-president while retaining his role as FOCA commander. Colonel Laurent 'Rumbago' Ndagijimana, who had been the FDLR's primary liaison with the Congolese government,[48] replaced Callixte Mbarushimana as the FDLR's executive secretary. According to satellite telephone records, the Hutu rebels continued to have extensive contacts with their support networks in Zambia and Uganda.

In a foreshadowing of what many hoped awaited Murwanashyaka and Musoni, the trials of Germain Katanga and Mathieu Ngudjolo for war crimes and crimes against humanity opened at the ICC in The Hague that same month. Both men would plead innocent. Witnesses testifying against the two were threatened, and a senior investigator would confess that the court did not have the resources to protect them.[49]

Nor could the international financial system protect Congo's money for the benefit of its people. In mid-February 2010, a parliamentary commission discovered that US$23.7 million – nearly half of the US$50 million payment made by China Railway Engineering Corporation, China Metallurgical Group and Sino-hydro Corporation to Gécamines – had disappeared.[50] It would later transpire that, in April 2009, Gécamines was ordered to pay US$23.7 million of debt that it allegedly owed to Caprice Enterprises Limited, a British Virgin Islands-registered company that had been incorporated only two years before and which was previously unknown. The fact that the demand to pay the debt occurred only weeks before Gécamines received half of its US$100 million signature bonus in connection with the China–Congo deal raised many eyebrows. An appeal by Gécamines was rejected.[51] In another example of warlord entrepreneurship, FARDC General Gabriel Amisi Kumba, the former RCD-G commander known as Tango Fort, helped to install a mining firm, Geminaco, at the Omate mine in North Kivu in return for a 25 per cent cut of the profits. Geminaco head Rene Mwinyi was said to be a personal friend of Amisi's, who went as far as using FARDC units under his command to evict a rival company, Socagrimines, and put Geminaco in its place.[52]

While Amisi was digging for treasure, his former bosses in Rwanda were busy, in their way, mending fences. In Kigali on 7 January 2010, Minister of Foreign Affairs Louise Mushikiwabo, with her French counterpart Bernard Kouchner at her side, pledged that the two countries were 'beginning a new phase in our shared history'.[53] Subsequently, Nicolas Sarkozy became the first president to visit Rwanda in 25 years, saying at a joint press conference with Kagame that the nations would 'turn an extremely painful page' of their histories together. Five days later,

Agathe Habyarimana was arrested in Courcouronnes, south of Paris, on the strength of a Rwandan arrest warrant issued the previous year for her role in the 1994 genocide.[54]

Old habits die hard, however, and Paul Kagame once more revealed the steely authoritarian beneath the glad-handing international statesmen with the April 2010 appointment of James Kabarebe as minister of defence. The appointment of Kabarebe, who as much as any single individual was responsible for implementing Kigali's brutal campaign of ethnic cleansing in Congo during the 1990s, showed that Kagame had no intention of ceding even an inch from his previous political path at home or abroad. The same month as Kabarebe's appointment, Victoire Ingabire, the chairperson of the Unified Democratic Forces opposition party and a Hutu exile who had lived and worked in the Netherlands for many years, was arrested on charges of denying the genocide and of collaborating with the FDLR, charges that both she and the FDLR denied.[55] Ingabire's lawyer, the American attorney and fringe genocide denier Peter Erlinder, was also subsequently arrested once he arrived in the country,[56] but was later released on medical grounds.[57] Rwanda's electoral commission subsequently barred Ingabire from running for president.[58] The month following her arrest, two people were killed and 27 injured in grenade attacks in Kigali.[59]

In a changing of the guard that many greeted with relief, on 9 June, UN Secretary-General Ban Ki-moon announced that former US ambassador to Congo Roger A. Meece would replace Alan Doss as his Special Representative and head of MONUC, which would be re-christened MONUSCO (the UN Organization Stabilisation Mission in the Democratic Republic of the Congo).[60]

Despite the excesses of Umoja Wetu and Kimia II, the UN signed a joint operational directive with the FARDC as it launched yet another operation against the FDLR, this one dubbed Amani Leo ('Peace Today' in Swahili) during January 2010. MONUC's Force Commander, Lieutenant General Babacar Gaye, and the

MONUC commander in charge of North Kivu, Brigadier General Ajae Kumar Sharma, held a series of meetings with the FARDC's Major General Dieudonné Amuli and Colonel Bobo Kakudji, both of whom had commanding roles in Amani Leo.[61] One issue apparently not addressed was the extensive CNDP presence within the FARDC in the east, and the role of such former CNDP commanders as Lieutenant Colonel Innocent Zimurinda, based in Masisi territory. Zimurinda's presence had been denounced by a coalition of 51 human rights and civil society organisations due to his alleged participation in the Kiwanja massacre in November 2008, as well as in a series of other mass killings of civilians dating back at least to 2007.[62] Zimurinda would subsequently be the subject of a travel ban and asset freeze by the UN Security Council for his role in Congo's violence.[63] Former CNDP officers had also begun imposing illegal taxes on civilians working in and around the cassiterite mines in Bisie in North Kivu and at Muhinga in South Kivu.[64]

Despite UN assurances to the contrary, nothing – absolutely nothing – had changed. As Amani Leo continued, Immaculée Birhaheka of the Promotion et Appui aux Initiatives Feminines pleaded that 'the name of the military operation has changed, but the situation remains the same: women are still being killed, maimed, abused like animals'.[65] With MONUC having provided rations, logistical support and medical assistance to FARDC troops pushing towards the FDLR in North and South Kivu,[66] by mid-March 2010, the FARDC was claiming that 609 FDLR fighters had been 'neutralised since the start of the operation'.[67] With little fanfare, UN Under-Secretary-General Alain Le Roy announced after a meeting with Kabila that the UN had begun talks about when and how to begin withdrawing from Congo.[68]

Faced with this melancholy landscape, Congo looked towards its fiftieth anniversary of independence on 30 June. As a present for that anniversary, the government of Canadian Prime Minister Stephen Harper, as utterly in thrall to mining concerns and their money as any African head of state had ever been, delayed a US$8 billion of debt relief for Congo in order to do the bidding of First Quantum Minerals, a Vancouver-based mining company whose mining contract was cancelled following Congo's review of contracts signed during the First and Second Congo Wars.[69] Eventually, the International Monetary Fund (IMF) and the World Bank's International Development Association announced that they were supporting US$12.3 billion in debt relief to Congo, comprising US$11.1 billion under the enhanced Heavily Indebted Poor Countries Initiative and US$1.2 billion under the Multilateral Debt Relief Initiative. In its press release, the IMF cited Congo's:

> satisfactory implementation of the country's poverty reduction and growth strategy, maintenance of macroeconomic stability, improvements in public expenditure and debt management, and improved governance and service delivery in key social sectors such as health, education and rural development.[70]

With eloquent timing, in Brussels several prominent Belgian lawyers asked prosecutors to bring war crimes charges against Belgian officials implicated in the murder of Patrice Lumumba.[71]

Nothing, however, overshadowed Congo's independence celebrations as much as the discovery on 2 June of the body of Floribert Chebeya Bahizire, the director of Voix des Sans Voix (Voice of the Voiceless), one of Congo's most respected human rights organisations. A day after sending a text message to his family saying he was on his way home after meeting Kabila's adviser and PNC Inspector General John Numbi, Chebeya's body was found in his car in the Mont Ngafula district of Kinshasa. Chebeya's driver, Fidèle Bazana, was missing. The previous March, Chebeya had had a gun pointed to his head during an interrogation by the PNC.[72] Chebeya had been in the process of preparing a complaint to be lodged with the ICC about the massacres of BDK members in Bas-Congo, in which Numbi was directly implicated, and he had strenuously protested against

Vital Kamerhe's removal from the presidency of the National Assembly. The day after Chebeya's body was found, Philip Alston said that the circumstances of the killing 'strongly suggest official responsibility'. In a crude attempt to smear Chebeya, a PNC spokesman said that used condoms and other sexually suggestive material were found in Chebeya's car.[73] By 5 June, the PNC was saying that several police officers had been arrested in connection with Chebeya's killing but would give no details.[74]

When the big day of 30 June arrived, present at the ceremonies in Kinshasa along with Kabila – now celebrating nearly a decade in power – were Albert II of Belgium (the brother of King Baudouin, who had died in 1993), Belgian Prime Minister Yves Leterme, Paul Kagame and Yoweri Museveni. One Kinshasa resident who saw footage of the ceremonies said that it was like watching a police line-up.

In the east, MONUSCO seemed to stumble from disaster to disaster. In an attack that began on 30 July and lasted for four days, the FDLR and their local Mai-Mai Cheka allies gang-raped over 200 women and children, some of whom were only infants, in the village of Luvungi, North Kivu, only a few miles away from a MONUSCO base in Kibua. At one point, a force of only 25 peacekeepers managed to drive up to 400 rebels back into the forest, but when the peacekeepers left the rebels returned.[75] Local civil society leaders said that they had warned the UN civil affairs bureau in Walikale and the FARDC the day before the attack that the absence of troops in the area had put the civilian population at grave risk, and that the FDLR was moving into the area.[76] Residents claimed that midway through the attacks, Indian MONUSCO peacekeepers had escorted commercial vehicles through Luvungi. As in many remote areas of Congo, there was a great dispute as to whether MONUSCO forces had sufficient interpreters on hand to understand local requests.[77] Two months later, Mai-Mai Cheka commander Sadoke Kokunda Mayele was handed over to UN troops by other fighters in his group, who said that the rapes 'had tarnished their name and [they] wanted to get rid of him'.[78] In the early hours of 18 August, three Indian MONUSCO peacekeepers were slain when attackers lured them out of their base in the North Kivu town of Kirumba and assailed them with machetes, spears and automatic weapons in an assault thought to be linked to the FDLR.[79]

History, however distant, had a way of continuing to beat a path back to the region's door. Try as it might, Kigali in particular could never entirely escape the echoes of the screams of those its forces had killed across Congo more than a decade earlier.

When a leaked draft of a US$3 million UN High Commissioner for Human Rights report on the Congo wars (known as the Mapping Exercise) made it clear that investigators had concluded that Rwandan troops may have committed genocide against Hutu refugees, Kigali responded by threatening to pull its 3,200 troops from UN peacekeeping operations in Sudan's western Darfur region,[80] Paul Kagame denounced the accusations of atrocities, which had been scrupulously documented by journalists and human rights organisations for over a decade, as 'absurd',[81] and Rwanda's Minister of Foreign Affairs Louise Mushikiwabo called the Mapping Exercise 'a moral and intellectual failure, as well as an insult to history'.[82] In a greatly toned-down version, the final report supinely referred to 'countervailing factors' arguing against acts of genocide having taken place in Congo.[83] The final version nevertheless also referred to 'a number of inculpatory elements that, if proven before a competent court, could be characterised as crimes of genocide'.[84] Although Rwandan troops assigned to UN peacekeeping duties stayed in place, Louise Mushikiwabo announced that Rwanda was 'reserving the right to review our various engagements with the UN' at a future date.[85]

Throughout 2010 in Goma, Rwanda's man in eastern Congo, Bosco Ntaganda, could be seen playing tennis on the red clay courts of Goma's Hotel Karibu, apparently without a care in the world despite the ICC's warrant against him and the presence of an international peacekeeping mission in the city.[86] Meanwhile, in and around the city, someone was settling accounts against his enemies. One CNDP supporter of Laurent Nkunda, Denis Ntare Semadwinga, was stabbed to death in his home in Gisenyi, just across the border in Rwanda.[87] Another Nkunda partisan, Lieutenant Colonel Antoine Balibuno, was murdered after meeting Ntaganda loyalists Lieutenant Colonel Kabakule Kennedy and Lieutenant Colonel John Asiki at a Goma bar. Balibuno had told people in the preceding months that Ntaganda had threatened to have him killed for not supporting the latter's leadership of the CNDP. As was obvious to anyone in Goma at the time, the CNDP would play a key role in Kabila's re-election plans, with a ballot having been announced for 27 November 2011. Opposition politicians charged that the date was unconstitutional as it was less than 90 days before the end of the president's term in office, in contravention of electoral law.[88]

In reaction to the profiteering of such warlords as Ntaganda, on 21 July, US President Barack Obama had signed into law H. R. 4173, known colloquially as the Dodd–Frank Act after its two main sponsors, congressmen Chris Dodd of Connecticut and Barney Frank of Massachusetts; in Congo, H. R. 4173 was referred to as the *loi Obama*, or Obama law. The law, which chiefly targeted financial regulation in the United States, nevertheless also contained several provisions relating to minerals mined in eastern Congo and assurances to be put in place that they did not benefit the various armed groups in the country. Although well intentioned, the law, which was strenuously supported by groups such as the Enough Project and Global Witness, proved a somewhat thornier matter when implemented on the ground. On a 9 September visit to Goma, Kabila announced a total ban on mining activities in the Kivus and Maniema (although, strangely, he ignored Ituri, Katanga and Kasai), a ban that was formalised 11 days later by ministerial decree. The ban lasted six months, and reaction to it among the people it was supposed to help was mixed: one Goma-based think tank asserted that 'if the government had been aiming for economic strangulation [of the region] it could not have found a better rope'.[89] The ban, some said, amounted to a 'de facto boycott', cutting off one of the region's few sources of income and laying off thousands of miners who were then unable to pay school fees for their children or buy basic necessities.[90] Many local observers felt that the sector should be regularised, not closed down or marginalised.[91]

The regime, however, was in no mood to brook further dissent. On 2 October, Armand Tungulu Mudiandambu, a Belgian resident of Congolese descent, was pronounced to have committed suicide in his cell using his pillowcase. Tungulu had been arrested three days earlier after allegedly throwing a stone at Kabila's convoy, and had been hauled off to Camp Tshatshi, the notorious Republican Guard torture centre where many of Jean-Pierre Bemba's followers had been killed in the March 2007 violence. Unfortunately for the state security forces, everyone knew that there were no pillows, let alone pillowcases, in Congolese jails.[92] Tungulu's death became a rallying cry for Kabila's Brussels-based opposition and the large Congolese diaspora there.[93] Anti-Kabila protesters in Brussels clashed with Belgian police during a chaotic demonstration against Tungulu's fate.[94] Less than 200 kilometres away from the scenes of chaos on the streets of Congo's former imperial power, at the start of Jean-Pierre Bemba's trial at The Hague, observers heard from witnesses testifying behind screens of how MLC fighters raped schoolgirls in a Bangui suburb as they fought in the Central African Republic's capital.[95] Bemba himself pleaded not guilty to the charges levelled against him.[96] Shortly before the trial, one of Bemba's deputies, MLC Deputy President Michel Nsimba Bayela, claimed that Congolese security agents had attempted to kidnap him from his home in Johannesburg, where he was in exile. The Kabila government dismissed Nsimba's claims, contemptuously referring to him as 'just an asylum seeker seeking sympathy'.[97]

After arriving in Kinshasa for a late October meeting with his Congolese counterpart Charles Mwando Nsimba, Rwanda's Minister of Defence James Kabarebe co-signed a statement where the two powers 'recognised with satisfaction advances made in the neutralisation and gradual eradication of armed groups and residual negative forces which still plunder the Great Lakes region'.[98]

The FDLR – whose forces raped at least 110 people and displaced some 40,000 during incursions into villages between November 2010 and January 2011[99] – had finally begun to feel the net closing around them. FDLR Executive Secretary Callixte Mbarushimana was arrested in October by French authorities acting on a sealed ICC warrant dating from September 2010 in which Mbarushimana was accused of participation in war crimes and crimes against humanity committed by the FDLR in the Kivus.[100] In early December, Ignace Murwanashyaka and Straton Musoni, who had been arrested a year earlier, were indicted at a court in Stuttgart for having 'directed FDLR actions, strategy and tactics' between January 2008 and November 2009.[101]

Congo looked towards a new year and a new vote. But before Congo could vote, Rwanda would hold its own election, and the atmosphere surrounding the ballot said much about the state that Paul Kagame and his loyalists had created since 1994.

In June 2010, Lieutenant General Faustin Kayumba Nyamwasa – former chief of staff of the RDF, head of military intelligence, Rwandan ambassador to India and Kagame confidant – was shot and wounded in Johannesburg in an attack that his wife attributed to an assassination plot directed from Kigali.[102] Nyamwasa had been in the process of forming a political group, the Rwandan National Congress, to oppose Kagame, and the South African police subsequently arrested ten people in connection with the shooting.[103] During the trial of three Rwandans and three Tanzanians accused in the attack, Kalisa Mubarak, a Rwandan immigrant who had lived in South Africa since 2003, said that he had been recruited to kill Nyamwasa by Rwandan soldiers offering vast sums of money and logistical support.[104] Speaking to a South African newspaper, Nyamwasa himself would later say of Kagame: 'Don't be surprised if we extract him from a pipe like the Libyans did with Muammar Gaddafi' (a reference to the Arab dictator slain in October 2011). Nyamwasa referred to Kagame as a 'vicious, spiteful, erratic, insensitive, greedy and murderous' man who wanted him dead because he knew too much. Nyamwasa also claimed that Kagame had ordered the assassination of Laurent Kabila at a meeting of the military high command at which Nyamwasa was present.[105] In Rwanda itself, Nyamwasa's brother, Lieutenant Colonel Rugigana Ngabo, was arrested for 'acts of destabilisation' against the country.[106]

Being a Rwandan journalist had become every bit as dangerous as it had been during the Habyarimana regime. The same month as the Nyamwasa shooting, Jean-Léonard Rugambage, the editor of Rwanda's *Umuvugizi* newspaper, was gunned down in Kigali just as his paper began an investigation into the Nyamwasa attack. His colleagues laid the crime at the feet of the Kagame government.[107] In the run-up to the August presidential elections, Agnes Uwimana, director of the *Umurabyo* newspaper, was arrested for 'contempt of the head of state' and denying the 1994 genocide.[108] Beyond the press, in the world of politics, the nearly decapitated body was found of André Kagwa Rwisereka, another RPF dissenter who had become the vice-chairman of the Democratic Green Party of Rwanda.[109] Following Kagwa's slaying, Louise Mushikiwabo was trotted out as per usual on the international stage to deny government involvement in the killing.[110]

Finally, in an 11 August ballot devoid of any meaningful opposition, and in a brazen echo of African dictators of old, Paul Kagame claimed 93 per cent of the vote.[111] The US National Security Council expressed its concern about the 'disturbing events' surrounding the ballot, but no move was made to cut off aid.[112] For the method if not for the man, one could almost see Joseph Kabila looking on approvingly from Kinshasa.

9 | ELECTIONS, ENCORE

As elections loomed, between December 2010 and January 2011, unmindful of the lessons of Kimia II, MONUSCO again joined forces with the FARDC in a joint operation dubbed Hatua Yamana ('Formidable Reach' in Swahili). The campaign was launched in areas of North Kivu, chiefly in Masisi territory, to flush out armed groups operating there, especially the FDLR. MONUSCO contributed logistical and technical support to the five FARDC battalions taking part.

On 31 December 2010, at least 100 uniformed men identified as FARDC soldiers invaded the isolated, mainly Hunde village of Bushani. The area was one with an active FDLR presence, and the FDLR maintained a base at nearby Bitoyi. The inhabitants of Bushani were interrogated about where they were hiding weapons, and beaten and abused by men in uniform. At least 47 women were the victims of sexual violence. The uniformed men left the next day after receiving radio messages in Kinyarwanda instructing them to proceed immediately to Kailenge, about three hours away on foot. They then returned to Bushani between 4 and 5 January, and the population fled into the bush while the uniformed men looted the town. UN investigators subsequently found packaging bearing references to food rations distributed to battalions that had received MONUSCO support during Operation Hatua Yamana. Some said that one of the battalions was composed of ex-CNDP members reporting to Bosco Ntaganda.[1]

On the judicial front, the beginning of the year saw four policemen sentenced to death by a military judge for the murder of human rights activist Floribert Chebeya Bahizire the previous year.[2] Most of the Congolese public, however, saw the four as simply scapegoats for a much broader conspiracy. One of the men sentenced, Major Paul Mwilambwe, had fled Congo before the ruling and later claimed that Chebeya had been killed on John Numbi's orders[3] and that the body of Chebeya's driver, which had never been recovered, was in fact buried at one of Numbi's farms.[4] In faraway Europe, as he arrived at the ICC in The Hague, former FDLR Executive Secretary Callixte Mbarushimana, who stood accused of 11 counts of crimes against humanity and war crimes, told the judges there that 'all my life I have fought injustice, hatred of other people and all forms of exploitation of human beings and I will continue to fight that in all its forms'.[5] Back in Congo itself, a mobile court programme, partially underwritten by the American Bar Association's Rule of Law Initiative and the Open Society Initiative for Southern Africa, finally began convicting and imprisoning soldiers for the crime of rape in South Kivu.[6]

As the elections approached, strange things appeared to be afoot. On 4 February, a lightly armed group took control of the Lubumbashi airport for several hours and raised a Katangese flag. On the evening of 27 February, gunmen attacked Kabila's residence in Kinshasa. Government spokesman Lambert Mende denounced the incident as 'an act of terrorism' and a possible coup attempt.[7] The tally of those killed ranged from seven to ten of the assailants, with UN personnel stating that gunmen had also targeted an army camp in the capital.[8] The group was said to be the previously little known Armée de Résistance Populaire, led by the former chief of staff of the FARDC, General Faustin Munene, who had fled Kinshasa for Brazzaville in October 2010.

The same month as the attacks on his residence and the airport at Lubumbashi, Kabila announced that the head of the CENI for the upcoming elections would be none other than his close confidant Pastor Daniel Ngoy Mulunda. Like so many of his confidants, Ngoy hailed from Katanga and had been touted by Kabila as his 'spiritual adviser'. In 2005, Ngoy had launched a curious NGO, the Programme Œcuménique de Paix, Transformation des Conflits et Réconciliation, and had organised the disastrous 'bicycle exchange' in Katanga that same year. He was also said to have at one time run a scheme repatriating alleged FDLR members to Rwanda who later turned out to be Congolese.[9] Perhaps more practically for Kabila's aims, Ngoy had been a founding member of the PPRD and had actively campaigned for the president in the 2006 elections. A more compromised and less neutral choice would have been hard to come up with.

As Congo prepared for its rendezvous with electoral destiny, Uganda's Yoweri Museveni, who in 1986 told his country that 'the problem of Africa in general and Uganda in particular is not the people but leaders who want to overstay in power',[10] entered his twenty-sixth year as that country's president, determined to secure a victory over his former personal physician, former soldier and Forum for Democratic Change leader Kizza Besigye.

Although not averse to using violence when it suited his aims, unlike Kagame in Rwanda, Museveni's default mode was to flatter and cajole. The EU observer mission for Uganda's February 2011 ballot concluded that 'the power of incumbency was exercised to such an extent as to compromise severely the level playing field between the competing candidates and political parties ... the distribution of money and gifts by candidates, especially from the ruling party, [is] a practice inconsistent with democratic principle.'[11]

On 20 February, Uganda's electoral commission declared Uganda's president the winner, with 68 per cent of the vote to 26 per cent for Besigye; at one point Museveni would rather bizarrely threaten his opponent by stating that 'we will catch him and eat him like a cake'.[12] In the following months, Besigye and his supporters would take to the streets, staging raucous protests in Kampala against fuel price hikes during which he and other opposition figures were arrested by security forces.[13] Besigye's arrest would spark unrest that would claim at least two lives when police opened fire on crowds protesting against his detention.[14]

At the end of April, the CENI announced that elections would be held on 28 November, with provisional results to be known by 6 December.[15] Around 18,500 people would be running for the 500 seats in parliament.[16] The second round of elections, so pivotal in 2006, had been eliminated, leaving a winner-take-all situation in the first round.

On the presidential slate there would be an interesting assemblage. Kabila's former ally Vital Kamerhe had left the PPRD after his ousting from the National Assembly presidency and had formed his own party, the Union pour la Nation Congolaise (UNC), under whose banner he would run for president. The former Ituri warlord Antipas Mbusa Nyamwisi quit his job in Kabila's government to also run for president, at the head of the RCD. Somewhat deluded, Jean-Pierre Bemba even announced from his cell at The Hague that he also wanted to compete in the elections as the MLC's presidential candidate, saying that his candidacy would be 'one that can deliver certain victory'.[17] His offer was declined by the party he had founded.[18]

There was little doubt that Kabila's chief rival would be veteran opposition figure and UDPS leader Étienne Tshisekedi, who this time seemed inclined to take part in the electoral process that he had thus far shunned. Although he had been away from Congo in South Africa and Belgium for three years being treated for an unspecified ailment, Tshisekedi and the UDPS still boasted the most extensive political organisation in the country save for that of Kabila himself. Despite Tshisekedi's years in opposition to Mobutu, Kabila could not have been presented with a more appealing rival. A snarling demagogue whose sense of entitlement to the role of president was palpable, Tshisekedi would prove himself, as he had in the past, ill suited to the rigours of democracy and of statesmanship.

Throughout the late spring and summer, the region remained

in flux. On 1 May, former UPC commander and Bosco Ntaganda confidant General Floribert Kisembo Bahemuka was killed by FARDC soldiers after he had gone to visit his home village of Lonyo in Ituri without authorisation to do so, allegedly to try and organise a rebellion.[19] Around the same time, former *interahamwe* leader Bernard Munyagishari was seized by the FARDC in North Kivu.[20] In London, which would see its share of central Africa-related drama in the coming months, two Rwanda exiles – Rene Mugenzi and former RPF officer Jonathan Musonera – were warned by the city's Metropolitan Police that they faced an 'imminent threat' of assassination by the Rwandan government.[21] On 9 July, South Sudan, whose territory had been so impacted by the cross-border incursions of the LRA, became an independent nation.

By mid-July, the CENI's Daniel Ngoy Mulunda announced that more than 30 million people had registered to vote in the November elections,[22] just as Minister of Communications Lambert Mende issued a decree indefinitely banning the Tshisekedi-supportive Radio Lisanga Télévision due to its broadcasting programmes 'that are promoting violence and contribute to disturbing public order'.[23] The 78-year-old Tshisekedi, appearing full of life despite his long absence from the public stage, addressed an overflowing crowd of 80,000 at a stadium in Kinshasa in early August.[24] That same month, militants of the Luba supremacist UNAFEC party (which had close links with Kabila's adviser John Numbi) attacked the UDPS office in Lubumbashi, shouting that they could 'smell the odour of Kasaians'.[25] It was not a promising opening salvo for the campaign to come.

In one of the great ironies for a country where so much conflict had been caused by mineral resources, on 18 August the Kabila government sold the state mining company Sodimico's 30 per cent stake in the Frontier and Lonshi mines in Katanga to a Hong Kong-registered shell company, Fortune Ahead, for US$30 million. Frontier was Congo's third largest copper mine, and the sale was ostensibly to help fund the upcoming ballot, but represented barely 6 per cent of the estimated market value of the government's stake. The mines had been owned by Canada's First Quantum until being confiscated in 2009.[26]

Tshisekedi formally submitted his candidacy on 5 September, and the same day UDPS militants attacked the headquarters of Kabila's PPRD in Kinshasa, ransacking the premises and setting several cars on fire. Pro-Kabila attackers then looted Tshisekedi's headquarters the following day. Police dispersed the crowd that gathered outside the Tshisekedi base with gunfire in which one person was killed.[27]

Two days after Tshisekedi registered, the dreaded Mai-Mai leader Gédéon Kyungu Mutanga was among nearly 1,000 prisoners who escaped from jail in Lubumbashi.[28] Two days later, Katanga's provincial interior minister, Dikanga Kazadi, announced a US$100,000 reward for anyone who brought Gédéon back into custody.[29]

The tension in neighbouring Burundi had also begun to spill over into Congo in a more profound way. On 19 September, gunmen wearing military fatigues and shouting 'Make sure there's no survivors' burst into a pub in Gatumba, west of the Burundian capital Bujumbura, and killed 36 people.[30] A defendant accused of taking part in the massacre later implicated Burundian police at his trial, saying the shooting was an attempt to kill Hutu rebel FNL commander Claver Nduwayezu gone awry.[31] (Nduwayezu himself would be slain in South Kivu the following year.[32]) Gatumba had been the site of the August 2004 killing of 152 Congolese refugees by the FNL. By 2011, Burundi's Observatoire de l'Action Governmentale, a coalition of civil society groups, said that government-backed death squads there had killed at least 300 demobilised FNL fighters.[33] In early October 2011, the FNL and its allies in the Mai-Mai Yakutumba militia (whose membership was largely drawn from the Bembe ethnic group) were blamed for an attack that killed five Congolese aid workers and two other civilians in Fizi in an assault where the group was apparently specifically targeting Banyamulenge.[34] Led by 'General' William Amuri, alias Yakutumba (hence the group's name), the Mai-Mai Yakutumba's 300 to 400 combatants had resisted joining the FARDC and had formed a close partnership with the FNL. Yakutumba's chief sponsor was said to be General Dunia Lengwama, a former Mai-Mai leader integrated into the FARDC.[35]

After the LRA carried out 120 separate attacks during the first four months of 2011, a coalition of nearly 40 human rights groups noted that there were fewer than 1,000 MONUSCO troops deployed in Haut-Uélé and none at all in Bas-Uélé, and called for intensified efforts to arrest the LRA leadership.[36] MONUSCO said that the Ugandan rebels had forced 300,000 people from their homes.[37] In October, US President Barack Obama announced that he was sending 100 special forces soldiers to help the UPDF hunt down the LRA, to be deployed in combat teams, as well as headquarters, communications and logistics personnel. Beyond Uganda, the forces would eventually deploy into South Sudan, the Central African Republic and Congo.[38] By the end of the year, the Ugandan army confirmed that the troops had moved along with the UPDF to the Central African Republic and South Sudan. What, if any, safeguards were in place to protect civilians and to avoid a repeat of the disastrous outcome of previous campaigns against the LRA was never made clear. As if in response, in November the LRA began raiding the rice crops of the commune of Bangadi in Orientale province.[39]

In Ituri, the still-active old-line FRPI of Cobra Matata attacked the towns of Aveba and Getty Etat on 20 October, sending some 30,000 people fleeing to nearby communities.[40]

Looking with concern at the climate in which the upcoming vote was to be held, the US-based Carter Center, which had been assessing the electoral situation in the country since August, issued a press release on 17 October where it said that there were 'serious threats to holding the election' and that 'serious incidents of intimidation and violence have occurred during campaigning'.[41] As if to underline that point, an attempted demonstration by Tshisekedi supporters in the capital's Gombe quarter on 20 October was brutally suppressed by the PNC, who beat the demonstrators with batons.[42] The following day, two PNC officers were assaulted in the city's Limete district, allegedly by UDPS partisans.[43]

'Who will win the elections?' a confident Kabila asked at a rare press conference in Kinshasa on 18 October. 'There is one thing of which I am sure and certain, and that is that I will not lose them.'[44]

As October drew to a close, things got worse. Despite Daniel Ngoy Mulunda's declaration that the CENI was 'more than ready' to conduct the vote,[45] whereas in 2006 there had been 2,528 compilation centres for ballot boxes, for the 2011 vote there would be only 168. Whereas before there had been 300 EU observers, this time there would be only 148. While in 2006 there had been 2,250 UN observers, this time there would be none. The Open Society Initiative for Southern Africa and the Enough Project warned in a joint statement that Congo could not 'afford for fraudulent or poorly conducted elections to spark violence and set back development'.[46] When members of the opposition-oriented Parti Travailliste attempted to celebrate the beginning of the electoral campaign in Tshisekedi's home base of Mbuji-Mayi, police responded by opening fire, killing one and injuring three. The demonstrators then set two buildings thought to belong to Kabila partisans ablaze.[47]

Both Kabila and Tshisekedi visited Goma on 28 October. Tshisekedi spoke first, promising free education for the young, free medicine for the old, and, provocatively, that he would kick 'Rwandans' and their sympathisers out of the country. In a more measured tone, Kabila promised to bring economic development to the east and implement his five-point plan for national development: reviving Congo's dilapidated roadways; pushing for universal access to healthcare and education; ensuring safe housing for all; regularising the delivery of water and electricity; and creating jobs.[48]

The rhetoric surrounding 2011's vote was, if anything, even more poisonous than that which had surrounded Kabila's contest with Jean-Pierre Bemba in 2006. Gabriel Kyungu, the president of Katanga's provincial assembly and a former governor, railed against people from Kasai, Tshisekedi's home base, telling a rally in Likasi that 'there are too many mosquitos in the living room; now is the time to apply insecticide'.[49] To the east, speaking in Rubaya in North Kivu's Masisi territory, parliamentarian Sylvain Seninga Ntamukunzi urged the Rwandaphone population of the area to 'liberate themselves of this domination, this slavery' by 'a small people who don't even know the origins of their ancestors'.[50] Bosco Ntaganda and the CNDP had endorsed Kabila's run for the presidency and were applying significant pressure in the zones they controlled for the inhabitants to toe the line come voting day, especially with regard to CNDP-affiliated candidate Bahati Ibatunganya.[51] Fabrice Mumpfiritsa, a well-known Hunde singer, was kidnapped in Goma and found days later, injured but alive. Formerly a Kabila partisan, Mumpfiritsa had grown disenchanted with the president and had begun vocally supporting Kabila's local opposition.

Given the violence committed by his supporters, Kabila made quite an unappealing candidate. Tshisekedi's behaviour and rhetoric, however, were themselves hardly reassuring. Speaking on the opposition-oriented RLTV on 6 November from South Africa (where he spent a total of two weeks immediately before the vote), Tshisekedi declared that 'since the majority of the Congolese people are with Tshisekedi and trust Tshisekedi, from now on I am the head of state'. For good measure, he added: 'If Ngoy Mulunda does not listen to what we are saying, he will be weeping in his native language.'[52] He later urged his followers to 'terrorise those who have terrorised us for so long', adding, somewhat puzzlingly: 'This is not a call for violence.'[53] Kabila's advisers could not have scripted it any better. Speaking to Voice of America, Lambert Mende said that Tshisekedi's statements were potentially criminal and that an investigation had been launched into them.[54] Running brawls erupted between PPRD and UDPS supporters in Lubumbashi that injured at least 15.[55] During a helicopter-borne visit to the Fizi town of Baraka, Kabila told those assembled that he would address the violence brought to the region by the fighting between the FARDC and the FNL-allied Mai-Mai Yakutumba.[56]

The international community, which had appeared to turn a blind eye to the Kabila government's abuses for so long, finally grew concerned as those abuses combined with Tshisekedi's calls to violent action. On 8 November, the EU released a statement saying that it was 'concerned at recent developments in the electoral campaign' and that 'a climate of violence and political, social and ethnic tension' existed in the country.[57] In its own statement, the US State Department condemned 'incendiary speech' as well as 'irresponsible actions, such as calls to violence and the proclaiming of victory prior to the vote, [which] undermine the electoral process and are inherently undemocratic'.[58] The UN Joint Human Rights Office criticised the 'continued repression of human rights and fundamental freedoms in the pre-electoral period'.[59]

These entreaties had little effect. In Kamina, north-east of Lubumbashi, UNAFEC militants attacked UDPS supporters on 17 November after they had burned Kabila's portrait, resulting in a number of injuries.[60] On the evening of 22 November, Marius Gangale, a deputy for the MLC in the provincial assembly, was shot to death by unknown gunmen as he was stuck in traffic in Kinshasa.[61] A UN investigation found credible allegations that former North Kivu governor Eugène Serufuli Ngayabaseka had provided funds to FDLR representatives in exchange for assurances of security for the electoral campaign of his Union des

Congolais pour le Progrès, which supported Kabila's presidential coalition.[62]

On 26 November – two days before the vote – the capital's N'djili airport witnessed a chaotic scene when both Kabila and Tshisekedi partisans gathered to welcome their respective candidates back to the city. Kabila's Republican Guard troops fired into the air to disperse the crowd but several also fired towards the esplanade of the airport, and blazed away along Boulevard Lumumba as the president's convoy made its way back. At least four people were killed.[63] Six UDPS supporters seized by government security forces subsequently disappeared. At least 69 people, some with no political affiliation, were wounded by gunfire.[64] During a 48-hour period between 25 and 27 November, the bodies of seven men (two of whom had been beheaded) were found along a riverbank in the area of the capital's Ngaliema commune. A month later, in the same area, five bodies were seen floating on the river. Witnesses told UN investigators that men in uniform had been throwing bodies into the river behind the Palais de la Nation.[65]

With elections less than 48 hours away, the CENI announced that 33 of the 80 aircraft scheduled to transport ballots and equipment had been grounded by bad weather.[66]

Election day – a Monday – saw menacing black clouds hanging over Kinshasa. In Lubumbashi, gunmen opened fire on a truck carrying ballots and assaulted a polling station in attacks that killed five.[67] In Mbuji-Mayi, three polling stations were burned down and demonstrators protesting that they did not know how to vote were dispersed by police firing live ammunition.[68] Speaking to reporters at the UN, US Ambassador Susan Rice said that the US was 'concerned by reports of violence and indeed some deaths today in various parts' of Congo, as well as by 'reported anomalies in the conduct of the election'.[69] Voting was extended for a second day as government spokesman Matthieu Mpita advised the population to 'stay calm and await further instructions'.[70] By Wednesday, four candidates – Vital Kamerhe, Léon Kengo Wa Dondo, Mbusa Nyamwisi and Adam Bombole – called for the results to be annulled before they were announced. CENI president Daniel Ngoy Mulunda claimed that more than 99 per cent of voting districts had functioned normally on election day.[71] By Saturday, Ngoy was announcing that Kabila was leading the vote count with 50.3 per cent of roughly a third of votes cast. As Tshisekedi supporters began attacking foreign journalists in the capital, accusing them of conspiring to return Kabila to power,[72] Vital Kamerhe accused Kabila of preparing 'carnage'.[73]

The same day as the Kabila government announced straight-faced that it was opening an inquiry into the violence surrounding the election,[74] Tshisekedi ratcheted up the rhetoric even further by saying that Kabila and the CENI would be committing 'suicidal acts' if they did not 'respect the will of the Congolese people', adding that UDPS partisans should 'stay vigilant so that if needed they can execute the orders I will give them'.[75] Noting that the population of the province had 'long suffered from the war', North Kivu's governor Julien Paluku appealed for calm.[76]

As tension grew, Congo's mobile phone providers suspended text messages and airlines cancelled flights in and out of the capital. Speaking at a press conference, Bishop Nicolas Djombo likened the situation to 'a high-speed train that is barrelling straight toward a wall'.[77] In Johannesburg, South African police fired rubber bullets at a group of protesters who had gathered in front of the headquarters of the governing African National Congress party and arrested several who tried to storm the Congo embassy in Pretoria.[78] Anti-Kabila demonstrators in London also clashed with police during a protest outside the residence of British Prime Minister David Cameron.[79]

In Kinshasa itself, police repeatedly doused UDPS partisans gathered outside the party's headquarters with tear gas.[80] After the CENI had been granted a 48-hour extension to publish the final total, police roamed the city, violently dispersing any attempted gathering of Tshisekedi supporters.[81] In the days that followed the publication of the provisional result, the Republican Guard and the PNC fired live ammunition at protesters in the communes of Bandalungwa, Kalamu, Kasa-Vubu, Kimbanseke, Limete and Ngaliema, killing at least eight people.[82] Finally, on 9 December, Kabila was declared the winner with 49 per cent of the 18.14 million votes cast to Tshisekedi's 32 per cent.[83]

Following the announcement of the results, at least six people were killed by gunfire in the capital.[84] In Rutshuru in North Kivu, civil society leader Willy Wabo, who had denounced the irregularities in the election, was slain.[85] Police in Kinshasa went door to door in opposition neighbourhoods seizing suspected Tshisekedi supporters.[86] As was usual, security forces also took the opportunity to loot anything that took their fancy.[87] PNC Inspector General Charles Bisengimana (who had replaced Kabila confidant John Numbi after the Floribert Chebeya murder) promised to 'punish' the perpetrators of any crimes within the force's ranks.[88] In London, police arrested nearly 150 people when a pro-Tshisekedi protest disintegrated and a faction of the marchers attacked cars and shops and 'threatened' members of the public, according to the police.[89]

The ballot met with widespread condemnation. In a statement, the Carter Center said it found that 'the quality and integrity of the vote tabulation process has varied across the country, ranging from the proper application of procedures to serious irregularities'. These irregularities included the loss of nearly 2,000 polling station results in the Tshisekedi stronghold of Kinshasa. The statement concluded that multiple locations, especially in Kabila's home base of Katanga, 'reported impossibly high rates of 99 to 100 per cent voter turnout with all, or nearly all, votes going to [the] incumbent'.[90] The 147 observers sent by the EU released a statement deploring 'the lack of transparency and irregularities in the collection, compilation and publication of the results'.[91]

A subsequent investigation by the UN found that, in the capital alone between 26 November and 25 December, at least 33 people were killed, 83 injured, 16 disappeared and 265 arrested – mostly illegally and/or arbitrarily after encounters with Kabila's security forces.[92] Once again, the Republican Guard played a leading role in the repression, although it was supported enthusiastically by specialised units of the PNC such as the Légion Nationale d'Intervention and the Groupe Mobile d'Intervention.

At a 12 December press conference, Kabila said that 'the credibility of these elections cannot be put in doubt'.[93] Tshisekedi's adviser Valentin Mubake claimed that the candidate was under house arrest, his house surrounded by Republican Guard troops.[94] On 16 December, Congo's Supreme Court upheld Kabila's victory, dismissing Vital Kamerhe's complaint regarding the flaws in the ballot.[95]

All was not quiet, though. In the town of Gungu in Bandundu province, partisans of Antoine Gizenga's PALU and those of the Alliance Démocratique pour le Développement – both nominal members of Kabila's governing coalition – clashed over alleged vote-rigging in PALU's favour.[96] At a press conference in the capital two days after the Supreme Court decision, Tshisekedi declared himself 'the president elected by the Congolese people' and announced that Kabila's government was 'dismissed starting today'.[97] How he intended to implement such declarations remained a mystery. Speaking on a Sunday, Tshisekedi also stated that he would inaugurate himself as president that coming Friday in the capital's Stade des Martyrs.[98] Police in Bukavu dispersed an attempted joint march by UPDF, MLC and UNC activists against the election results on 20 December.[99] That same day, Joseph Kabila was sworn in to another term as Congo's president in Kinshasa, telling a crowd of supporters (with noticeably few foreign dignitaries among them) that he would 'safeguard national unity and allow himself to be guided only by the general interest and the respect of human rights'.[100] Three days later, Tshisekedi attempted to hold his own 'swearing in' ceremony at the Stade des Martyrs, while police lathered his supporters with tear gas and fired live volleys into the air.[101] Police surrounded Tshisekedi's home and the UDPS headquarters in the Limete district of the capital, while Republican Guard soldiers brandished Kalashnikovs and rocket launchers as they criss-crossed Boulevard Lumumba.[102] In a final, somewhat pathetic gesture, Congo's longest-lasting and most visible opposition figure declared himself president of a country he did not govern and whose institutions he did not control at a private ceremony attended by about a dozen colleagues.[103]

If they could not assert their will in the streets of Kinshasa, Tshisekedi's supporters decided that they would do so elsewhere. Despite running against Kabila in the election for president, following the vote Léon Kengo wa Dondo fell more or less back into line, again supporting the governing coalition and attending Kabila's inauguration. This did not sit at all well with a group of UDPS 'fighters' who cornered the lawmaker at a Paris train station at the end of the year, battering him to the ground, knocking out his teeth and trampling on him. Some said they were angry because he had not withdrawn and thrown his support behind Tshisekedi.[104] After several days in the hospital, the 76-year-old parliamentarian was released.

And how, one may ask, were all of the machinations of Kinshasa viewed in the volatile east? Despite multiple offences against them and the attendant terrible human toll, and despite serious internal tensions over the authoritarian leadership style of Sylvestre Mudacumura, the FDLR remained a militarily potent force in eastern Congo, despite its international political leadership having largely gone to ground after FDLR-related arrests in Europe over the preceding two years. The FDLR had been under pressure connected to its mining concerns and, as a result, had begun to extract a larger chunk of its revenue from trade in commercial products in mining areas that it controlled, as well as from taxation and sales of agricultural products such as palm oil and cannabis.[105] As if the elections had changed nothing, residents fled more than a dozen villages in the Masisi and Walikale territories in early December as fighting erupted between the FDLR and a new Mai-Mai group referring to itself as 'Guides'.[106] On the night of 19 December, seven people were slain by the FDLR in Walikale territory in revenge for the killing of an FDLR commander by local militias the previous month.[107] A day later, suspected FDLR fighters abducted five people from the South Kivu village of Kamakombe, while a clash between the FDLR and FARDC killed two.[108] In mid-December 2011, much to the FDLR's glee, the ICC declined to charge Callixte Mbarushimana for the war crimes and crimes against humanity committed in the Kivus, the charges that had led to his arrest the previous October.[109]

And Bosco Ntaganda? Through his Rwandan patrons and his new alliance with the government in Kinshasa, Ntaganda had fared perhaps the best of anyone involved in the election save Kabila and his cadre themselves. With his CNDP loyalists now inserted into the FARDC and with the ability to lord it over Goma as a conquering chieftain, Ntaganda took full advantage of his new mobility. Despite a travel ban and an arrest warrant against him, Ntaganda crossed from Goma to Gisenyi at least three times in 2011. Neither Rwandan nor Congolese officials made any attempt to detain or arrest him.[110] Through the Great Lakes Mining Company of his associate Edson Musabarura, Ntaganda exercised significant control over North Kivu's Mungwe and Fungamwaka mines, and actively collaborated with east African regional dealer networks to sell real and counterfeit gold on the international market. When the Congolese basketball great Dikembe Mutombo, for many years resident in the United States, attempted to buy 4.5 tons of gold for US$10 million from 'a village in Kenya', his intermediary, a diamond trader named Carlos St Mary, ended up forking out over US$5 million, only to be whisked away aboard a Gulfstream jet to Goma. Before realising that he had been scammed, St Mary had a memorable meeting with a leather hat- and vest-wearing Ntaganda, during which this following exchange figured:

> St Mary: Give me just one reason to trust any of you in this room.
>
> Ntaganda: We didn't kill you this morning.[111]

Several million dollars lighter, St Mary finally left Congo, defeated. Ntaganda later claimed he had been working on Kinshasa's behalf to ensnare gold smugglers. Another individual integral to the Mutombo side of the deal, the Nigerian-born US oil tycoon Kase Lawal, had previously served on a US advisory committee for trade and policy negotiations.[112]

The UN Security Council adopted Resolution 2021 in November 2011, which condemned the illicit flow of weapons into Congo, expressed its support for due diligence guidelines for importers, processing industries and consumers of mineral products originating in Congo, and specifically demanded that the FDLR, LRA, FNL, Allied Democratic Forces (ADF) and Mai-Mai Yakutumba lay down their arms, but nowhere did it mention Ntaganda.[113] Although more than 80 staff members of the Rwanda Geology and Mines Authority had been set to work tagging minerals in more than 100 mine locations across the country, and although Kigali was the first government in the region to implement the Tin Supply Chain Initiative tagging system – which also forbade the import of untagged material from other countries – the regulations did not apply to sealed minerals that transited through Rwanda itself.[114]

On the ground in eastern Congo, it was a strange tableau the chilly détente between Kinshasa and Kigali had created. Travelling through North Kivu shortly after the elections, one could see red-beret-wearing soldiers – youthful to the point of resembling children – hauling shoulder-mounted grenade launchers through crowded marketplaces. Not far beyond Goma, one was almost immediately surrounded by vaulting green hills as far as the eye could see, steady rains turning the pitted roads to red clay rivulets. The green hills and valleys were shrouded in a ghostly mist that seemed to further emphasise the remoteness of the area, and from the mist herds of cattle would emerge, led by tall, gaunt herders. Sprawling camps for displaced people engulfed and dwarfed Masisi and other towns.[115]

After winning a convincing legitimate election in 2006, like Mobutu, Museveni and Kagame before him, Kabila and his advisers had decided that he was indispensable. Triumphing over the forces arrayed against it in 2011, the ruling clique no doubt believed itself to be settling in for another decade of uninterrupted rule. Between its alliance with the CNDP in the east, Kinshasa's détente with Kigali and Kampala, the government's grip on Katanga and the billion-dollar deals that had been negotiated by Kabila's key adviser Augustin Katumba Mwanke, the champagne would have tasted colder and more delicious in the halls of the Palais de la Nation, a palace that, like so many others, would turn out to be only a castle made of sand.

10 | REBELLION AFTER REBELLION

Victory though it was, Kabila's defeat of Tshisekedi was not an unqualified triumph. The PPRD had won an absolute majority in Congo's National Assembly, but the results still signified a haemorrhaging of 45 per cent of the seats that had belonged to the coalition previously and further undermined the regime's legitimacy.[1] Nor did all the president's opponents appear disposed to go quietly. Kinshasa felt threatened enough by the possibility of disturbance in the east that, on 20 January, the provincial assembly of North Kivu was shuttered two days after it opened 'to avoid disturbing public order'.[2] On 2 February, a shoot-out in Goma between the FARDC and the bodyguards of a UNC candidate for deputy, Dieudonné Bakungu Mitondeke, killed two soldiers and two policemen.[3] Bakungu was subsequently flown to Kinshasa where he was placed under 'house arrest'.[4]

As 2012 got under way, the consensus among many observers on the ground in North Kivu was that there was a great deal of alienation among non-CNDP groups, many of which had not been happy before the elections. Having given Kabila time to change his strategy in the Kivus, it rapidly became evident that the status quo – meaning that the most important positions in the army would go to ex-CNDP members – would remain.[5] One high-ranking official in an international organisation that had long had a presence in the province referred to the system of governance that had been put in place as being 'like a mafia ... Whoever doesn't side with [the CNDP], doesn't agree or says something in opposition will be intimidated, or eventually put under house arrest or killed.'[6] On a visit to Goma, another person told me that 'abductions, targeted killings, forced labour, extortions, sexual violence ... It's happening every single day. The international community has spent billions of dollars for years to reach where we are today, at the door of a new conflict.'[7]

Far from the elections quietening things down, in early February a new, largely Hunde Mai-Mai group dubbed Raïa Mutomboki arose around Shabunda in South Kivu, proclaiming its desire to defend the population there from attacks by the FDLR.[8] For its part, the FDLR's relations with the local population had deteriorated to the point that the group was beating villagers to death who refused to take part in FDLR-sanctioned forced labour.[9]

The government in Kinshasa no doubt saw little need to pay undue attention to these fits and starts. But then one clear afternoon on 12 February, a private jet carrying Kabila's trusted adviser Augustin Katumba Mwanke began its descent into the airport in Bukavu. Katumba Mwanke, the man responsible for the key 2007 and 2008 investment deals with China and who had proved so invaluable in the late 2008 negotiations with Kigali to end the Kivu crisis, was at the height of his power and influence. Joseph Kabila, a man upon whose shoulder Katumba Mwanke's hand had rested since the day Kabila had taken office, was again president. A cold peace was continuing with Rwanda. There would be many more deals, many more negotiations, to oversee in the years to come. Flying in good weather, the Gulfstream 200 apparently misjudged the length of the runway and skidded into a ditch. Katumba Mwanke, the plane's two American crew members and two people on the ground were killed.[10] Minister of Finance Matata Ponyo was seriously injured.[11] It was a shattering blow to the regime, and with the exception of appearing at Katumba Mwanke's funeral, Kabila would all but disappear from public view for the next few months.

Despite Mwanke's death, on the surface little had changed and the government reverted to type when confronted with even the most trivial threat. A group of Christians attempting to march in Kinshasa to protest at Kabila's theft of the elections – their display co-ordinated to happen on the twentieth anniversary of the *marche d'espoir* against the Mobutu dictatorship – was met with tear gas and physical assault by both the police and bussed-in government partisans.[12] Following the march, three senior diplomats from the Congolese embassy in London resigned, denouncing what they said was the 'climate of terror' the Kabila government had created in the country.[13] The UDPS and its allies in the Christian Democrats boycotted the National Assembly. Those associated with Kabila also remained fair game abroad, as Katanga governor Moïse Katumbi found out when he dined at the Hilton Hotel in Brussels. His table was charged by a group of anti-Kabila protesters who were then repelled by the politician's bodyguards.[14]

In February, Cobra Matata's FRPI looted several towns in Orientale province's Irumu territory.[15] At a meeting with the government security committee of Ituri in the village of Bukiringi, Matata presented a list of demands and said that, if they were met, the group would be persuaded to lay down its arms. These demands included a national amnesty, international protection, entrance into the FARDC and the recognition of the FRPI as a political party.[16] The request for amnesty was one supported by many in Ituri's civil society weary of years of war and ever shifting 'taxes' paid to both the government and the militia.[17] Tribal elders in the area also supported the call.[18] With little response coming from Kinshasa, the FRPI announced only a few months later that it was uniting with three other smaller military groupings to form a new coalition, the Coalition des Groupes Armés de l'Ituri.[19] It was a union that many believed had been engineered by Kigali.[20] As suspected FDLR fighters burned at least four people to death in the territory of Kabare in South Kivu over the night of 25–26 February,[21] a group of NGOs sent a letter to the government stating that there had been more than 300 murders in the province over the previous 12 months.[22]

During March, armed groups ranging from the Raïa Mutom-boki to the FDLR to the FARDC itself besieged the South Kivu territory of Kalehe, killing villagers and looting their dwellings and cattle.[23] Violent clashes with heavy weapons between the FARDC and both General Janvier Karairi's APCLS and the PARECO militias occurred in North Kivu throughout the month, especially in Masisi territory.[24] Speaking to Radio Okapi on 22 March, Janvier said that the movement might demobilise, but only in return for cash, stating that 'the Kinshasa government has neglected us, which is why we fight'. Janvier also added that Kabila had not responded to the group's overtures for dialogue.[25] On 6 March, PALU's Adolphe Muzito resigned as prime minister, to be replaced in the interim by government minister Louis Koyagialo.

Bosco Ntaganda's former comrade-in-arms in the UPC, Thomas Lubanga, was convicted by the ICC on 14 March of recruiting child soldiers during the conflict in Ituri. It was the first verdict in the court's decade of existence.[26] During the course of the trial, Lubanga's lawyer Catherine Mabille had lambasted the former child soldiers who had testified against the warlord, claiming that 'all the individuals presented as child soldiers, as well as their parents in some cases, deliberately lied before this court', hardly an approach likely to win sympathy for her client.[27] Two years earlier, the ICC had suspended the trial, accusing the prosecution of refusing to disclose the name of an intermediary involved in marshalling testimony against Lubanga.[28] The court then ruled that Lubanga's detention was no longer legal given the suspension of the trial, a decision later reversed on appeal.[29] Lubanga would subsequently be sentenced to 14 years in jail.[30] Former FNI/FRPI commander Mathieu Ngudjolo Chui fared better, however, and was acquitted of war crimes charges at the end of the year.[31]

While the ICC was praised to its face, many human rights and victims' groups criticised the court and chief prosecutor Luis Moreno-Ocampo in particular for refusing to hold Lubanga accountable for the sexual violence and multitude of other crimes committed by his troops.[32] At a post-conviction press conference at The Hague, Moreno-Ocampo demanded that Kabila turn Bosco Ntaganda over to the court for trial,[33] an appeal that was soon seconded by US ambassador to Congo James Entwistle.[34] Following Lubanga's conviction, civil society leaders in Katanga appealed for a tribunal to prosecute 'economic crimes' as well.[35] The government of Congo's new prime minister, Augustin Matata Ponyo Mapon (who had survived the plane crash that had killed Katumba Mwanke the previous February), was installed on 18 April, nearly five months after elections and over a month since his predecessor, Adolphe Muzito, had resigned – and it looked as if it had its work cut out for it.

Pressure had been growing for Bosco Ntaganda to break the parallel chains of command within the FARDC-integrated CNDP units, and, with a chorus of calls demanding his arrest, the warlord finally decided that the pressure was too much.

By early April, former CNDP members who had been integrated into the FARDC's 804th Regiment began to desert their posts in Rutshuru and head south towards Katale. Some of those closest to Bosco Ntaganda headed towards Kitshanga.[36] On the night of 7 April in Rutshuru, Colonel Innocent Kayina, the commander of the FARDC's 805th Regiment, also defected to the rebels, taking along with him several men and considerable ammunition and destroying two jeeps for good measure.[37] Despite Ntaganda's protestations that 'I am here, I'm not afraid' and that he was not involved in the mutiny, his aides handed out flyers with the deserters' list of grievances on them to anyone who wanted them.[38] As Kabila, MONUSCO head Roger Meece and the FARDC's Chief of Staff Didier Etumba all arrived in Goma on 10 April, Meece said that Ntaganda 'had posed a threat to the population of this region long enough'.[39] Kabila, however, demurred, saying that, although the Congolese state had 'more than a hundred reasons to arrest' Ntaganda, his government

would 'not work under pressure from the international community'.[40] Speaking in Goma on 11 April, Kabila announced
that he was 'suspending' all military operations in North Kivu.[41]
Shortly before the trio's arrival, 128 deserters had unexpectedly
returned to their posts in Uvira.[42] A little over a week later,
more deserters, having based themselves between Uvira and Fizi,
expressed their desire to do the same but said they would return
only in the presence of MONUSCO.[43] In some of the most intense
clashes that year, 27 people were killed during fighting between
the FARDC and the CNDP-allied Mai-Mai Cheka in Walikale
territory from 11 to 14 April.[44] By the end of the month, the
Mai-Mai Cheka would succeed in seizing Luvungi, scene of the
group's ghastly campaign of mass rape two years earlier when it
was allied with the FDLR.[45]

Fighting between the FARDC and deserters killed at least 15
in Masisi territory on 30 April.[46] By early May, the rebels controlled at least seven towns in North Kivu's Masisi and Walikale
territories.[47] Finally, speaking at a press conference in Goma on
2 May, North Kivu governor Julien Paluku gave voice to what
everyone knew all along, stating that 'everything that is happening
currently in Masisi is under the responsibility of General Bosco
Ntaganda and ... if our units catch hold of him, he will have to
answer for all his actions before Congolese jurisdictions'.[48]

Later, saying that he was speaking to reporters from his farm
in the countryside about 50 kilometres west of Goma, Ntaganda
denied involvement in the unrest, saying: 'My superiors in the
army know I'm here.'[49] Nearly 25 tonnes of arms, including
mortars, were recovered from one of Ntaganda's abandoned farms
in Masisi by the FARDC on 8 May.[50] The rebels announced
that same day in a communiqué to Radio Okapi that they would
henceforth be known as the Mouvement du 23 Mars (or M23),
a reference to the date of the 2009 peace accords between the
CNDP and the Kabila government. It was also announced that
Colonel Sultani Makenga, one of the former commanders of the

Amani Leo campaign as well as a former CNDP commander and Nkunda loyalist, would serve as the group's titular head.[51] (Makenga's troops had joined the uprising slightly later than the initial rebellion.) Many saw the placement of Makenga as an attempt to deflect attention from Ntaganda.

As had been the case with so much of the violence in eastern Congo since 1996, Kigali's fingerprints were all over the rebellion. A subsequent UN report would conclude that Rwanda had violated the April 2008 arms embargo on rebel groups in the country by transporting weapons and soldiers through Rwandan territory, recruiting Rwandan youth and demobilised ex-combatants as well as Congolese refugees for M23, providing weapons and ammunition to the rebels, and violating the assets freeze and travel ban by its support of sanctioned individuals such as Ntaganda.[52] Those press-ganged into serving with M23 by the Rwandan authorities even included, ironically, a number of former FDLR fighters who had completed the Rwandan government's demobilisation and reintegration programme. Between mid-April and mid-May, it was believed that Ntaganda's forces had recruited at least 149 boys and young men into the new rebel movement.[53] In a 14 May statement, the ICC announced that it was adding further crimes against humanity (murder, persecution based on ethnic grounds and rape/sexual slavery) and war crimes (intentional attacks against civilians and pillaging) to the charges it had already levied against him.[54] In a 25 May op-ed in *Le Monde*, the French human rights activist Clément Boursin noted that 'at least two war criminals' – Laurent Nkunda and Jules Mutebutsi – were 'staying unmolested' in Rwanda.[55]

The M23 was not the only armed group causing displacement and suffering in the east. On 14 May, elements of the Raïa Mutomboki infiltrated a crowd protesting about MONUSCO's failure to stop FDLR attacks at a base in Kamananga in South Kivu and opened fired, wounding 11 Pakistani peacekeepers.[56] Around 19 May, the FDLR and its Mai-Mai allies were believed to have killed more than 100 civilians in massacres carried out in close proximity within Masisi territory.[57] In late May, the FARDC succeeded in pushing the Mai-Mai Cheka out of a number of localities in Walikale.[58]

By early June, it was believed that Rwanda had provided at least 200 to 300 fighters – some of them recruited by force or in public places such as markets – to support the M23 rebellion. Ntaganda also managed to enter Rwanda on several occasions after the rebellion started, and there met with Rwandan military personnel.[59] The charges of Rwandan recruitment and press-ganging into military service on M23's behalf were later attested to by numerous press reports[60] and interviews with former combatants.[61] At the same time, Congolese Chief of Staff Didier Etumba claimed that over 200 mutineers had been killed by the FARDC since April.[62]

Outrunning the Kabila government, a group of opposition activists held a press conference in Kinshasa on 7 June where they denounced the new conflict in the east as 'a war from Rwanda with its army, an assault pure and simple'; they went on to denounce 'the complicity of those in power in the destabilisation of this part of the country'.[63] The Kabila government's instincts had grown so automatically repressive by this point that even a march in Kinshasa organised by opposition politician Clement Kanku in support of the FARDC was broken up by security personnel.[64] Inspecting the border town of Bunagana in the presence of the FARDC and MONUSCO peacekeepers, Prime Minister Matata Ponyo excluded negotiations as a way of ending the crisis and said that 'the government would make available to the FARDC all military means' to defeat the rebels.[65] Finally, in Goma on 9 June, Kabila's spokesman Lambert Mende said that there was 'overwhelming' evidence of Kigali's role in the rebellion.[66]

On the night of 11 June, the M23 sabotaged a water pipe in Rutshuru, cutting off the water supply to at least five towns.[67] On 17 June, the rebels laid siege to the nearby towns of Tarika,

Ruseke and Murambi.[68] North Kivu civil society leaders called on the international community to 'suspend all aid to Rwanda in order to force it to contribute to the stability of the region and opt for a policy of good neighbourliness.'[69] Soon after, community leaders in North Kivu's Rutshuru and Lubero territories attempted to raise the alarm about the presence of 'foreign troops' in their districts.[70] Later still, civil society leaders in Goma would denounce what they said was the presence of Ugandan as well as Rwandan troops on Congolese territory.[71] Uganda denied the charge, with acting Minister of Foreign Affairs Henry Okello Oryem calling the claim 'rubbish'.[72]

Beyond the M23, the Congolese had other things to fear. The LRA had conducted a spate of murders, rapes and abductions in Orientale province in early to mid-February[73] and had kidnapped 30 adults in late March.[74] Between January and March, the group's attacks had displaced more than 4,200 people.[75] Between March and June, the LRA killed eight and kidnapped 50 in the districts of Haut- and Bas-Uélé.[76]

The FDLR was still levying 'taxes' in North Kivu[77] and fatally battling its former allies in the FARDC throughout the province.[78] Searching for leaders of the Mai-Mai Cheka, the FDLR killed at least 20 people in the villages of Erobe and Misau in Walikale territory during 21–22 June.[79] Nine died in fighting between the FARDC and the FDLR and its Mai-Mai allies when the latter groups attacked the village of Luofu on 1 July.[80]

And yet the Congolese themselves never stopped trying to find a better way. In late June, leaders of the Hutu and Tembo communities in the South Kivu territory of Kalehe, where clashes between the FDLR and its allies against Raïa Mutomboki had severely disrupted the lives of the population, met to demonstrate that 'they are all animated by a desire for peace'.[81]

Their forbearance and efforts were not reflected in their leaders. Having cancelled the country's 30 June independence celebrations, in a televised address to the nation Kabila said that he would 'defend the country until the end, in order to obtain peace in the province of North Kivu'.[82] Instead, after a ten-day pause, fighting commenced again between the FARDC and M23 at Bweza in Rutshuru territory near Virunga National Park.[83]

During 5–6 July, the village of Jambo and then the important town of Bunagana on the Ugandan border fell to the M23 in fighting that also claimed the life of an Indian MONUSCO peacekeeper.[84] The Ugandan army estimated that at least 600 Congolese troops had fled into the country after the assault.[85] Following the fall of Bunagana, residents of the town of Rutshuru waited in fear for the arrival of the rebels.[86] By 8 July, with the FARDC again abandoning the civilian population and looting what it could on the way out, Rutshuru had fallen. The rebels stayed for several days before mysteriously withdrawing.[87] Parliamentarians from North Kivu would subsequently call on Kabila to change 'the entire chain of command' of the army following the FARDC's behaviour.[88]

In the wake of the M23 advance, both MONUSCO and the FARDC moved additional troops into Goma to defend the city.[89] On 12 July, a dual FARDC/MONUSCO operation bombarded M23 positions along the road between Goma and Rutshuru.[90] Roger Meece said that the UN mission would do 'everything possible' to protect civilians.[91] Following the offensive, the M23 pledged to respond to attacks against its forces, 'regardless of who is the author'.[92]

At a meeting of the African Union (AU) in the Ethiopian capital of Addis Ababa, the group's chairman, Gabonese diplomat Jean Ping, said that the AU was 'prepared to contribute to the establishment of a regional force to put an end to the activities of armed groups' in Congo.[93]

After a face-to-face meeting on the sidelines of the AU conference, Kabila and Kagame, absurdly, said that they mutually agreed in principle to an 'international force' to neutralise the M23.[94] In a 16 July statement, the 15-member UN Security

Council demanded 'that all forms of support to [the M23] cease immediately'.[95] On 24 July, MONUSCO helicopters again rained down fire on M23 positions, this time near Rugari and Kimumba, north of Goma.[96]

The Western powers appeared to have arrived at a parting of the ways with their former star client. Saying that the Obama administration had 'decided it can no longer provide foreign military financing appropriated in the current fiscal year to Rwanda', on 22 July the United States finally announced – for the first time since 1994 – that it was suspending military aid to the Kagame regime. The reason was given as 'evidence that Rwanda is implicated in the provision of support to Congolese rebel groups, including M23'.[97] Six years after they had helped craft Senate Bill 2125, Obama and Hillary Clinton had finally found themselves in a position to implement it. On 26 July, the Netherlands announced that it was suspending €5 million (US$6.2 million) in aid to Rwanda, a decision it said was directly linked to the contents of the UN report and Kigali's support of M23.[98] The following day, the British government also announced the freezing of £16 million of aid to Rwanda.[99]

A further shift in US rhetoric was evident when Stephen Rapp, head of the Office of Global Criminal Justice within the US Department of State, told reporters in reference to Paul Kagame that:

> there is a line that one can cross under international law where you can be held responsible for aiding a group in a way that makes possible their commission of atrocities ... [There could be] a situation where individuals who were aiding [the M23] from across the border could be held criminally responsible.[100]

Rapp had previously served as a lead prosecutor at the Rwanda genocide tribunal and was a driving force behind the prosecution of former Liberian President Charles Taylor for the latter's crimes backing rebel movements in Sierra Leone.

While the world's attention was focused on the M23, in its attempts to thwart the FDLR the Raïa Mutomboki continued to cut a brutal swathe through North Kivu, invading communities in Walikale territory.[101] After an attack by the militia claimed the lives of ten people in the town of Ngungu, residents denounced what they called the FARDC's 'passivity' with regard to the group.[102]

Having failed to hold Callixte Mbarushimana to account, on 13 July the ICC issued an arrest warrant for FDLR leader Sylvestre Mudacumura on nine counts of war crimes committed in the Kivus.[103] Despite all the chest-thumping of the campaigns against the FDLR, its ability to victimise Congolese civilians had scarcely been diminished; the group killed 11 people in the South Kivu town of Kabare on 10 August[104] and spread its zone of influence further along Lake Edward.[105] In the coming weeks, at least seven people were killed in fighting between the FARDC and the Raïa Mutomboki in Kalehe.[106] In late July, Cobra Matata's FRPI took the opportunity to kill five members of the Hema ethnic group near the Ituri community of Kasenyi.[107]

By late July, while speaking on state television, Kabila himself was saying that Rwanda's presence at the heart of the M23 rebellion was an 'open secret', and he repeated his call for a 'neutral' buffer force between the rebels and the FARDC.[108] Speaking to the UN Security Council in late July, MONUSCO head Roger Meece was said to have given a grim assessment of an FARDC running out of ammunition and suffering substantial casualties at the hands of the rebels.[109] In a toothless statement, the UN Security Council demanded that unspecified 'outside countries' halt their support for M23, declining to mention Rwanda or Uganda by name.[110] In Kinshasa, thousands of Catholics, clutching Bibles and waving signs saying 'No to the Balkanisation' of Congo, marched through the city calling for an end to the fighting in the east.[111]

An early August summit at a lakeside resort in Munyonyo in Uganda, attended by Kabila, Kagame and Museveni, ended with no substantive resolution beyond an agreement to keep talking via the 11-member International Conference on the Great Lakes Region.[112] Following the summit, Congo's Minister of Foreign Affairs Raymond Tshibanda said there would be 'no negotiation' with the rebels.[113] At the conclusion of a meeting of the Southern African Development Community in Maputo, the group managed to display more backbone than the UN had, saying that the M23 rebellion and attendant violence were 'being perpetrated by rebel groups with the assistance of Rwanda' and that the 'summit mandated a mission to Rwanda to urge them to stop support for the M23'.[114]

By November, the M23 would overrun Goma. The FARDC fled in the face of the rebel advance, raping and looting as it did so. Appearing to have learned nothing from the mission's refusal to defend Kisangani in August 2002 and Bukavu in May 2004, as the M23 marched into town, MONUSCO troops never fired a shot in defence of Goma and its inhabitants. The M23 would then leave Goma two weeks later. It was part of a deal, they said, hammered out by Kabila, Kagame, Museveni and the international community.

EPILOGUE

When I first returned to Goma after a long absence, shortly before the M23 rebellion erupted, I found the town much as I remembered it. Passing through the lush tea plantations that line the road from Ruhengeri, I crossed the border from Rwanda into Congo on foot at Gisenyi. A solicitous and bespectacled older FARDC soldier perused my passport and visa in a fairly cursory fashion before waving me on my way. A light rain had begun to fall, the droplets shimmering against Lake Kivu just in the distance as I climbed upon the back of a motorcycle taxi to take me to my guest house.

The city pulsed with the life of central Africa. In contrast to the austere atmosphere of Rwanda, where spit-and-polish RDF troops served as the most visible face of a tightly centralised state and conversed in vaguely martial-sounding Kinyarwanda, Goma, despite the presence of the CNDP, was palpably more relaxed. By the roadside, ubiquitous vendors of mobile phone cards pulled tarpaulin over themselves to shield their businesses from the rain and joked in the rather more lilting cadences of Swahili. Other merchants stacked bags of charcoal four high on bicycles, staining the bikes and the rider's clothing an inky black as they pedalled through the drizzle. Despite the barely disciplined and rather menacing CNDP soldiers moving in convoys through the city, the local population seemed to think that, if things were calm, even for the moment, they would take what they could get.

'In Kinshasa, they think war and struggle are some kind of romantic thing,' said an acquaintance of mine as we drove through town later that day. 'But here they have seen war, they have seen how you die. They don't want that.'

In addition to travelling to the camps in Masisi, one of my local meetings was with a resident European, a man who had once been in the military of his native country but who had recast himself as a businessman here in Goma. He had developed deep contacts with both the government and the armed groups operating in the east over the years, and spoke in a voice so quiet in the restaurant where we met that I had to lean close to catch his words. The restaurant was very near the Goma home of Bosco Ntaganda, and my companion kept changing SIM cards in his mobile phone in order to make calls.

'The presence of the state here is only symbolic; they don't control anything,' he told me. 'Bosco controls Goma.'

And indeed so it seemed.

The Kabila government did not, as it had hoped, rule the east through the CNDP. Rather, the CNDP ruled the east with an added sheen of officialdom provided by its association with faraway Kinshasa. By striking a deal with Kigali in March 2009, Kabila and his courtiers had bought themselves time to get through the election, but little else. After the plane crash that killed Katumba Mwanke, one of the pillars on which the regime rested, even that triumph had been thrown into doubt.

Joseph Kabila's government remains, in many ways, a younger, more sophisticated, more polished version of his father's, relying on an extremely narrow circle of trusted individuals and a network of international alliances to keep itself at the top of the heap of those scrambling for control of Congo. It is a power structure that has built a patronage base rather than a political base on which it can draw. It has not created institutional structures that will resolve Congo's underlying issues. As with Mobutu and Kabila *père*, the central government in Kinshasa has proven time and again that it views efforts to achieve local understandings about local issues as threatening to its hegemony of power. These efforts are systematically sabotaged and shut down, although no real process is put in place by the government itself as a substitute for them.

The regime's policy of integrating some of the country's worst human rights abusers into senior positions within the FARDC was one that was doomed to failure, and some of us even wrote as much at the time.[1] Likewise, the international community's refusal to hold the Kabila government to account for its most flagrant human rights abuses – the repeated sieges of the Bemba compound and murder of MLC partisans, the mass slaughter of BDK adherents and civilians in Bas-Congo, the violent repression of the UDPS and other opponents in the run-up to and aftermath of the 2011 elections – only served to embolden Congo's government in its belief that the path it had chosen was the correct one, and one that would bear very few negative consequences.

The international community's response to the great human tragedy of our time has been just as dismal. The brutally cynical realpolitik of the Cold War was replaced by a near-pathological deference to personal loyalty as shown by leaders such as François Mitterrand and Bill Clinton to successive African despots; this caused them to shut out overwhelming evidence of pogroms in favour of bonds that were at once intimate and geo-political. Although Mitterrand has been largely discredited on various counts, Clinton, a man whose immense innate charm more often than not overshadows some of the darker aspects of his personality, has not been. Clinton seemed to view his duty to Rwanda as one of atonement, and like many other aspects of his administration, he appeared to use policy as some sort of public therapy, an approach that led to disaster in Congo's case.

However convenient it may be as an emotional narrative, genocide guilt alone does not explain the repeated carte blanche given by the West to the manifestly undemocratic regimes in Rwanda and Uganda. As the government of Clinton's successor, US President George W. Bush, waged war on what it perceived as the threat of militant Islam in Afghanistan and Iraq following the attacks of 11 September 2001, it was Rwanda that demonstrated its willingness to send its soldiers on peacekeeping missions in Sudan and elsewhere. Uganda, for its part, came to the fore as the leader of the AU mission to Somalia, where the Islamist Al-Shabaab, affiliated to the Al-Qaeda terrorist organisation of Osama bin Laden, held sway. These were missions where, although the United States had a pronounced strategic interest, it could not take the lead for reasons of politics and optics. Rwanda and Uganda have thus proven themselves time and again to be useful surrogates to this end.

MONUSCO has been ludicrously understaffed and over-stretched for such an immense country, and at times in its history run by bureaucrats who seemed more interested in the perpetuation of the mission itself than the protection of the near-defenceless Congolese people. By this point, the UN body has become viewed by the population as little more than an arm of the Kabila government. Given the UN's chequered history in Congo, including its (at best) failure to stop the murder of Patrice Lumumba in 1961 (a failure still widely viewed in Congo as collusion), such a perception is the most unfortunate of outcomes for the UN's global prestige.

As the historian Theodore Trefon eloquently concluded, the international community, once Congo had held elections in 2006, 'fell into the trap of legitimizing what would rapidly become a corrupt and inefficient political machine'.[2]

In Uganda, Yoweri Museveni now appears as something of an ageing caricature of himself, and is believed by many to be busy preparing the way for the expected succession to the presidency of his son, UPDF commander Muhoozi Kainerugaba. Given the bouts of unrest in Kampala after Museveni's own disputed recent electoral victories, it is doubtful that this transition will go smoothly. Faced with ever eroding legitimacy, the thought that the lure of Congo's riches will prompt another lunge westwards is not beyond the realm of possibility.

Uganda's other contribution to Congo, Joseph Kony and his fighters in the LRA, are now a thousand miles from the cradle of their insurgency, and appear to have little hope of returning to Uganda, although their potential to wreak havoc on civilians remains undiminished. In both late 2009 and late 2010, LRA emissaries met Sudanese armed forces' representatives in the violence-wracked Sudanese territory of Darfur, asking for help with their continued struggle. Their Sudanese hosts sent them away with only token ammunition, and so there are no clear indications that the LRA is still getting significant support from Khartoum.[3] The likely best scenario for the LRA is that South Sudan, as of July 2011 a new nation but one beset by corruption and ethnic tension, implodes. For many years, South Sudan was the LRA's sanctuary, where the group survived, and even thrived in a sense, and there is some evidence that the group may be making forays back there again.[4] With its decampment to Congo and the Central African Republic, there is much debate as to what role, if any, the spiritual aspects of the LRA, so evident during its early history, play now in a totally foreign territory. People, including Ugandan soldiers, remain convinced that Joseph Kony has special powers and can foresee the future. But the LRA remains first and foremost a military force, and a very potent one at that. At this point, leaving the LRA is a very difficult proposition for those who remain. If local people catch isolated members trying to escape or to give themselves up, they have in the past killed them; nor is it clear whether the UPDF actually hands over all the LRA combatants who turn themselves in as per a promised amnesty. The best that Joseph Kony and his men – the cause of so much misery in central Africa – can do is continue to survive on the back of the civilian populations of Congo and the Central African Republic, something they have thus far proved themselves very adept at doing.

Rwanda remains governed by an RPF elite. Paul Kagame, having solidified his police state, appears to resemble Juvénal

Habyarimana – a development darling abroad and a ruthless despot at home – more and more with each passing year. The regime in Kigali has, if anything, grown more intolerant and destructive over time. In December 2011, Inyenyeri News editor Charles Ingabire, who had fled Rwanda in 2007, was gunned down in Kampala by unknown assailants; as a matter of form, the Kigali government denied it had any involvement in the event.[5] The UN findings of Kigali's continued backing of Bosco Ntaganda and the M23 rebels well into 2012 point to a sphere of power whose world view has remained essentially unchanged since the mid-1990s: Rwanda can do what it wants, when it wants, where it wants, with little fear of being held to account. That view is in large part an accurate reflection of reality as it has existed. Like an alcoholic staggering back to the bar for one more drink, Kagame simply cannot restrain himself from ceaseless intriguing against his neighbours. Recent moves by the international community to sanction the government in the face of overwhelming evidence of its duplicity are perhaps a sign that, at long last, things are beginning to change. The FDLR, that awful spawn of the 1994 genocide, remains marginal in terms of broad political issues but terribly destructive in terms of its impact on the daily lives of people in the areas it occupies.

The powers that rule Congo today consist of a still-youthful president who learned statecraft during one of history's most brutal wars, during which virtually any atrocity committed was accepted and greeted with at best a shrug and at worst a wink by the international community, a cadre of advisers who have themselves been linked to gross human rights abuses and illicit enrichment and appear not even to understand the most basic elements of democratic liberties, and an assortment of power brokers, insurrectionists and other potential spoilers.

Against this dismal litany are arrayed the Congolese people.

The Congolese – from the street-side vendors in Kinshasa to the dock workers in sweltering Kisangani, from the schoolmistress

in Bunia to the farmers, herders and matrons emerging from the
cool mist of the mountains of the Kivus – carry within themselves
the idea of a nation, a nation stitched together out of a patchwork
of tribal kingdoms that was never meant to be one but that has
persisted. Despite what might seem like overwhelming odds, the
Congolese continue. They persevere. Somehow, thanks largely
only to themselves, they survive.

A few days after Katumba Mwanke's plane crashed into the
earth of eastern Congo, I was having dinner with a group of
people in Goma. We had travelled there over roads facing ob-
sidian volcanic soil, where green shoots of vegetation struggled
through hopefully towards the warmth of the sky. We were sitting,
a mix of Congolese and foreigners, after the sun had set, in a
rather refined French restaurant whose grounds sloped down
towards Lake Kivu. When conversation lulled, you could hear
water lapping against the shore through the black night. The
discussion was animated. Almost everyone agreed that Kabila
was a nightmare but that Tshisekedi would have been worse,
and that if Kabila thought that he could ever control Bosco
Ntaganda, he was totally wrong (which proved to be the case).
There was disagreement about Jean-Pierre Bemba, with some
arguing that he had been no more criminal in his behaviour
than most of the political grandees currently striding across the
national stage, and others thinking that prison was exactly where
he belonged. When we began talking about in what direction the
country might be heading in the immediate future, now that it
seemed that Kabila had succeeded in returning himself to office
for another full term, there was much discussion of the almost
mystical synchronicity of Katumba Mwanke's death only three
months after the rigged elections, and how deeply such a seemingly random, unforeseeable occurrence had shifted the political
geography of the country's powerful elite.

One of my companions was a doctor, a brilliant surgeon who
had been born and raised in Congo and had been working for

years to aid victims of sexual violence and other misfortune in North Kivu and elsewhere. As the night gathered around us, he looked up at me when I asked what he thought about Katumba Mwanke's passing.

'You see,' he told me, smiling broadly from ear to ear as the dark lake splashed on to the shore near our table. 'I told you. God is protecting us.'

Postscript

A violent rift would develop between Bosco Ntaganda and the M23's public face, Sultani Makenga, with the former vigorously opposed to the group's withdrawal from Goma. The tension between the two sides grew ever greater, leading to armed confrontations between their loyalists, with the Makenga faction stating plainly that they wanted Ntaganda dead. On 18 March 2013, Bosco Ntaganda appeared before startled employees at the US embassy in Kigali, announcing that he was giving himself up and wanted to surrender and be transferred to the ICC in The Hague to stand trial for the charges against him. Apparently, he felt more confident trusting himself to justice there than to the tender mercies of his former allies. Bosco Ntaganda arrived at the ICC on 22 March 2013.

NOTES

Prologue

1 Alex Veit argues that the Lendu as a distinct ethnic group did not exist before colonial times and that, in any event, they did not become largely cattle farmers until after a cattle plague of the 1890s decimated their herds. See Veit, Alex (2011) *Intervention as Indirect Rule: Civil war and statebuilding in the Democratic Republic of Congo*. Frankfurt: Campus Verlag.

2 Ibid., pp. 58–9.

3 Author interviews, Bunia, April 2008.

4 Turnbull, Colin (1961) *The Forest People*. New York, NY: Touchstone, pp. 11–12.

5 'Special report on the events in Ituri, January 2002–December 2003'. United Nations Organization Mission in the Democratic Republic of the Congo, 16 July 2004.

6 'La loi Bakajika face à la souveraineté: un vrai-faux débat'. *Le Potentiel*, 30 December 2005.

7 Human Rights Watch (2003) *Ituri: 'Covered in blood'. Ethnically targeted violence in northeastern DR Congo*. New York, NY: Human Rights Watch.

8 'Ituri in eastern DRC: chronology of key events'. IRIN, 14 December 2002.

9 'Emergency in Ituri, DRC: political complexity, land and other challenges in restoring food security'. Presentation by Johan Pottier to Food and Agriculture Organization of the United Nations workshop, 23–25 September 2003.

10 'Democratic Republic of the Congo: ICRC assists the wounded in Bunia'. International Committee of the Red Cross, 1 February 2001.

11 Warrant of arrest for Germain Katanga, International Criminal Court, 2 July 2007.

12 Human Rights Watch (2005) *The Curse of Gold: Democratic Republic of Congo*. New York, NY: Human Rights Watch.

13 'DRC: Who's who in Ituri – militia organisations, leaders'. IRIN, 20 April 2005.

14 Human Rights Watch, *Ituri: 'Covered in blood'. Ethnically targeted violence in northeastern DR Congo*.

15 'DRC: ICC Warrant of Arrest unsealed against Bosco Ntaganda', International Criminal Court, 28 April 2008.

16 Author interview with Father Alfred Buju, Commission Justice et Paix, Bunia, April 2008.

17 Author interview with Sylvestre Sombo, Bunia, April 2008.

18 Author interview with Adamo Bedijo, Manyidaa, April 2008.

1 Kingdom of Congo

1 Vansina, Jan (1966) *Kingdoms of the Savanna*. Madison, WI: University of Wisconsin Press, p. 37.

2 Ibid., p. 42.

3 Thornton, John K. (1999) *Warfare in Atlantic Africa 1500–1800*. New York, NY: Routledge, pp. 104–14.

4 Vansina, Jan, *Kingdoms of the Savanna*, pp. 45–6.

5 Ibid., p. 46.

6 Hochschild, Adam (1999) *King Leopold's Ghost: A story of greed, terror, and heroism in colonial Africa*. New York, NY: Mariner Books, p. 11.

7 Vansina, Jan, *Kingdoms of the Savanna*, p. 66.

8 Ibid., pp. 64–7.

9 Thornton, John K., *Warfare in Atlantic Africa 1500–1800*, p. 103.

10 Ibid., p. 118.

11 Vansina, Jan (2010) *Being Colonized: The Kuba experience in rural Congo 1880–1960*. Madison, WI: University of Wisconsin Press, p. 16.

12 Ibid., pp. 46–8.

13 Ibid., p. 22.

14 Reefe, Thomas Q. (1981) *The Rainbow and the Kings: A history of the Luba empire to 1891*. Berkeley, CA: University of California Press, p. 5.

15 Ibid., pp. 24–39.

16 Vansina, Jan, *Being Colonized: The Kuba experience in rural Congo 1880–1960*, p. 30.

17 Vansina, Jan, *Kingdoms of the Savanna*, p. 160.

18 Ibid., pp. 242–4.

19 Ibid., p. 81.

20 Thornton, John K., *Warfare in Atlantic Africa 1500–1800*, p. 104.

21 Vansina, Jan, *Kingdoms of the Savanna*, p. 161.

22 Boyles, Denis (1988) *African Lives*. New York, NY: Ballantine Books, p. 86.

23 Hochschild, Adam, *King Leopold's Ghost: A story of greed, terror, and heroism in colonial Africa*, p. 36.

24 Ibid., p. 49.

25 It was one of history's great ironies that Leopold's powers at home were severely curtailed, as Belgium had been a constitutional monarchy since 1830.

26 Vansina, Jan, *Being Colonized: The Kuba experience in rural Congo 1880–1960*, pp. 70–5.

27 Bradford, Phillips Verner (1992) *Ota Benga: The pygmy in the zoo*. New York, NY: St Martin's Press, p. 218.

28 Hochschild, Adam, *King Leopold's Ghost: A story of greed, terror, and heroism in colonial Africa*, pp. 164–5.

29 Ibid., p. 180.

30 Casement, Roger (2003) *The Eyes of Another Race: Roger Casement's Congo report and 1903 diary*. Dublin: University College Dublin Press, p. 71.

31 Ibid., p. 58.

32 Ibid., pp. 93–5.

33 Ibid., p. 71.

34 Ibid., p. 72.

35 Ibid., pp. 254–63.

36 Stearns, Jason (2011) *Dancing in the Glory of Monsters: The collapse of the Congo and the great war of Africa*. New York, NY: PublicAffairs, pp. 71–2.

37 Young, Crawford and Thomas Turner (1985) *The Rise and Decline of the Zairian State*. Madison, WI: University of Wisconsin Press, p. 38.

38 MacGaffey, Janet (1991) *The Real Economy of Zaire: The contribution of smuggling and other unofficial activities to national wealth*. Philadelphia, PA: University of Pennsylvania Press, p. 27.

39 'Order restored in Congo capital after riots fatal to 34 Africans'. Associated Press, 6 January 1959.

40 '24 Killed in Riot in Belgian Congo'. Reuters, 31 October 1959.

41 'Congo festivities marred'. *The Guardian*, 1 July 1960.

42 MacGaffey, Janet, *The Real Economy of Zaire: The contribution of smuggling and other unofficial activities to national wealth*, p. 27.

43 de Witte, Ludo (2001) *The Assassination of Lumumba*. London: Verso, p. 38.

44 Urquhart, Brian (1994) *Hammarskjold*. New York, NY: W. W. Norton and Company, p. 407.

45 As quoted in de Witte, Ludo, *The Assassination of Lumumba*, p. 9.

46 Devlin, Larry (2008) *Chief of Station, Congo: Fighting the Cold War in a hot zone*. New York, NY: Public Affairs, pp. 49–50; 54.

47 Ibid., p. 66.

48 Ibid., pp. 79–80.

49 de Witte, Ludo, *The Assassination of Lumumba*, p. 27.

50 Ibid., p. 54.

51 Ibid., p. 55.

52 Ibid., pp. 93–124.

53 Noll, Michel (2001) *Une mort de style colonial: l'assassinat de Patrice Lumumba*. Documentary film.

54 'La dernière lettre de Patrice Lumumba à sa femme'. *Jeune Afrique*, 17 January 2011. Author's translation.

55 Young, Crawford and Thomas Turner, *The Rise and Decline of the Zairian State*, p. 49.

56 Ibid., p. 52.

2 Fire in his wake

1 Close, William T. (2006) *Beyond the Storm: Treating the powerless and the powerful in Mobutu's Congo/Zaire*. Marbleton, WY: Meadowlark Springs Productions, pp. 113.

2 Mobutu's pseudonym of choice was De Banzy. Duvalier's had been Abderrahman.

3 See Devlin, Larry (2008) *Chief of Station, Congo: Fighting the Cold War in a hot zone*. New York, NY: Public Affairs; Young, Crawford and Thomas Turner (1985) *The Rise and Decline of the Zairian State*. Madison, WI: University of Wisconsin Press.

4 Young, Crawford and Thomas Turner, *The Rise and Decline of the Zairian State*, p. 52.

5 Ibid., p. 55.

6 'DRC: elections under the Second Republic'. Electoral Institute for Sustainable Democracy in Africa. Available at www.eisa.org.za/WEP/drcsecondrepublic.htm (accessed 26 March 2013).

7 Immigration and Refugee Board of Canada (1997) *The Student Movement*. 1 August. Available at www.unhcr.org/refworld/docid/3ae6a8654.html (accessed 26 March 2013).

8 Schatzberg, Michael G. (1991) *The Dialectics of Oppression in Zaire*. Bloomington, IN: Indiana University Press, p. 25.

9 Close, William T., *Beyond the Storm: Treating the powerless and the powerful in Mobutu's Congo/Zaire*, p. 250.

10 Author interviews, Goma, February 2008 and February 2012. As happened with many of Mobutu's advisers, Bisengimana would fall out of favour with Mobutu in 1977.

11 Young, Crawford and Thomas Turner, *The Rise and Decline of the Zairian State*, p. 64.

12 Ibid., p. 66.

13 Autesserre, Séverine (2010)

The Trouble with the Congo: Local violence and the failure of international peacebuilding. Cambridge: Cambridge University Press, p. 136.

14 This is vividly illustrated in the director Thierry Michel's 1999 documentary *Mobutu, roi du Zaïre*.

15 World Bank (2008) *Democratic Republic of Congo: Growth with governance in the mining sector*. Washington, DC: The World Bank.

16 Mailer, Norman (1975) *The Fight*. New York, NY: Vintage, p. 20.

17 MacGaffey, Janet (1991) *The Real Economy of Zaire: The contribution of smuggling and other unofficial activities to national wealth*. Philadelphia, PA: University of Pennsylvania Press, pp. 15–17.

18 Schatzberg, Michael G., *The Dialectics of Oppression in Zaire*, p. 24.

19 Young, Crawford and Thomas Turner, *The Rise and Decline of the Zairian State*, p. 116.

20 Pole Institute (2002) *The Coltan Phenomenon: How a rare mineral has changed the life of the population of war-torn North Kivu province in the East of the Democratic Republic of Congo*. Goma: Pole Institute.

21 Lamb, David (1982) *The Africans*. New York, NY: Random House, p. 46.

22 Schatzberg, Michael G., *The Dialectics of Oppression in Zaire*, p. 138.

23 Ibid., pp. 40–4.

24 A good example of the former is the PRP's rather tedious hymn, *Mapiganoya wanao dhulimiwa* (The Struggle of the Oppressed), which continues along the lines of *PRP – hii ni mwanga, wa wakulima, no wafanyakazi, pia wanyonge wote/Hatuna budi kufyeka unonyaji na kuunda jamii la uja maa, nadhiri yetu kweli kushindwa muhali* ('The PRP is a torch for peasants and workers, and for all the oppressed. We spare no effort to halt the exploitation and to build a communal society'). See Cosma, Wilungula B. (1997) *Fizi, 1967–1986: le maquis Kabila*. Paris: L'Harmattan, p. 67. Translation from the French translation of the Swahili original by the author.

25 Lamb, David, *The Africans*. p. 46.

26 'Freddy Kibassa Maliba est mort'. Digitalcongo.net, 5 April 2003.

27 Prunier, Gérard (2009) *Africa's World War: Congo, the Rwandan genocide, and the making of a continental catastrophe*. New York, NY: Oxford University Press, p. 172.

28 Muyumba, Frank Mayundo (2006) *Exploitation Minière au Sud-Kivu: De la responsabilité des entreprises et de l'état*. Bakavu: Université du Cepromad.

29 Kongulo Mobutu would die, reportedly of AIDS, in exile in Monaco in September 1998.

30 'Zaire: violence against democracy'. Amnesty International, 16 September 1993.

31 Trefon, Theodore (ed.) (2005) *Reinventing Order in the Congo: How people respond to state failure in Kinshasa*. London: Zed Books, p. 143.

32 'Zaire: violence against democracy'. Amnesty International, 16 September 1993.

33 Immigration and Refugee Board of Canada, *The Student Movement*.

34 'Zaire: IRIN Briefing Part II, 02/27/97'. UN Integrated Regional Information Network (IRIN), 27 February 1997.

35 Berkeley, Bill (1993) 'Zaire: an

African horror story'. *The Atlantic*, 1 August.

36 'Zaire: IRIN Briefing Part III, 02/27/97'. IRIN, 27 February 1997.

37 'Zaire: violence against democracy'. Amnesty International, 16 September 1993.

38 Ibid.

39 Ibid.

40 Ibid.

41 Ibid.

42 Hodges, Tony (2001) *Angola: From Afro-Stalinism to petro-diamond capitalism*. Oxford: James Currey.

43 'Republic of Congo profile'. BBC News, 19 July 2011.

44 'Profile: Sudan's Islamist leader'. BBC News, 15 January 2009.

45 Author interviews, Gulu, February 2012.

46 Lemarchand, René (1994) *Burundi: Ethnic conflict and genocide*. Cambridge: Cambridge University Press, p. 55.

47 United Nations International Commission of Inquiry, June 2002.

48 Ibid.

49 Prunier, Gérard, *Africa's World War: Congo, the Rwandan genocide, and the making of a continental catastrophe*, pp. 13–14.

50 Prunier, Gérard (1995) *The Rwanda Crisis: History of a genocide*. New York, NY: Columbia University Press, p. 15.

51 For an authoritative history of Yuhi V's reign, see des Forges, Alison Liebhafsky (2011) *Defeat is the Only Bad News: Rwanda under Musinga, 1896–1931*. Madison, WI: University of Wisconsin Press.

52 Prunier, Gérard, *The Rwanda Crisis: History of a genocide*, p. 25.

53 Ibid., p. 28.

54 Ibid., p. 31.

55 Mutara III's wife, Rosalie Gicanda, would later be murdered during the Rwandan genocide.

56 Prunier, Gérard, *The Rwanda Crisis: History of a genocide*, p. 56.

57 Ibid., p. 109.

58 'Beyond the rhetoric: continuing human rights abuses in Rwanda'. Human Rights Watch, 1 June 1993, Vol. 5, No. 7.

59 Prunier, Gérard, *The Rwanda Crisis: History of a genocide*, p. 147.

60 Reed, William Cyrus (1998) in Clapham, Christopher S. (ed.) *African Guerrillas*. Oxford: James Currey, p. 137.

3 The great Congo wars

1 In 2006, French judge Jean-Louis Bruguière accused Paul Kagame of orchestrating the attack, but a subsequent French investigation concluded that the missile that shot down Habyarimana's plane was fired from up to 1 kilometre away, an area held by a unit of the FAR. See 'Rwanda leader accused of ordering attack', Associated Press, 21 November 2006 and 'Rwanda genocide: Kagame "cleared of Habyarimana crash"', BBC News, 10 January 2012. In October 2011, Kagame's former aide Theogene Rudasingwa claimed that Kagame had personally told him 'with characteristic callousness and much glee' that he ordered Habyarimana's plane shot down. See 'Rwanda president ordered Habyarimana plane shot: ex-aide', Agence France-Presse, 22 October 2011.

2 Despite being perhaps the most widely and scrupulously documented atrocity of the last decade of the twentieth century, the events of 1994 in Rwanda have nevertheless given birth to a grotesque subculture of

genocide deniers, who include Edward Herman (a US-born economist with no background in Africa who has similarly denied the Serbian policy of ethnic cleansing during the Bosnian Wars of the 1990s and the atrocities of the Khmer Rouge in 1970s Cambodia) and David Peterson, a Chicago-based 'independent writer and researcher'. Anointing with glowing endorsements the book in which such revisionism appears, *The Politics of Genocide*, are such individuals as American linguist Noam Chomsky (a long-time Herman collaborator) and the Australian journalist John Pilger.

3 Reed, William Cyrus (1998) in Clapham, Christopher S. (ed.) *African Guerrillas*. Oxford: James Currey, p. 137.

4 Thanks to the efforts of Roméo Dallaire and his deputy, Major General Henry Anyidoho, several hundred UNAMIR soldiers did remain in Rwanda and succeeded in saving thousands of lives. One UNAMIR officer in particular, Mbaye Diagne of Senegal, helped save the lives of hundreds of people before being killed by a mortar shell at a Kigali roadblock on 31 May 1994. See 'Ghosts of Rwanda'. *Frontline* (PBS), 1 April 2004.

5 Rice has since said that she does not remember uttering the sentence. Rice subsequently served as ambassador to the UN for the government of President Barack Obama, while Power also worked for the Obama administration as Senior Director of Multilateral Affairs. See Power, Samantha (2001) 'Bystanders to genocide'. *The Atlantic*, 1 September.

6 Terry, Fiona (2002) *Condemned to Repeat? The paradox of humanitarian action*. Ithaca, NY: Cornell University Press, p. 171.

7 Ibid., p. 164.

8 Ibid., p. 157.

9 Destexhe, Alain (1994) 'Hurry to prevent a Cambodian epilogue in Rwanda'. *International Herald Tribune*, 11 August.

10 Ogata, Sadako (2005) *The Turbulent Decade: Confronting the refugee crises of the 1990s*. New York, NY: W. W. Norton and Company, pp. 176–7.

11 Terry, Fiona, *Condemned to Repeat? The paradox of humanitarian action*, p. 193.

12 Ogata, Sadako, *The Turbulent Decade: Confronting the refugee crises of the 1990s*, pp. 191–2.

13 Destexhe, Alain, 'Hurry to prevent a Cambodian epilogue in Rwanda'.

14 Stearns, Jason (2011) *Dancing in the Glory of Monsters: The collapse of the Congo and the great war of Africa*. New York, NY: PublicAffairs, p. 272.

15 Pickard, Terry (2010) *Combat Medic: An eyewitness account of the Kibeho massacre*. Newport, Australia: Big Sky Publishing, pp. 63–6.

16 Ibid., p. 64.

17 Prunier, Gérard (2009) *Africa's World War: Congo, the Rwandan genocide, and the making of a continental catastrophe*. New York, NY: Oxford University Press, pp. 40–3.

18 Ibid., p. 42.

19 Kinzer would go on to lambast minutely documented reports on Kagame's human rights record as Rwanda's president as a 'new form of imperialism'. See Kinzer, Stephen (2010) 'End human rights imperialism now'. *The Guardian*, 31 December. Kinzer also went on to declare that 'this authoritarian regime is the best thing that has happened to Rwanda since colonialists arrived a century ago'.

20 Stearns, Jason, *Dancing in the Glory of Monsters: The collapse of the Congo and the great war of Africa*, p. 87.

21 Prunier, Gérard, *Africa's World War: Congo, the Rwandan genocide, and the making of a continental catastrophe*, p. 113.

22 'James Kabarebe: "Kabila n'est pas fait pour le commandement"'. Jeune Afrique, 29 April 2002.

23 'What Kabila is hiding: civilian killings and impunity in Congo'. Human Rights Watch, 1 October 1997.

24 'James Kabarebe: "Kabila n'est pas fait pour le commandement"'. Jeune Afrique, 29 April 2002.

25 'Zaire: IRIN update on the conflict in South Kivu'. UN Department of Humanitarian Affairs Integrated Regional Information Network (IRIN), 11 October 1996.

26 Ibid.

27 Ibid.

28 'Report of the Mapping Exercise documenting the most serious violations of human rights and international humanitarian law committed within the territory of the Democratic Republic of the Congo between March 1993 and June 2003' (original draft). UN High Commissioner for Human Rights, September 2010.

29 Ibid.

30 'What Kabila is hiding: civilian killings and impunity in Congo'. Human Rights Watch, 1 October 1997.

31 Ibid.

32 'US reduces number of troops for central African mission'. United States Information Agency, 19 November 1996.

33 'Mobutu returns to Zaire, but reveals no solutions'. *Los Angeles Times*, 18 December 1996.

34 'Forced flight: a brutal strategy of elimination in eastern Zaire'. MSF, 16 May 1997.

35 Ibid.

36 Ibid.

37 Ibid.

38 Amnesty International (1998) *Amnesty International Report 1998 – Congo (Democratic Republic of the)*. London: Amnesty International. Available at www.unhcr.org/refworld/docid/3ae6a9ef9o.html (accessed 8 April 2013).

39 'What Kabila is hiding: civilian killings and impunity in Congo'. Human Rights Watch, 1 October 1997.

40 Terry, Fiona, *Condemned to Repeat? The paradox of humanitarian action*, p. 205.

41 'Report of the Mapping Exercise documenting the most serious violations of human rights and international humanitarian law committed within the territory of the Democratic Republic of the Congo between March 1993 and June 2003' (original draft). UN High Commissioner for Human Rights, September 2010.

42 French, Howard (2005) *A Continent for the Taking: The tragedy and hope of Africa*. New York, NY: Vintage, p. 142.

43 'What Kabila is hiding: civilian killings and impunity in Congo'. Human Rights Watch, 1 October 1997.

44 Prunier, Gérard, *Africa's World War: Congo, the Rwandan genocide, and the making of a continental catastrophe*, p. 130.

45 French, Howard, *A Continent for the Taking: The tragedy and hope of Africa*, p. 140.

46 Terry, Fiona, *Condemned to Repeat? The paradox of humanitarian action*, p. 151.

47 'Albright urges leader of Congo to honor vows'. Associated Press, 12 December 1997.

48 Kempster, Norman (1997) 'In Africa, Albright vows "new chapter" in ties'. *Los Angeles Times*, 10 December.

49 Drogin, Bob (1997) 'Zaire's Kabila Keeps Grip on Power with New Cabinet'. *Los Angeles Times*, 23 May.

50 Author interview with former USAID official in Democratic Republic of Congo, January 2012.

51 'Ces enfants-soldats qui ont tué Kabila'. *Le Monde*, 9 February 2001.

52 'Disarmament in the Congo: Jump-starting DDRRR to prevent further war'. Africa Report No. 38. International Crisis Group, 14 December 2001.

53 Prunier, Gérard, *Africa's World War: Congo, the Rwandan genocide, and the making of a continental catastrophe*, p. 173.

54 Telephone interview with former official in Democratic Republic of Congo, 24 January 2012.

55 Simmons, Ann M. (1997) 'Many in Congo disdain new rulers'. *Los Angeles Times*, 27 December.

56 Tribune News Services (1998) 'Congo's recalcitrance cited in recall of rights team'. *Chicago Tribune News*, 18 April.

57 'Text of President Clinton's address to genocide survivors at the airport in Kigali, Rwanda, as provided by the White House'. CBS News (accessed 11 February 2009).

58 Prunier, Gérard, *Africa's World War: Congo, the Rwandan genocide, and the making of a continental catastrophe*, p. 365.

59 Plummer, Comer (2007) 'The Kitona operation: Rwanda's African odyssey'. MilitaryHistoryOnline.com.

Available at www.militaryhistoryon line.com/20thcentury/articles/kitona. aspx (accessed 8 April 2013).

60 'Report on the situation of human rights in the Democratic Republic of the Congo'. UN Human Rights Commission, 8 February 1999.

61 Ibid.

62 'Hate messages on East Congolese radio'. BBC News, 12 August 1998.

63 Erlanger, Steven (1998) 'US sees Rwandan role in Congo revolt.' *The New York Times*, 5 August.

64 Author interview with Joseph Sebarenzi, President of the Parliament of Rwanda, 1997–2000, December 2011. Sebarenzi, a Tutsi who lost most of his family in the 1994 genocide, also penned a memoir, *God Sleeps in Rwanda*, that is terrifying and surreal, featuring among other details the fact that the particular rhythm of a drum across the hillsides during anti-Tutsi pogroms would sometimes determine who would live and who would die.

65 Prunier, Gérard, *Africa's World War: Congo, the Rwandan genocide, and the making of a continental catastrophe*, p. 204.

66 'DRC: who's who – key members of the rebellion'. IRIN, 20 August 1998.

67 'IRIN Update No. 435 for Central and Eastern Africa'. IRIN, 11 June 1998.

68 'Rapport du COJESKI – Part III/V'. Collectif des Organisations des Jeunes Solidaires du Congo-Kinshasa (COJESKI). Available at www.con gonline.com/Forum1/Forum02/Kam baleo5.htm (accessed 8 April 2013).

69 Stearns, Jason, *Dancing in the Glory of Monsters: The collapse of the*

Congo and the great war of Africa, p. 251–66.

70 'Rapport du COJESKI – Part III/V'. Collectif des Organisations des Jeunes Solidaires du Congo-Kinshasa (COJESKI). Avalable at www.congonline.com/Forum1/Forum02/Kambale05.htm (accessed 8 April 2013).

71 'Report of the Mapping Exercise documenting the most serious violations of human rights and international humanitarian law committed within the territory of the Democratic Republic of the Congo between March 1993 and June 2003' (original draft). UN High Commissioner for Human Rights, September 2010.

72 Ibid.

73 Report of the Panel of Experts, UN Security Council, 2002.

74 'Report of the Mapping Exercise documenting the most serious violations of human rights and international humanitarian law committed within the territory of the Democratic Republic of the Congo between March 1993 and June 2003' (original draft). UN High Commissioner for Human Rights, September 2010.

75 'Crisis talks for former African allies'. BBC News, 16 August 1999.

76 'Kazini removed from Kisangani'. *The Monitor*, 13 September 1999.

77 MONUC mandate according to UN Security Council Resolution 1291 (2000).

78 'Katanga: the Congo's forgotten crisis'. Africa Report No. 103. International Crisis Group, 9 January 2006.

79 'Grenada bank boss settles in Kampala'. *New Vision*, 8 September 1999.

80 Adusei, Lord Aikins (2009) 'Small arms in Africa: where does the buck stop'. *The African Executive*, 18–25 March.

81 Report of the Panel of Experts, UN Security Council, 2002.

82 Ibid.

83 Sebarenzi, Joseph (2009) *God Sleeps in Rwanda: A journey of transformation*. New York, NY: Atria Books, pp. 183–207.

84 'Rwanda: opposition politician shot, others detained'. Human Rights Watch, 10 January 2002.

85 Author interviews, Kinshasa, April and May 2008.

86 'Ces enfants-soldats qui ont tué Kabila'. *Le Monde*, 9 February 2001.

87 'Murder in Kinshasa'. Al Jazeera, 8 June 2011.

4 **Enter his father's house**

1 Evans, Leslie (2003) 'Acting Assistant Secretary of State for African Affairs surveys the continent'. UCLA African Studies Center, 3 December.

2 Borzello, Anna (2001) 'Uganda's Museveni leads in "rigged" elections'. *The Guardian*, 14 March.

3 'Ituri: "covered in blood"'. Ethnically targeted violence in northeastern DR Congo'. Human Rights Watch, July 2003.

4 'Interahamwe chief-of-staff captured'. UN Office for the Coordination of Humanitarian Affairs Integrated Regional Information Network (IRIN), 16 July 2001.

5 Romkema, Hans (2007) *Opportunities and Constraints for the Disarmament & Repatriation of Foreign Armed Groups in the Democratic Republic of Congo: The cases of the FDLR, FNL and ADF/NALU*. Washington, DC:

Multi-Country Demobilization and Reintegration Program, The World Bank.

6 Pole Institute (2010) *Guerillas in the Mist: The Congolese experience of the FDLR war in Eastern Congo and the role of the international community*. Goma: Pole Institute.

7 Ibid.

8 'War crimes in Kisangani: the response of Rwandan-backed rebels to the May 2002 mutiny'. Human Rights Watch, August 2002.

9 Ibid.

10 Ibid.

11 MONUC mandate according to UN Security Council Resolution 1291 (2000).

12 Author interviews, Bunia, October 2008.

13 Author interviews, Bunia, April 2008; Kinshasa, March 2008.

14 'Kampala to withdraw troops, bilateral relations to be normalised'. IRIN, 16 August 2002.

15 'Ituri: "covered in blood". Ethnically targeted violence in north-eastern DR Congo'. Human Rights Watch, July 2003.

16 Ibid.

17 Author interviews, Mongbwalu, April 2008.

18 Human Rights Watch (2005) *The Curse of Gold: Democratic Republic of Congo*. New York, NY: Human Rights Watch.

19 'UN condemns DR Congo cannibalism'. BBC News, 15 January 2003.

20 'DRC: MONUC confirms cannibalism in Mambasa, Mangina'. IRIN, 15 January 2003.

21 'Ituri: "covered in blood". Ethnically targeted violence in north-eastern DR Congo'. Human Rights Watch, July 2003.

22 'DRC: Shabunda reported calm following Mayi-Mayi takeover'. IRIN, 4 October 2002.

23 'Katanga: the Congo's forgotten crisis'. Africa Report No. 103. International Crisis Group, 9 January 2006.

24 'Ituri: "covered in blood". Ethnically targeted violence in north-eastern DR Congo'. Human Rights Watch, July 2003.

25 Human Rights Watch, *The Curse of Gold: Democratic Republic of Congo*.

26 'DRC: IRIN interview with Ituri militia leader Thomas Lubanga'. IRIN, 29 August 2003.

27 Human Rights Watch, *The Curse of Gold: Democratic Republic of Congo*.

28 '966 massacred in Congo'. *The Telegraph*, 7 April 2003.

29 Human Rights Watch, *The Curse of Gold: Democratic Republic of Congo*.

30 'Ituri: "covered in blood". Ethnically targeted violence in north-eastern DR Congo'. Human Rights Watch, July 2003.

31 'Est de la RDC: l'armée rwandaise attaque un leader tutsi ennemi du RCD'. Agence France-Presse, 2 April 2002.

32 'Second special report of the Secretary-General on the United Nations Organization Mission in the Democratic Republic of the Congo'. UN Security Council, 27 May 2003.

33 'Central African Republic: hundreds raped and neglected'. Amnesty International, 10 November 2004.

34 Watchlist on Children and Armed Conflict (2006) *Struggling to Survive: Children in armed conflict in the Democratic Republic of the Congo*.

New York, NY: Watchlist on Children and Armed Conflict.

35 Ibid.

36 'Rwandan poll "not entirely fair"'. BBC News, 27 August 2003.

37 'Text of Kagame's victory speech'. BBC News, 26 August 2003.

38 'Mayi-Mayi, RCD-Goma begin reconciliation efforts'. IRIN, 11 September 2003.

39 'IRIN interview with Mayi-Mayi political leader Marcel Munga'. IRIN, 11 September 2003.

40 'Mayi-Mayi, RCD-Goma sign ceasefire in Shabunda'. IRIN, 3 October 2003.

41 Kodi, Muzong W. (2007) *Anti-Corruption Challenges in Post-Election Democratic Republic of Congo*. Africa Programme Report. London: Chatham House.

42 'D.R. Congo: war crimes in Bukavu'. Human Rights Watch Briefing Paper, June 2004.

43 Autesserre, Séverine (2010) *The Trouble with the Congo: Local violence and the failure of international peacebuilding*. Cambridge: Cambridge University Press, p. 89.

44 Ibid. p. 159.

45 'DR Congo army "massacred Tutsis"'. BBC News, 17 August 2004.

46 'Mediators go to DR Congo hotspot'. BBC News, 16 December 2004.

47 'Congo troops battle Rwandan Hutu militia in border region'. Associated Press, 27 December 2004.

48 'UN troops adopt warriors' tactics'. Associated Press, 28 December 2004.

49 Ibid.

50 Carroll, Rory (2004) 'Violence threatens to engulf Congo'. *The Guardian*, 26 November.

51 'UN checks on thousands fleeing Congo fighting'. Reuters, 27 December 2004.

52 Christophe Boulierac/MONUC (2004) DR Congo: Rape in Ituri – Kpandroma under a law of silence'. MONUC, 17 December 2004.

53 'Congo mutineers say they are holding fire pending pullout by regular forces'. Agence France-Presse, 23 December 2004.

54 'Warlord "arrest" for UN killings'. BBC News, 1 March 2005.

55 'Profile: DR Congo militia leader Thomas Lubanga'. BBC News, 23 January 2009.

56 'Women killed and mutilated in Congo attack – UN'. Reuters, 7 April 2005.

57 Ibid.

58 Lacey, Marc (2005) 'Rebels in Congo say they'll end cross-border raids in Rwanda'. *The New York Times*, 1 April.

59 Watchlist on Children and Armed Conflict (2006) *Struggling to Survive: Children in armed conflict in the Democratic Republic of the Congo*.

60 Ibid.

61 'The US Congress and the crisis in the Congo'. United States Congress, made available by the offices of Senator Mike DeWine, 10 June 2005.

62 'DR Congo: UN reports peaceful constitutional referendum, with few incidents'. UN News Centre, 19 December 2005.

63 MONUSCO chronology of events. Available at http://monusco.unmissions.org/Default.aspx?tabid=10672&language=en-US (accessed 8 April 2013).

64 'DR Congo voters approve new constitution'. Associated Press, 12 January 2006.

65 'Kabila could benefit from

election boycott'. *Business Day* (Johannesburg), 6 April 2006.

5 Hundred per cent Congolese

1 'Worries in the east: hopes for quiet elections this year may dwindle once again'. *The Economist*, 2 February 2006.

2 'DRC: rape on the rise in North Kivu, as fighting displaces 70,000'. UN Office for the Coordination of Humanitarian Affairs Integrated Regional Information Network (IRIN), 10 February 2006.

3 'Rutshuru, DR Congo: attacks on civilians cause thousands to flee'. Médecins Sans Frontières, 6 February 2006.

4 'Democratic Republic of Congo: alarming resurgence in recruitment of children in North-Kivu'. Amnesty International, 31 March 2006.

5 'Renewed crisis in North Kivu'. Human Rights Watch, 24 October 2007.

6 'Opposition vows to block Congo vote'. Associated Press, 3 April 2006.

7 Author interviews, Kinshasa, March–June 2008.

8 'Special investigation mission into human rights violations and abuses committed in the Territory of Mitwaba, Katanga Province, 13–19 February 2006'. MONUC Human Rights Division, 6 July 2006.

9 Ibid.

10 'Katanga: the Congo's forgotten crisis'. Africa Report No. 103. International Crisis Group, 9 January 2006.

11 Ibid.

12 'Congo Catholic Church warns of flawed elections'. Reuters, 21 July 2006.

13 Prunier, Gérard (2009) *Africa's World War: Congo, the Rwandan genocide, and the making of a continental catastrophe*. New York, NY: Oxford University Press, p. 311.

14 Gettleman, Jeffrey (2006) 'Congo holds first multiparty election in 46 years'. *The New York Times*, 31 July.

15 'Congo's capital is restless as election results tilt toward president'. Reuters, 14 August 2006.

16 'Kabila gets 44.8 pct in Congo poll, goes to run-off'. Reuters, 20 August 2006.

17 Human Rights Watch (2008) *'We Will Crush You': The restriction of political space in the Democratic Republic of Congo*. New York, NY: Human Rights Watch.

18 'Twenty-second report of the Secretary-General on the United Nations Organization Mission in the Democratic Republic of the Congo'. UN Security Council, 21 September 2006.

19 Human Rights Watch, *'We Will Crush You': The restriction of political space in the Democratic Republic of Congo*.

20 Author's interviews, Kinshasa, February and March 2008.

21 Human Rights Watch, *'We Will Crush You': The Restriction of Political Space In the Democratic Republic of Congo*.

22 Gettleman, Jeffrey (2006) 'Kidnapping and turmoil ahead of Congo vote'. *The New York Times*, 28 October 2006.

23 'AU hails DRC polls, appeals for calm'. *Mail & Guardian*, 31 October 2006.

24 'DRC observers seek transparency in vote counting'. Voice of America, 31 October 2009.

25 'Congo's election: Congo on a knife edge'. *The Economist*, 15 November 2006.

26 McGreal, Chris (2006) 'Congo faces danger of new civil war as opposition rejects election result'. *The Guardian*, 15 November.

27 McGreal, Chris (2006) 'Opposition objects as Kabila named Congo election winner'. *The Guardian*, 16 November.

28 'Part of the Supreme Court burnt amid gunshots'. IRIN, 21 November 2006.

29 'Bemba accepts DR Congo poll loss'. BBC News, 28 November 2006.

30 'Renewed crisis in North Kivu'. Human Rights Watch, 24 October 2007.

31 'S. 2125 (109th): Democratic Republic of the Congo Relief, Security, and Democracy Promotion Act of 2006'. Text, 22 December 2006.

32 'Renewed crisis in North Kivu'. Human Rights Watch, 24 October 2007.

33 'Last Ituri warlord signs peace deal in DR Congo'. Agence France-Presse, 29 November 2006.

34 Ngwawi, Joseph (2007) 'Kabila names coalition government for DRC'. Southern African News Features, 11 February.

35 Human Rights Watch, *'We Will Crush You': The restriction of political space in the Democratic Republic of Congo*.

36 Author interviews, Kinshasa, May 2008.

37 'The human rights situation in the Democratic Republic of Congo (DRC): during the period January to June 2007'. MONUC Human Rights Division, 27 September 2007.

38 Human Rights Watch, *'We Will Crush You': The restriction of political space in the Democratic Republic of Congo*.

6 Glittering demons

1 'Assemblée Nationale commission spéciale chargée de l'examen de la validité des conventions à caractère économique et financier. Conclues pendant les guerres de 1996–1997 et de 1998'. Democratic Republic of Congo, June 2005.

2 World Bank (2008) *Democratic Republic of Congo: Growth with governance in the mining sector*. Washington, DC: The World Bank.

3 Ibid.

4 'Katanga: the Congo's forgotten crisis'. Africa Report No. 103. International Crisis Group, 9 January 2006.

5 Johnson, Dominic and Aloys Tegera (2005) *Digging Deeper: How the DR Congo's mining policy is failing the country*. Goma: Pole Institute.

6 Veit, Alex (2011) *Intervention as Indirect Rule: Civil war and statebuilding in the Democratic Republic of Congo*. Frankfurt: Campus Verlag, p. 68.

7 Kodi, Muzong W. (2007) *Anti-Corruption Challenges in Post-Election Democratic Republic of Congo*. Africa Programme Report. London: Chatham House.

8 'Final report of the United Nations Panel of Experts on the illegal exploitation of natural resources and other forms of wealth of the Democratic Republic of the Congo'. UN Security Council, October 2002.

9 World Bank, *Democratic Republic of Congo: Growth with governance in the mining sector*.

10 'Report of the Panel of Experts'. UN Security Council, 2002.

11 Global Witness (2005) *Under-Mining Peace: The explosive trade in cassiterite in eastern DRC*. Washington, DC: Global Witness Publishing.

12 Ibid.

13 Johnson, Dominic and Aloys Tegera, *Digging Deeper: How the DR Congo's mining policy is failing the country*.

14 Global Witness, *Under-Mining Peace: The explosive trade in cassiterite in eastern DRC*.

15 'Report of the Panel of Experts'. UN Security Council, 2002.

16 Global Witness, *Under-Mining Peace: The explosive trade in cassiterite in eastern DRC*.

17 'Report of the Panel of Experts'. UN Security Council, 2002. Bout, who also supplied weapons to Jean-Pierre Bemba's MLC, was arrested in Thailand in November 2008, and was subsequently extradited to the United States. He was convicted of conspiring to supply weapons to the Fuerzas Armadas Revolucionarias de Colombia (FARC) rebel group and of conspiring to kill US citizens and officials. See 'Russian Viktor Bout convicted over Colombian arms deal'. Associated Press, 2 November 2011.

18 Global Witness, *Under-Mining Peace: The explosive trade in cassiterite in eastern DRC*.

19 Ibid.

20 Ibid.

21 Ibid.

22 'Report of the Panel of Experts'. UN Security Council, 2002.

23 'Report of the Panel of Experts'. UN Security Council, 2001.

24 Human Rights Watch (2005) *The Curse of Gold: Democratic Republic of Congo*. New York, NY: Human Rights Watch.

25 Global Witness (2004) *Same Old Story: Natural resources in the Democratic Republic of Congo*. Washington, DC: Global Witness Publishing.

26 'Report of the Panel of Experts'. UN Security Council, 2002.

27 Ibid.

28 Author interviews, Kampala, January 2012.

29 'Profile: Major General James Kazini'. BBC News, 13 November 2009.

30 'Final report of the United Nations Panel of Experts on the illegal exploitation of natural resources and other forms of wealth of the Democratic Republic of the Congo'. UN Security Council, October 2002.

31 'Disarmament in the Congo: jump-starting DDRRR to prevent further war'. Africa Report No. 38. International Crisis Group, 14 December 2001.

32 'Report of the Panel of Experts'. UN Security Council, 2002.

33 'Final report of the United Nations Panel of Experts on the illegal exploitation of natural resources and other forms of wealth of the Democratic Republic of the Congo'. UN Security Council, October 2002.

34 'Report of investigation'. UN Office of Internal Oversight Services Investigations Division, 2 July 2007.

35 'Final report of the United Nations Panel of Experts on the illegal exploitation of natural resources and other forms of wealth of the Democratic Republic of the Congo'. UN Security Council, October 2002.

36 'Report of the Panel of Experts'. UN Security Council, 2002.

37 'Final report of the United Nations Panel of Experts on the illegal

exploitation of natural resources and other forms of wealth of the Democratic Republic of the Congo'. UN Security Council, October 2002.

38 Global Witness, *Same Old Story: Natural resources in the Democratic Republic of Congo*.

39 Morrison, Kevin (2006) 'Global investors push up commodities prices'. *Financial Times*, 9 April.

40 Clark, Campbell (2011) 'Nuclear worries behind failed Forsys deal'. *The Globe and Mail*, 17 January.

41 'Recent allegations of uranium trafficking in the Democratic Republic of Congo'. George Forrest International Group, 20 December 2001.

42 'Report of the Panel of Experts'. UN Security Council, 2001.

43 'DR Congo uranium mine collapses'. BBC News, 12 July 2004.

44 'DRC: UN mission denied access to collapsed uranium mine'. UN Office for the Coordination of Humanitarian Affairs Integrated Regional Information Network (IRIN), 21 July 2004.

45 'DR Congo "uranium ring" men freed'. BBC News, 13 March 2007.

46 'Final report of the United Nations Panel of Experts on the illegal exploitation of natural resources and other forms of wealth of the Democratic Republic of the Congo'. UN Security Council, October 2002.

47 'Zimbabwe: President Robert Mugabe's money men'. IRIN, 4 February 2009.

48 Ibid.

49 Author interviews, Mongbwalu, April 2008.

50 Global Witness (2006) *Reforming the DRC diamond sector*. Washington, DC: Global Witness Publishing.

51 Human Rights Watch, *The Curse of Gold: Democratic Republic of Congo*.

52 Ryan, Brendan (2005) 'Anglo-Gold Ashanti acts on DRC allegations'. www.miningmx.com, 1 June.

53 Author interview with Jean-Paul Lonema, Mongbwalu, April 2008.

54 Author interview with Guy-Robert Lukama, country manager for AngloGold Ashanti, Kinshasa, April 2008.

55 Author interview with Jean-Claude Kanku, community development and relationship manager for AngloGold Ashanti, Mongbwalu, April 2008.

56 Global Witness (2006) *Digging in Corruption: Fraud, abuse and exploitation in Katanga's copper and cobalt mines*. Washington, DC: Global Witness Publishing.

57 Johnson, Dominic and Aloys Tegera, *Digging Deeper: How the DR Congo's mining policy is failing the country*.

58 Global Witness, *Digging in Corruption: Fraud, abuse and exploitation in Katanga's copper and cobalt mines*.

59 'Katanga: the Congo's forgotten crisis'. Africa Report No. 103. International Crisis Group, 9 January 2006.

60 Global Witness, *Digging in Corruption: Fraud, abuse and exploitation in Katanga's copper and cobalt mines*.

61 'Kilwa trial: a denial of justice. A chronology: October 2004–July 2007.' Global Witness, Rights & Accountability in Development, Action Against Impunity for Human Rights, and African Association for the Defence of Human Rights,17 July 2007.

62 Ibid.

63 Ibid.

64 UN Human Rights Council

(2008) *Report of the Independent Expert on the Situation of Human Rights in the Democratic Republic of the Congo, Mr. Titinga Frédéric Pacéré.* Geneva: UN Human Rights Council.

65 'Moïse katumbi, un Ovni en politique'. *Le Soir*, 31 March 2009.

66 'Final report of the Group of Experts on the Democratic Republic of the Congo'. UN, December 2008.

67 Global Witness (2011) *China and Congo: Friends in need*. London: Global Witness.

68 Ibid.

69 Cropley, Ed (2009) 'China, others shove U.S. in scramble for Africa'. Reuters, 6 August.

70 Holslag, Jonathan (2010) 'China's true intentions in Congo'. *Harvard International Review*, 19 April.

71 Romkema, Hans (2007) *Opportunities and Constraints for the Disarmament & Repatriation of Foreign Armed Groups in the Democratic Republic of Congo. The cases of the FDLR, FNL and ADF/NALU.* Washington, DC: Multi-Country Demobilization and Reintegration Program, The World Bank.

72 Ibid.

73 Ibid.

74 Author interview with photojournalist Andrew McConnell, who had spent time in FDLR camps in South Kivu, April 2012.

75 'Final report of the Group of Experts on the Democratic Republic of the Congo'. UN Security Council, 13 February 2008.

76 Author interviews, Congo, February–June 2008.

77 'Final report of the Group of Experts on the Democratic Republic of the Congo'. UN Security Council, 13 February 2008.

78 'Renewed crisis in North Kivu'. Human Rights Watch, 24 October 2007.

79 'MONUC monthly human rights assessment: May 2007'. MONUC Human Rights Division, 19 June 2007.

80 Romkema, Hans, *Opportunities and Constraints for the Disarmament & Repatriation of Foreign Armed Groups in the Democratic Republic of Congo. The cases of the FDLR, FNL and ADF/NALU.*

81 UN Human Rights Council (2007) *Report of the Special Rapporteur on Violence against Women, its Causes and Consequences, Yakin Ertürk: Indicators on violence against women and state response*. Geneva: UN Human Rights Council.

82 'Final report of the Group of Experts on the Democratic Republic of the Congo'. UN Security Council, 13 February 2008.

83 UN Human Rights Council, *Report of the Independent Expert on the Situation of Human Rights in the Democratic Republic of the Congo, Mr. Titinga Frédéric Pacéré.*

84 Harvard Humanitarian Initiative (2010) *'Now, the World is without Me': An investigation of sexual violence in eastern Democratic Republic of Congo*. Cambridge, MA: Harvard Humanitarian Initiative and Oxfam International.

85 'MONUC monthly human rights assessment: May 2007'. MONUC Human Rights Division, 19 June 2007.

86 Human Rights Watch (2010) *Always on the Run: The vicious cycle of displacement in eastern Congo*. New York, NY: Human Rights Watch.

87 'UNESCO Director-General

condemns murder of Congolese journalist Serge Maheshe'. UNESCO, 19 June 2007.

88 'Bapuwa Mwamba. Freelance journalist'. Committee to Protect Journalists, 6 July 2005.

89 'Franck Kangundu: La Référence Plus'. Committee to Protect Journalists, 3 November 2005.

90 UN Human Rights Council, *Report of the Independent Expert on the Situation of Human Rights in the Democratic Republic of the Congo, Mr. Titinga Frédéric Pacéré.*

91 'Renewed crisis in North Kivu'. Human Rights Watch, 24 October 2007.

92 'Goma situation report'. US Embassy Kinshasa cable, 22 December 2007.

93 'Organizers say DRC Goma peace conference on course'. Voice of America, 15 January 2008.

94 'Rebels vow no let up at DR Congo peace conference'. Agence France-Presse, 13 January 2008.

95 'Congo's Kabila flies to eastern peace conference'. Reuters, 15 January 2008.

96 'Warrant of arrest against Bosco Ntaganda unsealed'. ICC, 8 April 2008.

97 'MONUC welcomes the success of the Goma conference and the signing of its acts of engagement'. MONUC press release, 24 January 2008.

98 Author visit, Kibumba, February 2008.

99 Author interviews, Rutshuru, February 2008.

100 Author interview, Rutshuru, February 2008.

101 Author interview with Muiti Muhindo, Goma, February 2008.

102 Author telephone interview with General Vainqueur Malaya, February 2008.

103 International Rescue Committee (2008) *Mortality in the Democratic Republic of Congo: An ongoing crisis.* New York, NY: International Rescue Committee. In the author's view, subsequent criticisms, such as those levelled at the study by the Human Security Report Project at Simon Fraser University, do not rise to a level to significantly impact the field sampling and baseline mortality rate methodology of the IRC report.

7 Threats

1 'DRC signs a $390 million five year governance programme with the UNDP'. MONUC press release, 14 February 2008.

2 After his stint with Kabila, Kasongo would return to the anchor's chair with the Congo Média Channel, a station that he also owned.

3 Hodges, Tony (2001) *Angola: From Afro-Stalinism to petro-diamond capitalism.* Oxford: James Currey, p. 22.

4 Prunier, Gérard (2009) *Africa's World War: Congo, the Rwandan genocide, and the making of a continental catastrophe.* New York, NY: Oxford University Press, p. 90.

5 Thornton, John K. (1998) *The Kongolese Saint Anthony: Dona Beatriz Kimpa Vita and the Antonian movement, 1684–1706.* Cambridge: Cambridge University Press, p. 10.

6 'Simon Kimbangu: The Church of Jesus Christ on Earth'. Dictionary of African Christian Biography. Available at www.dacb.org/stories/demrepcongo/kimbangu1_simon.html (accessed 17 April 2013).

7 'Ne Muanda Nsemi, chef spirituel de Bundu dia Kongo'. *Le Potentiel*, 15 May 2006.

8 'Democratic Republic of the Congo: information on the Bundu dia Kongo (BDK) movement, including its political program, location of its offices, the number of its members, its situation with respect to other political parties, and the attitude of government authorities toward its leaders and members'. Immigration and Refugee Board of Canada, 6 April 2011.

9 Kabwe, Willy (2002) 'Affaire Bundu Dia Kongo: éviter la répétition de la situation de l'est'. Paris: Institute Panos.

10 'Congo: consolidating the peace'. Africa Report No. 128. International Crisis Group, 5 July 2007.

11 Human Rights Watch (2008) *'We Will Crush You': The restriction of political space in the Democratic Republic of Congo*. New York, NY: Human Rights Watch.

12 'Bundu dia Kongo revendique l'indemnisation des victimes des événements sanglants du Bas-Congo'. *Le Potentiel*, 20 February 2007.

13 'The human rights situation in the Democratic Republic of Congo (DRC): during the period January to June 2007'. MONUC Human Rights Division, 27 September 2007.

14 Author interviews, Matadi and Luozi, March 2008.

15 Human Rights Watch, *'We Will Crush You': The restriction of political space in the Democratic Republic of Congo*.

16 'Special inquiry into the Bas Congo events of February and March 2008'. MONUC Human Rights Division, May 2008.

17 Author interview, Matadi, March 2008.

18 Author interview, Matadi, March 2008.

19 Author interview, Matadi, March 2008.

20 'Special inquiry into the Bas Congo events of February and March 2008'. MONUC Human Rights Division, May 2008.

21 Ibid.

22 Ibid.

23 'Après trois folles journées à l'assemblée nationale'. *Le Potentiel*, 31 March 2008.

24 Covington, Yolanda Denise (2008) 'Embodied histories, danced religions, performed politics: Kongo cultural performance and the production of history and authority'. Dissertation submitted to University of Michigan.

25 'Joint meeting between Belgium and the Democratic Republic of Congo'. Belgian Development Cooperation press release, 19 March 2007.

26 'Paul Wolfowitz: arrival statement, Democratic Republic of Congo [DRC]'. World Bank, 8 March 2007.

27 'Statements made by the Ministry of Foreign Affairs spokesperson'. 26 March 2007.

28 'UN fully exempts Congo government from arms ban'. Reuters, 31 March 2008.

29 Gersony, Robert (2007) 'The anguish of Northern Uganda: results of a field-based assessment of the civil conflicts in Northern Uganda'. Report submitted to United States Embassy, Kampala, and USAID Mission, Kampala, August 1997.

30 Behrend, Heike (2000) *Alice Lakwena & the Holy Spirits: War in*

northern Uganda 1986–97. Athens, OH: Ohio University Press, p. 24. Author's note: I saw much the same phenomenon while reporting on the attempted reintegration into civilian society of former members of the Autodefensas Unidas de Colombia in the department of Antioquia in Colombia in early 2010. See 'Like Colombia, iconic city remains a place of promise and peril'. Inter Press Service, 3 June 2010.

31 Gersony, Robert, 'The anguish of Northern Uganda: results of a field-based assessment of the civil conflicts in Northern Uganda'.

32 Author interviews, Kampala and Gulu, February 2012.

33 Gersony, Robert, 'The anguish of Northern Uganda: results of a field-based assessment of the civil conflicts in Northern Uganda'.

34 Mutaizibwa, Emma (2011) 'The roots of war: Atiak massacre, new wave of LRA brutality'. *The Observer* (Uganda), 3 October.

35 Gersony, Robert, 'The anguish of Northern Uganda: results of a field-based assessment of the civil conflicts in Northern Uganda'.

36 'Uganda: UN DHA IRIN humanitarian situation report'. UN Department of Humanitarian Affairs Integrated Regional Information Network (IRIN), 15 March 1997.

37 Klein, Alice (2012) 'Northern Uganda's displaced people are left to fend for themselves'. *The Guardian*, 24 January.

38 Finnström, Sverker (2008) *Living with Bad Surroundings: War, history, and everyday moments in Northern Uganda*. Durham, NC: Duke University Press, p. 141.

39 Author interview with Francis Odongyoo, Executive Director of Human Rights Focus, Gulu, 9 February 2012.

40 Finnström, Sverker, *Living with Bad Surroundings: War, history, and everyday moments in Northern Uganda*, p. 142.

41 Pros. v. D. Ongwen: Warrant of Arrest, 8-7-2005. ICC, 8 July 2005.

42 Human Rights Watch (2009) *The Christmas Massacres: LRA attacks on civilians in Northern Congo*. New York, NY: Human Rights Watch.

43 'Guatemalan blue helmet deaths stir Congo debate'. Reuters, 31 January 2006.

44 'Guatemala losing patience over Congo troops' deaths probe'. Reuters, 4 April 2006.

45 Author interviews, Kampala and Gulu, February 2012.

46 Human Rights Watch, *The Christmas Massacres: LRA attacks on civilians in Northern Congo*.

47 Downie, Richard (2011) 'The Lord's Resistance Army'. Center for Strategic and International Studies, 18 October.

48 Human Rights Watch, *The Christmas Massacres: LRA attacks on civilians in Northern Congo*.

49 Ibid.

50 'EU slams rebel calls for Congolese to fight govt'. Agence France-Presse, 7 October 2008.

51 Charbonneau, Louis (2008) 'Congo gives U.N. council "proof" of Rwanda incursion'. Reuters, 10 October.

52 McGreal, Chris (2008) 'Rwanda president accuses UN of betrayal and denies backing Tutsi rebels in Congo'. *The Guardian*, 15 November.

53 'Final report of the Group of Experts on the Democratic Republic

of the Congo'. UN Security Council, December 2008.

54 Pole Institute (2010) *Guerillas in the Mist: The Congolese experience of the FDLR war in Eastern Congo and the role of the international community*. Goma: Pole Institute.

55 'Special report by the United Nations Joint Human Rights Office (UNJHRO)'. 7 September 2009.

56 Tran, Mark (2008) 'Angolan troops "reinforcing Congo army against rebels"'. *The Guardian*, 7 November.

57 'DR Congo president names new prime minister: report'. Agence France-Presse, 10 October 2008.

58 'Mbusa Nyamwisi: yesterday's man?' VZCZCXRO3813. Cable from US Embassy Kinshasa, 19 June 2009.

59 Ibid.

60 'Congo opposition leader says life still in danger'. Reuters, 1 April 2008.

61 Warrant of Arrest in the Case of the Prosecutor v. Jean-Pierre Bemba. ICC, 10 June 2008.

62 'Final report of the Group of Experts on the Democratic Republic of the Congo'. UN Security Council, December 2008.

63 'International court unseals arrest warrant against Bosco Ntaganda'. Human Rights Watch, 30 April 2008.

64 'Final report of the Group of Experts on the Democratic Republic of the Congo'. UN Security Council, December 2008.

65 Ibid.

66 Ibid.

67 'Report of the High Commissioner for Human Rights on the situation of human rights and the activities of her Office in the Demo-

cratic Republic of the Congo'. UN Human Rights Council, 1 March 2009.

68 Human Rights Watch (2008) *Killings in Kiwanja: The UN's inability to protect civilians*. New York, NY: Human Rights Watch.

69 'UN: army raping civilians in Congo'. Associated Press, 12 November 2008.

70 'Refugees must relocate to flee rebels, says UN'. France 24, 14 November 2008.

71 Perhaps the worst example of the media's sometimes fawning and credulous treatment of Nkunda came from the American self-styled 'investigative journalist' Georgianne Nienaber, whose videotaped interview with Nkunda is disturbing both for Nienaber's bizarre focus on the fate of two gorillas as opposed to the atrocities that Nkunda's men had been committing in the Congo and for Nkunda's ability to lie with such brazen conviction. See 'Interview with General Laurent Nkunda, Parts 1–5'. Available at www.youtube.com/watch?v=K9tiu-1ig58.

72 'Congo rebel backs U.N. peace plan, fighting persists'. Reuters, 16 November 2008.

73 Holland, Hereward and Finbarr O'Reilly (2008) 'Defiant Congo rebels stage rally in captured town'. Reuters, 22 November.

74 O'Reilly, Finbarr (2008) 'Congo rebel pullback raises hopes for peace talks,' Reuters, 19 November.

75 'Congo rebels advance despite ceasefire'. Associated Press, 17 November 2008.

76 'Why Rwanda turned against Nkunda'. Al Jazeera, 24 January 2009.

77 Author interviews, Goma, February 2012.

78 Bavier, Joe (2008) 'Congo, Rwanda agree plan to disband FDLR militia'. Reuters, 4 December.

79 'DR Congo rebel leader faces fresh call to step down'. Agence France-Presse, 8 January 2009.

80 'Congo rebels in truce with government'. Associated Press, 16 January 2009.

81 Human Rights Watch (2009) *'You Will Be Punished': Attacks on civilians in Eastern Congo*. New York, NY: Human Rights Watch.

82 Ibid.

83 'Rwanda arrests Congo rebel leader Laurent Nkunda'. Associated Press, 23 January 2009.

84 'Rebels begin joining DR Congo army'. Agence France-Presse, 29 January 2009.

85 Text of the peace agreement between the government and the CNDP, Goma, 23 March 2009.

86 Human Rights Watch (2010) *Always on the Run: The vicious cycle of displacement in Eastern Congo*. New York, NY: Human Rights Watch.

8 A false peace

1 McGreal, Chris (2008) '"We have to kill Tutsis wherever they are"'. *The Guardian*, 16 May.

2 Callimachi, Rukmini (2010) 'One by one, rebels desert from army in Congo'. Associated Press, 6 February.

3 'Report of the High Commissioner for Human Rights on the situation of human rights and the activities of her Office in the Democratic Republic of the Congo'. UN Human Rights Council, 1 March 2009.

4 Ibid.

5 Human Rights Watch (2009) *'You Will Be Punished': Attacks on civilians in Eastern Congo*. New York, NY: Human Rights Watch.

6 Author interviews, Goma, February 2012.

7 Human Rights Watch, *'You Will Be Punished': Attacks on civilians in Eastern Congo*.

8 Ibid.

9 Author telephone interview with former diplomat, January 2012.

10 Doss, Alan (2009) 'These outrageous slurs undermine our mission in Congo'. *The Guardian*, 3 July.

11 Human Rights Watch, *'You Will Be Punished': Attacks on civilians in Eastern Congo*.

12 'DR Congo: militia leader guilty in landmark trial'. Human Rights Watch, 10 March 2009.

13 '30,000 Congolese flee to escape fresh conflict in Ituri district'. UNHCR, 7 April 2009.

14 'ICC's first war crimes defendant denies charges'. Agence France-Presse, 26 January 2009.

15 Mushizi, Charles M. (2009) 'For RFI, static in Kinshasa'. Committee to Protect Journalists blog, 4 August.

16 'At least 60 killed in Congolese rebel attacks: UN'. Agence France-Presse, 15 May 2009.

17 Pole Institute (2010) *Guerillas in the Mist: The Congolese experience of the FDLR war in Eastern Congo and the role of the international community*. Goma: Pole Institute.

18 Bavier, Joe (2009) 'Thirty-two killed in eastern Congo clashes'. Reuters, 19 June.

19 'Some 35,000 flee renewed clashes in DRCongo: UNHCR'. Agence France-Presse, 24 July 2009.

20 Lee, Matthew (2009) 'Clinton demands end to sexual violence in Congo'. Associated Press, 11 August.

21 Olukya, Godfrey and Rukmini Callimachi (2009) 'Top Rwanda genocide suspect caught in Uganda'. Associated Press, 6 October.

22 'DR Congo: civilian cost of military operation is unacceptable'. Congo Advocacy Coalition, 13 October 2009.

23 Charbonneau, Louis (2009) 'U.N. should continue Congo ops despite criticism: envoy'. Reuters, 16 October.

24 McCrummen, Stephanie (2009) 'U.N. official assails Congo operation'. *The Washington Post*, 16 October.

25 'UN: Congolese army killed 62 civilians in E. Congo'. Associated Press, 2 November 2009.

26 Tran, Mark (2009) 'UN denies complicity in Congo war crimes'. *The Guardian*, 11 November.

27 Holslag, Jonathan (2010) 'China's true intentions in Congo'. *Harvard International Review*, 19 April.

28 Global Witness (2011) *China and Congo: Friends in need*. London: Global Witness.

29 Bavier, Joe (2009) 'India grants Congo $263 mln in infrastructure loans'. Reuters, 30 October.

30 'Refugees return to Equateur province as UNHCR promotes reconciliation'. UNHCR, 19 October 2011.

31 'Dongo: spectacle désolant d'une cité déserte'. Radio Okapi, 16 November 2009.

32 'Congolese forces arrest 100 over police deaths'. Reuters, 8 November 2009.

33 'DR Congo's Equateur governor announces end of Enyele rebellion'. Xinhua, 31 March 2010.

34 'Enyele rebels enter major city in Equateur province'. Xinhua, 4 April 2010.

35 'U.N. failed civilians during Congo rebel attack'. Associated Press, 9 April 2010.

36 Chaco, Emmanuel (2010) 'Kinshasa rejects report of Congolese army atrocities'. Inter Press Service, 3 May.

37 M'Putu, Edouardin (2009) 'Deported Congolese tell of Angolan terror'. Agence France-Presse, 14 October.

38 Gettleman, Jeffrey (2010) 'Hundreds were raped on Congo–Angola border'. *The New York Times*, 5 November.

39 'Top rebel commander "surrenders" to Uganda troops'. Agence France-Presse, 5 November 2009.

40 Ngoupana, Paul-Marin (2009) 'Dozens dead in Ugandan rebel attack in CAR: sources'. Reuters, 25 November.

41 'CAR/DR Congo: LRA conducts massive abduction campaign'. Human Rights Watch, 11 August 2010.

42 Mukiibi, Hellen (2008) 'Uganda: Museveni's son graduates from U.S. college'. New Vision, 14 June.

43 'Doctors: Uganda riots death toll rises to 21'. Associated Press, 14 September 2009.

44 'Hundreds arrested in deadly Uganda riots'. CNN, 13 September 2009.

45 Rice, Xan and Barbara Among (2010) 'Three killed in Kampala clashes after royal mausoleum destroyed by fire'. *The Guardian*, 17 March.

46 Broadcast on NTV Uganda, 12 November 2009.

47 'Rwandan Hutu rebel leaders held in German jail: official'. Agence France-Presse, 18 November 2009.

48 'Final report of the Group of

Experts on the Democratic Republic of the Congo'. UN Security Council, 2 December 2011.

49 'Report: Congo massacre witnesses were threatened'. Associated Press, 25 November 2009.

50 Kavanagh, Michael (2010) 'Congo commission says half of copper signing bonus missing'. Bloomberg, 16 February.

51 Global Witness, *China and Congo: Friends in need*.

52 Fessy, Thomas (2010) 'Congo general "profits from blood gold"'. BBC News, 10 November.

53 Rater, Philippe (2010) 'Rwanda, France pledge to bolster ties'. Agence France-Presse, 7 January.

54 Davies, Lizzy and Chris McGreal (2010) 'Widow of assassinated Rwandan president arrested'. *The Guardian*, 2 March.

55 'Rwanda rebels deny link to opposition chief'. Reuters, 28 April 2010.

56 Erlinder, Peter (2009) 'Rwanda: no conspiracy, no genocide planning … no genocide?' Global Research, 24 January.

57 'Rwanda court grants medical release to US lawyer'. Associated Press, 17 June 2010.

58 'Rwandan opposition faces crackdown ahead of vote'. Associated Press, 25 June 2010.

59 'Two dead, 27 hurt in Rwanda grenade attacks: police'. Agence France-Presse, 16 May 2010.

60 'Secretary-General appoints Roger A. Meece Special Representative for Democratic Republic of Congo'. UN Department of Public Information, 9 June 2010.

61 'DR Congo: peacekeepers plan Operation Amani Leo with FARDC in North Kivu'. MONUC press release, 19 January 2010.

62 'Complaint against Lt. Col. Innocent Zimurinda'. Letter from non-governmental organisations to Major General Dieudonné Amuli Bahigwa, 1 March 2010.

63 Charbonneau, Louis (2010) 'Congo army commander hit with U.N. sanctions'. Reuters, 1 December.

64 'DR Congo: ex-rebels take over mineral trade extortion racket'. Global Witness, 11 March 2010.

65 Pichegru, Laure (2010) 'Pursuing rebels at what price'. Inter Press Service, 16 June.

66 'U.N.-backed mission launched against Congo rebels'. Reuters, 3 March 2010.

67 'Over 600 Rwandan rebels killed or captured: DR. Congo army'. Agence France-Presse, 17 March 2010.

68 Smith, David (2010) 'UN begins talks on withdrawal from Congo'. *The Guardian*, 4 March.

69 Manson, Katrina (2010) 'Canada blocks debt relief as Congo marks jubilee'. Reuters, 1 July.

70 'IMF and World Bank announce US$12.3 billion in debt relief for the Democratic Republic of the Congo'. IMF press release, 1 July 2010.

71 'Lawyers: murder of Congolese PM was war crime'. Associated Press, 21 June 2010.

72 DiLorenzo, Sarah (2010) 'Congo activist's death reflects power struggle'. Associated Press, 12 June.

73 Chaco, Emmanuel (2010) 'Rights defender's death renews calls to end impunity'. Inter Press Service, 3 June.

74 'Several arrested for Congo activist's death'. Associated Press, 5 June 2010.

75 'Some 200 women gang-raped near Congo UN base'. Associated Press, 22 August 2010.

76 Smith, David (2010) 'UN "ignored Congo rape warnings"'. *The Guardian*, 3 September.

77 Faul, Michelle (2010) 'Congo leaders: we begged UN to protect civilians'. Associated Press, 1 September.

78 'Rebels handed over man arrested over Congo rapes'. Associated Press, 6 October 2010.

79 'UN deplores deadly attack against blue helmets in DR Congo'. UN News Centre, 18 August 2010.

80 David, Kezio-Musoke (2010) 'Rwanda considers pulling its peacekeepers from Darfur'. Reuters, 31 August.

81 'Genocide accusations against Rwanda are "absurd": Kagame'. Agence France-Presse, 16 September 2010.

82 Holland, Hereward (2010) 'Rwanda: U.N. Congo report threat to region's stability'. Reuters, 30 September.

83 'UN tones down Congo "genocide" report'. Associated Press, 30 September 2010.

84 'UN claims possible genocide in DRCongo'. Agence France-Presse, 1 October 2010.

85 Holland, Hereward (2010) 'Rwanda: we reserve right to review U.N. relations'. Reuters, 1 October.

86 Smith, David (2010) 'Congo conflict: "The Terminator" lives in luxury while peacekeepers look on'. *The Guardian*, 5 February.

87 2010 country reports on human rights practices in the Democratic Republic of Congo. US State Department, Bureau of Democracy, Human Rights, and Labor.

88 'Congo sets date for 2011 presidential vote'. Associated Press, 10 August 2010.

89 'DRC: the mineral curse'. *Regards Croisés* No. 30. Pole Institute, October 2011.

90 Ibid.

91 Johnson, Dominic and Aloys Tegera (2005) *Digging Deeper: How the DR Congo's mining policy is failing the country*. Goma: Pole Institute.

92 'DR Congo: Joseph Kabila critic's "suicide" doubted'. BBC News, 4 October 2010.

93 'Qui était Armand Tungulu?' Jeune Afrique, 13 October 2010.

94 'Police, anti-Kabila protesters clash in Brussels'. Agence France-Presse, 23 October 2010.

95 Gray-Block, Aaron (2010) 'Witness recalls rapes, killings in Bemba ICC trial'. Reuters, 24 November.

96 Corder, Mike (2010) 'Congo's Bemba pleads not guilty to murder, rape'. Associated Press, 22 November.

97 Kwinika, Savious (2010) 'Congo opposition figure allegedly escapes kidnapping attempt'. *The Christian Science Monitor*, 1 October.

98 'DR Congo, Rwanda hail progress in eradicating rebels'. Agence France-Presse, 18 October 2010.

99 'Final report of the Group of Experts on the Democratic Republic of the Congo'. UN Security Council, 2 December 2011.

100 'Rwandan rebel group chief arrested in France: ICC'. Agence France-Presse, 11 October 2010.

101 'Rwandan Hutu rebel leaders indicted in Germany'. Agence France-Presse, 17 December 2010.

102 'Rwandan general shot in S. Africa'. Reuters, 19 June 2010.

103 '10 now arrested in shooting

of ex-Rwandan general'. Associated Press, 25 August 2010.

104 'Witness: Rwandan soldiers behind S Africa shooting'. Associated Press, 29 June 2011.

105 Smith, David (2012) 'Exiled Rwandan general attacks Paul Kagame as "dictator"'. *The Guardian*, 30 July.

106 'Rwandan army officer arrested for "destabilisation"'. Agence France-Presse, 22 August 2010.

107 Smith, David (2010) 'Editor blames security forces after Rwandan journalist shot dead'. *The Guardian*, 25 June.

108 'Rwanda arrests newspaper director'. Agence France-Presse, 9 July 2010.

109 'Rwanda party seeks "real motives" behind murder'. Agence France-Presse, 17 July 2010.

110 Lederer, Edith M. (2010) 'Rwanda minister denies government role in attacks'. Associated Press, 19 July.

111 Vesperini, Helen (2010) 'Kagame sweeps Rwanda's presidential polls'. Agence France-Presse, 11 August.

112 '"Disturbing events" marred Rwanda leader's re-election, U.S. says'. Reuters, 14 August 2010.

9 Elections, encore

1 'Report on the Investigation Missions of the United Nations Joint Human Rights Office into the mass rapes and other human rights violations committed in the villages of Bushani and Kalambahiro, in Masisi Territory, North Kivu, on 31 December 2010 and 1 January 2011'. MONUSCO and UN Office of the High Commissioner for Human Rights, July 2011.

2 'Congo: 4 death sentences over activist's death'. Associated Press, 23 June 2011.

3 'Plaintiffs accuse DR Congo police chief in murder case'. Agence France-Presse, 17 July 2012.

4 'Procès Chebeya: Fidèle Bazana aurait été enterré dans la ferme du général John Numbi à Kinshasa'. Radio Okapi, 25 July 2012.

5 Corder, Mike (2011) 'Rwandan rebel: I am innocent of Congo war crimes'. Associated Press, 28 January.

6 'On rape's front line'. *The Guardian* (South Africa), 20 November 2011.

7 'DR Congo leader's home attacked, six gunmen killed: official'. Agence France-Presse, 27 February 2011.

8 'Many targets in Sunday's DR Congo attacks: government'. Agence France-Presse, 1 March 2011.

9 Pompey, Fabienne (2011) 'Le pasteur Mulunda, l'homme qui murmurait à l'oreille de Kabila'. Jeune Afrique, 8 April.

10 Onyango-Obbo, Charles (2012) 'Museveni at 90: a practical guide for an African big man'. Daily Monitor, 22 February.

11 'Preliminary statement: Uganda 2011 elections'. EU Election Observation Mission, 20 February 2011.

12 'Uganda's president says he'll "eat" challenger'. Associated Press, 25 February 2011.

13 'Kizza Besigye held over Uganda "Walk to Work" protest'. BBC News, 12 April 2011.

14 'Uganda politician's arrest sparks deadly riot'. Al Jazeera, 29 April 2011.

15 'Congo to hold national elections on November 28'. Reuters, 30 April 2011.

16 'Counting starts in violence-hit

Congo poll'. Reuters, 29 November 2011.

17 'War crimes accused declares DR Congo poll candidacy'. Agence France-Presse, 22 July 2011.

18 'Congo former VP Bemba not running in elections'. Associated Press, 9 September 2011.

19 'Final report of the Group of Experts on the Democratic Republic of the Congo'. UN Security Council, 2 December 2011.

20 Smith, David (2011) 'Rwandan genocide mastermind captured in DRC'. *The Guardian*, 26 May.

21 Siddique, Haroon (2011) 'Rwandan exiles warned of assassination threat by London police'. *The Guardian*, 20 May.

22 '30M voters registered for Congo November elections'. Associated Press, 15 July 2011.

23 'DRC's Kabila government bans broadcaster favorable to rival'. Committee to Protect Journalists, 13 July 2011.

24 'Congo elections: fears of violence, unity doubts'. Associated Press, 14 August 2011.

25 'DR Congo: candidates should not incite violence'. Human Rights Watch, 28 October 2011.

26 Hogg, Jonny (2011) 'Congo sells mining assets to fund polls: MPs, docs'. Reuters, 18 August.

27 'Police shoot protesters in Congo; 1 dead'. Associated Press, 6 September 2011.

28 'Congo prison mass escape after attack by gunmen'. BBC News, 7 September 2011.

29 'DR. Congo offers $100,000 reward for militia chief'. Agence France-Presse, 9 September 2011.

30 'Gunmen from Congo kill 36 at pub in Burundi'. Associated Press, 19 September 2011.

31 'Police implicated in Burundi bar massacre trial'. Agence France-Presse, 14 December 2011.

32 'Burundi rebel killed in Democratic Republic of Congo'. South African Press Association, 4 May 2012.

33 Ndikumana, Esdras (2011) 'Burundi death squads killed 300: rights group'. Agence France-Presse, 22 November 2011.

34 'Rebels kill five aid workers, two others in DRCongo: UN'. Agence France-Presse, 7 October 2011.

35 'Final report of the Group of Experts on the Democratic Republic of the Congo'. UN Security Council, 2 December 2011.

36 'Uganda rebels continue central Africa attacks'. Associated Press, 24 May 2011.

37 'UN: 300,000 Congolese displaced by Ugandan rebels'. Associated Press, 12 May 2011.

38 Text of a letter from the President to the Speaker of the House of Representatives and the President Pro Tempore of the Senate, 14 October 2011.

39 'Ouganda: Province Orientale – les rebelles de la LRA pillent les récoltes de riz à Bangadi'. Radio Okapi, 13 November 2001.

40 'Ituri: une nouvelle attaque des FRPI fait 30 000 déplacés'. Radio Okapi, 20 October 2011.

41 'Carter Center calls for urgent steps by DRC's Election Commission to prepare for Nov. 28 elections'. Carter Center press release, 17 October 2011.

42 'Une nouvelle manifestation de l'UDPS et alliés réprimée à Kinshasa'. Radio Okapi, 20 October 2011.

43 'Kinshasa: des militants de l'UDPS agressent deux policiers à Limete'. Radio Okapi, 21 October 2011.

44 '"I will not lose" presidential vote: DR Congo's Kabila'. Agence France-Presse, 18 October 2011.

45 Hogg, Jonny (2011) 'Congo election campaign kicks off'. Reuters, 28 October.

46 'DR Congo: as electoral campaign starts, Congolese and international NGOs call for urgent measures to prevent escalating violence'. Open Society Initiative for Southern Africa et al., 28 October 2011.

47 'Le lancement de la campagne électorale fait un mort et des blessés'. Radio Okapi, 29 October 2011.

48 Zengg, Sarah (2011) 'Congo presidential candidates bring their campaigns to the east'. *The Christian Science Monitor*, 18 November.

49 'DR Congo: candidates should not incite violence'. Human Rights Watch, 28 October 2011.

50 Ibid.

51 Author interviews, Masisi, February 2012.

52 Stearns, Jason K. (2011) 'Congolese candidate Tshisekedi declares himself president'. *The Christian Science Monitor*, 8 November.

53 'DR Congo opposition leader urges voters to rise up'. Agence France-Presse, 11 November 2011.

54 'DRC minister warns opposition over jail break threats'. Voice of America, 7 November 2011.

55 'DR Congo tension mounts ahead of vote'. Agence France-Presse, 8 November 2011.

56 'Joseph Kabila promet d'éradiquer l'insécurité dans la cité d'Uvira'. Radio Okapi, 9 November 2011.

57 'EU concerned at pre-election violence in DR Congo'. Agence France-Presse, 8 November 2011.

58 'US slams "incendiary" speech in DRC'. Agence France-Presse, 10 November 2011.

59 'UN: repression endangers this month's Congo vote'. Associated Press, 9 November 2011.

60 'Des blessés dans des heurts opposition/majorité au Katanga'. Radio Okapi, 17 November 2011.

61 'Élections en RDC: un député du MLC tué par balles à Kinshasa'. Jeune Afrique, 23 November 2011.

62 'Final report of the Group of Experts on the Democratic Republic of the Congo'. UN Security Council, 2 December 2011.

63 'Congo opposition to defy meeting ban ahead of vote'. Associated Press, 27 November 2011.

64 'Report of the United Nations Joint Human Rights Office on serious human rights violations committed by members of the Congolese defense and security forces in Kinshasa in the Democratic Republic of the Congo between 26 November and 25 December 2011'. MONUSCO and UN Office of the High Commissioner for Human Rights, March 2012.

65 Ibid.

66 Berger, Joshua Howat (2011) 'Weather delays vote materials for DR Congo polls'. Agence France-Presse, 25 November 2011.

67 '5 dead in election clashes as Congolese vote'. Associated Press, 28 November 2011.

68 Lewis, David and Jonny Hogg (2011) 'Chaos, arson, violence mar Congo election'. Reuters, 28 November.

69 'Remarks by Ambassador

Susan E. Rice, U.S. Permanent Representative to the United Nations, following Security Council consultations on Libya'. 28 November 2011. Available at http://usun.state.gov/briefing/statements/2011/177826.htm (accessed 16 April 2013).

70 Callimachi, Rukmini (2011) 'Officials extend voting to 2nd day in Congo'. Associated Press, 29 November.

71 'Opposition candidates call on Congo to annul vote'. Associated Press, 30 November 2011.

72 'Congo's Kabila leading 50.3 percent, early results'. Associated Press, 3 December 2011.

73 Callimachi, Rukmini (2011) 'Congo's Kabila leads election in early results'. Associated Press, 3 December.

74 'DR Congo to open inquiry into vote violence'. Agence France-Presse, 3 December 2011.

75 'DR Congo bishops sound alarm as vote tensions build'. Agence France-Presse, 4 December 2011.

76 'Le gouverneur appelle la population à accepter les résultats des élections dans le calme'. Radio Okapi, 4 December 2011.

77 Callimachi, Rukmini (2011) 'Congo holds its breath, election results expected'. Associated Press, 5 December.

78 'DR Congo protesters clash with S. Africa police'. Agence France-Presse, 5 December 2011.

79 'DR Congo protesters clash with police in London'. Agence France-Presse, 6 December 2011.

80 'DR Congo on high alert ahead of vote results'. Agence France-Presse, 6 December 2011.

81 Berger, Joshua Howat (2011) 'DR Congo police clamp down as wait for vote result drags on'. Agence France-Presse, 7 December.

82 'Report of the United Nations Joint Human Rights Office on serious human rights violations committed by members of the Congolese defense and security forces in Kinshasa in the Democratic Republic of the Congo between 26 November and 25 December 2011'. MONUSCO and UN Office of the High Commissioner for Human Rights, March 2012.

83 Callimachi, Rukmini (2011) 'President Kabila declared winner of Congo election'. Associated Press, 9 December.

84 '6 morts, dont deux femmes, dans des tensions post-électorales'. Radio Okapi, 10 December 2011.

85 'Inquiétude après l'assassinat d'un responsable de la société civile de Rutshuru'. Radio Okapi, 10 December 2011.

86 'Police go door-to-door in Congo after poll results'. Associated Press, 10 December 2011.

87 Callimachi, Rukmini (2011) 'Congo police sweep capital day after poll results'. Associated Press, 10 December.

88 'Le général Bisengimana promet de sanctionner les coupables'. Radio Okapi, 11 December 2011.

89 'London police arrest 143 at DR Congo vote protest'. Agence France-Presse, 10 December 2011.

90 'Carter Center: DRC presidential election results lack credibility'. Carter Center press release, 10 December 2011.

91 Peuchot, Emmanuel (2011) 'EU joins mounting criticism of DR Congo vote'. Agence France-Presse, 13 December.

92 'Report of the United Nations

Joint Human Rights Office on serious human rights violations committed by members of the Congolese defense and security forces in Kinshasa in the Democratic Republic of the Congo between 26 November and 25 December 2011'. MONUSCO and UN Office of the High Commissioner for Human Rights, March 2012.

93 Nossiter, Adam (2011) 'Congo President Kabila denies reports of election fraud'. *The New York Times*, 12 December.

94 'Etienne Tshisekedi placé en "résidence surveillée", selon l'UDPS'. Radio Okapi, 13 December 2011.

95 'Congo supreme court upholds president's victory'. Associated Press, 16 December 2011.

96 'Bandundu: les partisans du PALU et de l'ADD s'affrontent à Gungu'. Radio Okapi, 18 December 2011.

97 'Congo opposition leader declares himself – not Kabila – election winner, urges calm'. Associated Press, 18 December 2011.

98 Bangre, Habibou (2011) 'DR Congo's Tshisekedi insists he is "president-elect"'. Agence France-Presse, 18 December.

99 'Bukavu: la police disperse une marche des partis de l'opposition'. Radio Okapi, 20 December 2011.

100 Peuchot, Emmanuel (2011) 'Kabila sworn in as president of divided DR Congo'. Agence France-Presse, 20 December.

101 'DR Congo fires tear gas to stop 'swearing in''. Agence France-Presse, 23 December 2011.

102 'Kinshasa: la police disperse les militants de l'UDPS dans la périphérie du stade des Martyrs'. Radio Okapi, 23 December 2011.

103 'Congo's opposition leader holds own inauguration ceremony'. *The Guardian*, 23 December 2011.

104 'DR Congo condemns attack on lawmaker in Paris'. Agence France-Presse, 31 December 2011.

105 'Final report of the Group of Experts on the Democratic Republic of the Congo'. UN Security Council, 2 December 2011.

106 'Les combats entre rebelles vident les villages de Walikale et Masisi'. Radio Okapi, 11 December 2011.

107 '7 personnes tuées par des présumées FDLR'. Radio Okapi, 19 December 2011.

108 'Plusieurs groupes armés sévissent dans la région de Kabare'. Radio Okapi, 19 December 2011.

109 'ICC declines to charge Rwandan rebel for DR Congo crimes'. Agence France-Presse, 16 December 2011.

110 'Final report of the Group of Experts on the Democratic Republic of the Congo'. UN Security Council, 2 December 2011.

111 Rosen, Armin (2012) 'The warlord and the basketball star: a story of Congo's corrupt gold trade'. *The Atlantic*, 1 March.

112 Jones, Pete (2012) 'Obama-appointed US trade adviser linked to illegal deal in Congolese gold'. *The Guardian*, 5 February.

113 'Security Council renews arms embargo, related sanctions against Democratic Republic of Congo amid illicit weapons flows within, into country'. UN Security Council Department of Public Information, 29 November 2011.

114 'Final report of the Group of Experts on the Democratic Republic of the Congo'. UN Security Council, 2 December 2011.

115 Author's notes, North Kivu, February 2012.

10 Rebellion after rebellion

1 'Congo leader's party loses 45 percent of its seats'. Associated Press, 2 February 2012.

2 'Nord-Kivu: des partis d'opposition demandent la réouverture de l'assemblée provinciale'. Radio Okapi, 5 February 2012.

3 'Goma: échange des tirs entre FARDC et gardes d'un député sortant, 4 morts'. Radio Okapi, 2 February 2012.

4 'Le député Bakungu Mytondeke assigné à résidence à Kinshasa'. Radio Okapi, 5 February 2012.

5 Author interviews, Goma, February 2012.

6 Author interview, Goma, February 2012.

7 Author interview, Goma, February 2012.

8 'Un nouveau groupe armé créé au Sud-Kivu'. Radio Okapi, 8 February 2012.

9 'Renewed atrocities threaten IDPs in Eastern DRC'. UNHCR, 3 February 2012.

10 'DR Congo president's aide killed in plane crash: official'. Agence France-Presse, 13 February 2012.

11 'RDC: un avion s'écrase à l'aéroport de Bukavu, 5 morts'. Radio Okapi, 13 February, 2012.

12 Hangre, Habibou (2012) 'DR Congo police teargas Christians'. Agence France-Presse, 16 February.

13 Taylor, Diane (2012) 'Congo embassy workers claim asylum in UK'. *The Guardian*, 20 February.

14 'Des Congolais de la diaspora ont tenté d'agresser Moïse Katumbi à Bruxelles'. Radio Okapi, 28 February 2012.

15 'Province Orientale: les miliciens de FRPI pillent bétail et argent à Irumu'. Radio Okapi, 23 February 2012.

16 'Ituri: le comité de sécurité entame des négociations avec le chef milicien Cobra Matata'. Radio Okapi, 27 February 2012.

17 'Ituri: la société civile invite Joseph Kabila à amnistier Cobra Matata et sa milice'. Radio Okapi, 9 March 2012.

18 'Les notables de l'Ituri demandent l'implication de Joseph Kabila pour la réintégration des miliciens FRPI dans l'armée'. Radio Okapi, 30 March 2012.

19 'RDC: une nouvelle coalition de groupes armés naît en Ituri'. Radio Okapi, 25 May 2012.

20 'Group of Experts report on the Democratic Republic of Congo'. UN Security Council, June 2012.

21 'Sud-Kivu: 4 personnes calcinées dans une attaque atribuée aux FDLR'. Radio Okapi, 27 February 2012.

22 'Sud-Kivu: les ONGDH enregistre plus de 300 cas d'assassinats en 12 mois'. Radio Okapi, 23 February 2012.

23 'Kalehe: la société civile dénonce le regain d'insécurité'. Radio Okapi, 14 March 2012.

24 'Masisi: de nouveaux combats opposent les FARDC aux Maï-Maï APCLS et Nyatura du Pareco Fort'. Radio Okapi, 14 March 2012.

25 'Nord-Kivu: la milice APCLS exige une indemnisation pour mettre fin à la rébellion à Masisi'. Radio Okapi, 23 March 2012.

26 Smith, David (2012) 'Congo warlord Thomas Lubanga convicted of using child soldiers'. *The Guardian*, 14 March.

27 '"Child soldiers" are liars,

Lubanga's lawyer tells court'. Agence France-Presse, 27 January 2010.

28 'ICC suspends DR Congo ex-militia chief's trial'. Agence France-Presse, 9 July 2010.

29 'Int'l court says Congo warlord must stay in jail'. Associated Press, 23 July 2010.

30 Hennop, Jan (2012) 'War crimes court hands DR Congo rebel 14 years' jail'. Agence France-Presse, 10 July.

31 'DR Congo: Mathieu Ngudjolo Chui acquitted of war crimes by ICC'. BBC News, 18 December 2012.

32 'Rights groups hail DR Congo warlord conviction'. Agence France-Presse, 14 March 2012.

33 'CPI: le procureur Luis Moreno demande à Joseph Kabila de livrer Bosco Ntaganda'. Radio Okapi, 16 March 2012.

34 'James Entwistle: "Bosco Ntaganda devrait être arrêté et livré à la CPI"'. Radio Okapi, 6 April 2012.

35 'La société civile du Katanga demande la création d'un tribunal économique international'. Radio Okapi, 19 March 2012.

36 'Rutshuru: la rumeur d'une défection des militaires issus de l'ex-rébellion du CNDP agite la population'. Radio Okapi, 3 April, 2012.

37 'Rutshuru: le colonel Innocent Kayina des FARDC fait défection'. Radio Okapi, 9 April 2012.

38 'Wanted Congo warlord says he has not fled'. Agence France-Presse, 6 April 2012.

39 'Insécurité aux Kivu: Joseph Kabila, Didier Etumba et Roger Meece à Goma'. Radio Okapi, 10 April 2012.

40 'Foreign "pressure" will not force Ntaganda arrest: DR Congo'. Agence France-Presse, 11 April 2012.

41 'Joseph Kabila suspend toutes les opérations militaires au Nord-Kivu'. Radio Okapi, 11 April 2012.

42 'FARDC: 128 militaires déserteurs sont rentrés dans le rang à Uvira'. Radio Okapi, 9 April 2012.

43 'Sud-Kivu: des déserteurs veulent rentrer dans le rang des FARDC'. Radio Okapi, 17 April 2012.

44 'Walikale: 27 morts dans les affrontements entre FARDC et Mai-Mai Cheka à Luvungi'. Radio Okapi, 18 April 2012.

45 'Nord-Kivu: les Maï-Maï Cheka contrôlent la localité de Luvungi'. Radio Okapi, 29 April 2012.

46 'Nord-Kivu: les combats entre FARDC et mutins font 15 morts à Ngungu'. Radio Okapi, 30 April 2012.

47 'Nord-Kivu: Julien Paluku nie la chute de certaines localités aux mains des insurgés'. Radio Okapi, 1 May 2012.

48 'Ex-rebel chief Ntaganda behind clashes: DR Congo governor'. Agence France-Presse, 2 May 2012.

49 'Ex-rebel leader Ntaganda "not involved" in Congo unrest: AFP'. Agence France-Presse, 1 May 2012.

50 'Masisi: les FARDC récupèrent 25 tonnes d'armes dans la ferme de Bosco Ntaganda'. Radio Okapi, 9 May 2012.

51 'Nord-Kivu: des déserteurs des FARDC créent un mouvement politico-militaire dénommé M23'. Radio Okapi, 9 May 2012.

52 'Group of Experts report on the Democratic Republic of Congo'. UN Security Council, June 2012.

53 'DR Congo: Bosco Ntaganda recruits children by force'. Human Rights Watch, 16 May 2012.

54 'Statement ICC prosecutor on new applications for warrants of arrest DRC situation'. ICC, 14 May 2012.

55 'Le Rwanda doit extrader et

livrer à la CPI les criminels de guerre congolais'. *Le Monde*, 25 May 2012.

56 'RDC: 11 casques bleus de la Monusco blessés à Kamananga'. Radio Okapi, 15 May 2012.

57 'Nord-Kivu: des rebelles FDLR et Maï-Maï assassinent plus de 100 civils à Ufamandu'. Radio Okapi, 23 May 2012.

58 'Nord-Kivu: les FARDC délogent les Maï-Maï Cheka dans une dizaine de localités de Walikale'. Radio Okapi, 1 June 2012.

59 'DR Congo: Rwanda should stop aiding war crimes suspect'. Human Rights Watch, 4 June 2012.

60 Hogg, Jonny (2012) 'East Congo mutiny rakes over regional, ethnic wounds'. Reuters, 8 June.

61 'Rwandan tells AP of training to fight Congo'. Associated Press, 12 August 2012.

62 'Congo army claims 200 mutineers killed since April'. Agence France-Presse, 6 June 2012.

63 'Mutinerie dans les Kivu: l'opposition dénonce une agression rwandaise'. Radio Okapi, 8 June 2012.

64 'Kinshasa: une marche de soutien aux FARDC et à la population de l'Est a été dispersée'. Radio Okapi, 2 June 2012.

65 'RDC: mutinerie aux Kivu, Matata Ponyo exclut les négociations'. Radio Okapi, 8 June 2012.

66 'Kinshasa confirme la présence des Rwandais au sein du M23'. Radio Okapi, 10 June 2012.

67 'RDC: les mutins du M23 sabotent une canalisation d'eau à Rutshuru'. Radio Okapi, 15 June 2012.

68 'Nord-Kivu: les rebelles du M23 assiègent les localités de Tarika, Ruseke et Murambi'. Radio Okapi, 17 June 2012.

69 'Mutinerie du M23: la société civile demande à la communauté internationale de suspendre toute aide au Rwanda'. Radio Okapi, 23 June 2012.

70 'RDC: la société civile préoccupée par la présence de troupes étrangères à Rutshuru et Lubero'. Radio Okapi, 3 July 2012.

71 'RDC: la société civile du Nord-Kivu dénonce la présence des militaires ougandais et rwandais au sein du M23'. Radio Okapi, 26 July 2012.

72 'Uganda denies backing DR Congo rebels'. Agence France-Presse, 3 August 2012.

73 'Dungu: plusieurs meurtres, vols et pillages attribués aux rebelles de la LRA'. Radio Okapi, 11 February 2012.

74 'Province Orientale: des présumés rebelles de la LRA se livrent à des exactions à Bondo'. Radio Okapi, 23 March 2012.

75 'Hundreds more flee continuing LRA attacks in north-east Congo'. UNHCR, 30 March 2012.

76 'Province Orientale: les LRA tuent 8 personnes et enlèvent 50 autres à Dungu'. Radio Okapi, 13 June 2012.

77 'Nord-Kivu: des FDLR prélèvent des taxes de "sécurisation" aux habitants de Rutshuru et Lubero'. Radio Okapi, 1 April 2012.

78 'Rutshuru: 6 morts lors d'un affrontement entre les FARDC et les FDLR'. Radio Okapi, 2 April 2012.

79 'Nord-Kivu: les FDLR tuent 20 personnes à Misau et Erobe'. Radio Okapi, 26 June 2012.

80 'Nord-Kivu: 9 morts après des combats entre FARDC et les groupes armés à Luofu'. Radio Okapi, 1 July 2012.

81 'Kalehe: les communautés Hutu et Tembo s'engagent à promouvoir la paix'. Radio Okapi, 20 June 2012.

82 'RDC: le chef de l'état annule les réjouissances de l'indépendance à cause de la guerre à l'Est'. Radio Okapi, 30 June 2012.

83 'Nord-Kivu: de nouveaux affrontements entre FARDC et M23 signalés à Bweza'. Radio Okapi, 2 July 2012.

84 'UN soldier dies as DR Congo rebels take Uganda border post'. Agence France-Presse, 6 July 2012.

85 'Official: 600 Congolese soldiers flee into Uganda'. Associated Press, 6 July 2012.

86 'Rutshuru: les habitants craignent une attaque des mutins du M23'. Radio Okapi, 7 July 2012.

87 'Congo rebels seize eastern town after army flees'. Associated Press, 8 July 2012.

88 'RDC: les députés du Kivu exigent le "changement de toute la chaîne de commandement de l'armée"'. Radio Okapi, 14 July 2012.

89 'DR Congo, UN troops reinforce Goma from rebel attack'. Agence France-Presse, 9 July 2012.

90 'Nord-Kivu: les FARDC et la Monusco bombardent des bases des rebelles du M23'. Radio Okapi, 12 July 2012.

91 'Rébellion du M23: la Monusco déterminée à "faire tout son possible" pour protéger les civils'. Radio Okapi, 13 July 2012.

92 Mwanamilongo, Saleh (2012) 'Congo rebels threaten to attack UN peacekeepers'. Associated Press, 15 July.

93 'AU ready to send peacekeepers to DR Congo'. Agence France-Presse, 15 July 2012.

94 Vesperini, Helen (2012) 'DR Congo, Rwanda agree on force to combat rebels'. Agence France-Presse, 15 July.

95 'U.N. Security Council condemns eastern Congo rebel attacks'. Reuters, 16 July 2012.

96 'UN helicopters fire on rebels in eastern DR Congo: UN'. Agence France-Presse, 24 July 2012.

97 'US halts military aid to Rwanda over DR Congo mutiny'. Agence France-Presse, 22 July 2012.

98 'Netherlands suspends aid to Rwanda over DR Congo unrest'. Agence France-Presse, 27 July 2012.

99 Smith, David (2012) 'UK blocks £16m aid to Rwanda'. The Guardian, 27 July.

100 McGreal, Chris (2012) 'Rwanda's Paul Kagame warned he may be charged with aiding war crimes'. The Guardian, 25 July.

101 'Nord-Kivu: les habitants d'une localité fuient la milice Raïa Mutomboki en brousse'. Radio Okapi, 16 July 2012.

102 'Nord-Kivu: les habitants de Ngungu dénoncent la passivité des FARDC face aux attaques des milices'. Radio Okapi, 26 July 2012.

103 'DRC situation: ICC issues an arrest warrant for Sylvestre Mudacumura'. ICC, 13 July 2012.

104 'Sud-Kivu: assassinat de 11 commerçants dans la localité de Kashuno'. Radio Okapi, 11 August 2012.

105 'Nord-Kivu: les FDLR et les Maï-Maï créent l'insécurité le long du Lac Edouard'. Radio Okapi, 13 August 2012.

106 'Sud-Kivu: 11 morts dans des affrontements entre FARDC et miliciens à Kalehe et Uvira'. Radio Okapi, 27 August 2012.

107 'Province Orientale: les
miliciens FRPI tuent 5 personnes à
Kasenyi'. Radio Okapi, 27 July 2012.

108 'DR Congo president accuses
Rwanda of aiding rebels'. Agence
France-Presse, 29 July 2012.

109 'DR Congo troops abandon
villages to rebels: envoys'. Agence
France-Presse, 31 July 2012.

110 'UN Council condemns "outside" backing for DR Congo rebels'.
Agence France-Presse, 2 August 2012.

111 'Thousands of Christians
march for peace in Congo'. Agence
France-Presse, 1 August 2012.

112 Declaration of the heads of
state and government. Press release,
8 August 2012.

113 Delany, Max (2012) 'DR Congo
says no negotiation with M23 rebels'.
Agence France-Presse, 9 August.

114 Jackson, Jinty (2012) 'Southern
Africa tells Rwanda to stop DR Congo
rebel support'. Agence France-Presse,
18 August.

Epilogue

1 Deibert, Michael (2012) 'DR
Congo: North Kivu's false peace'.
African Arguments, 29 February.

2 Trefon, Theodore (2011) *Congo
Masquerade: The political culture of aid
inefficiency and reform failure*. London:
Zed Books, p. 21.

3 Author interview, Gulu, February 2012.

4 'Group: Sudan army supporting
fugitive warlord Kony'. Associated
Press, 27 April 2013.

5 'Kagame denies any link to
Kampala journalist murder'. Agence
France-Presse, 12 December 2011.

BIBLIOGRAPHY

Autesserre, Séverine (2010) *The Trouble with the Congo: Local violence and the failure of international peacebuilding*. Cambridge: Cambridge University Press.

Behrend, Heike (2000) *Alice Lakwena & the Holy Spirits: War in northern Uganda 1986–97*. Athens, OH: Ohio University Press.

Boyles, Denis (1988) *African Lives*. New York, NY: Ballantine Books.

Bradford, Phillips Verner (1992) *Ota Benga: The pygmy in the zoo*. New York, NY: St Martin's Press.

Casement, Roger (2003) *The Eyes of Another Race: Roger Casement's Congo report and 1903 diary*. Dublin: University College Dublin.

Clapham, Christopher S. (ed.) (1998) *African Guerrillas*. Oxford: James Currey.

Close, William T. (2006) *Beyond the Storm: Treating the powerless and the powerful in Mobutu's Congo/Zaire*. Marbleton, WY: Meadowlark Springs Productions.

Cosma, Wilungula B. (1997) *Fizi, 1967–1986: le maquis Kabila*. Paris: L'Harmattan.

de Witte, Ludo (2001) *The Assassination of Lumumba*. London: Verso.

des Forges, Alison Liebhafsky (2011) *Defeat is the Only Bad News: Rwanda under Musinga, 1896–1931*. Madison, WI: University of Wisconsin Press.

Devlin, Larry (2008) *Chief of Station, Congo: Fighting the Cold War in a hot zone*. New York, NY: Public Affairs.

Finnström, Sverker (2008) *Living with Bad Surroundings: War, history, and everyday moments in northern Uganda*. Durham, NC: Duke University Press.

French, Howard (2005) *A Continent for the Taking: The tragedy and hope of Africa*. New York, NY: Vintage.

Gourevitch, Philip (1999) *We Wish to Inform You That Tomorrow We Will be Killed with Our Families: Stories from Rwanda*. New York, NY: Picador.

Hochschild, Adam (1999) *King Leopold's Ghost: A story of greed, terror, and heroism in colonial Africa*. New York, NY: Mariner Books.

Hodges, Tony (2001) *Angola: From Afro-Stalinism to petro-diamond capitalism*. Oxford: James Currey.

Lamb, David (1982) *The Africans*. New York, NY: Random House.

Lemarchand, René (1994) *Burundi: Ethnic conflict and genocide*. Cambridge: Cambridge University Press.

MacGaffey, Janet (1991) *The Real Economy of Zaire: The contribution of smuggling and other unofficial activities to national wealth*.

Philadelphia, PA: University of Pennsylvania Press.

Mailer, Norman (1975) *The Fight*. New York, NY: Vintage.

Ogata, Sadako (2005) *The Turbulent Decade: Confronting the refugee crises of the 1990s*. New York, NY: W. W. Norton and Company.

Pickard, Terry (2010) *Combat Medic: An eyewitness account of the Kibeho massacre*. Newport, Australia: Big Sky Publishing.

Prunier, Gérard (1995) *The Rwanda Crisis : History of a genocide*. New York, NY: Columbia University Press.

— (2009) *Africa's World War: Congo, the Rwandan genocide, and the making of a continental catastrophe*. New York, NY: Oxford University Press.

Reefe, Thomas Q. (1981) *The Rainbow and the Kings: A history of the Luba empire to 1891*. Berkeley, CA: University of California Press.

Schatzberg, Michael G. (1991) *The Dialectics of Oppression in Zaire*. Bloomington, IN: Indiana University Press.

Stearns, Jason (2011) *Dancing in the Glory of Monsters: The collapse of the Congo and the great war of Africa*. New York, NY: PublicAffairs.

Terry, Fiona (2002) *Condemned to Repeat? The paradox of humanitarian action*. Ithaca, NY: Cornell University Press.

Thornton, John K. (1998) *The Kongolese Saint Anthony: Dona Beatriz Kimpa Vita and the Antonian movement,* *1684–1706*. Cambridge: Cambridge University Press.

— (1999) *Warfare in Atlantic Africa 1500–1800*. New York, NY: Routledge.

Trefon, Theodore (ed.) (2005) *Reinventing Order in the Congo: How people respond to state failure in Kinshasa*. London: Zed Books.

— (2011) *Congo Masquerade: The political culture of aid inefficiency and reform failure*. London: Zed Books.

Turnbull, Colin (1961) *The Forest People*. New York, NY: Touchstone.

Urquhart, Brian (1994) *Hammarskjold*. New York, NY: W. W. Norton and Company.

Vansina, Jan (1966) *Kingdoms of the Savanna*. Madison, WI: University of Wisconsin Press.

— (2004) *Antecedents to Modern Rwanda: The Nyiginya kingdom*. Madison, WI: University of Wisconsin Press.

— (2010) *Being Colonized: The Kuba experience in rural Congo 1880–1960*. Madison, WI: University of Wisconsin Press.

Veit, Alex (2011) *Intervention as Indirect Rule: Civil war and statebuilding in the Democratic Republic of Congo*. Frankfurt: Campus Verlag.

Willame, Jean-Claude (1972) *Patrimonialism and Political Change in the Congo*. Stanford, CA: Stanford University Press.

Young, Crawford and Thomas Turner (1985) *The Rise and Decline of the Zairian State*. Madison, WI: University of Wisconsin Press.

INDEX